SERIAL KILLERS ARE GOOD PEOPLE

and other secrets for law enforcement

Published by E. Frost Media™

COPYRIGHT 2016
ELDON FROST

To improve future editions, please email any errors, omissions, or questions to:

efrostmedia@outlook.com

This document is geared toward providing exact and reliable information in regards to the topic and issue covered. The publication is sold with the idea that the publisher is not required to render accounting, officially permitted, or otherwise, qualified services. If advice is necessary, legal or otherwise, a practiced individual in the profession should be ordered.

- From a Declaration of Principles which was accepted and approved equally by a Committee of the American Bar Association and a Committee of Publishers and Associations.

2

TABLE OF CONTENTS

INTRODUCTION

This book will not be comfortable to read. I know that, because it certainly wasn't comfortable to write. The lives of serial killers are filled with chaos, abuse, and an inevitable trail of heartbreak and destruction. We want to know more about these people – they fascinate us. And yet, we tend not to examine them too closely. We keep our distance. We call them "monsters" to avoid thinking of them as human.

Through movies and the media, we're led to believe that serial killers look evil. They're presented either as psychotic madmen, or as expressionless intellectuals with sinister looks in their eyes. Certainly, there is some truth to these stereotypes. But it seems that audiences aren't ready for a more realistic depiction of a serial killer: a person who drives the kids to school, waves to the neighbors while mowing the lawn, and sings in the choir at the local church.

Though primarily written for law enforcement, anyone reading these pages may learn a thing or two about human nature, and about themselves. I hope it will be a fascinating journey.

Although many serial killers are featured in this work, about a dozen are used as examples throughout. For quick reference, short biographies of these killers can be found at the back of the book.

WHAT IS A SERIAL KILLER?

Until the mid-1970s, the term "serial killer" didn't even exist. It was coined by a streetwise FBI agent named Robert Ressler, after he recognized there was a type of killer – a cold-blooded, methodical murderer – for which no term then in use was accurate. Prior to Ressler's work, terms like "homicidal maniac," "serial murderer" and "mass murderer" had been thrown about loosely and without clear definition.

Today a serial killer is defined by the FBI as a person who murders two or more victims in two or more separate events, with an emotional cooling off period in between (NCAVC, 2005). This differs from a mass murderer, who kills several victims at a single location (such as a school shooting), or a spree killer who goes around madly killing in a single wild run. Yet, the standard definition of a serial killer is incomplete. Mobsters, gangsters and dictators may murder many people over the course of their careers, yet most people do not consider them to be serial killers. Only killers who hide their true personalities, or who murder for sexual reasons, really "count" as serial killers. Serial murder is a private affair.

The FBI estimates that, at any given moment, there are between thirty and fifty serial killers at large in the United States alone. Some disturbed individuals might believe that becoming a serial killer is a fast track to fame, but the statistics do not bear this out. For every well-known killer, there are a dozen more who have been forgotten. The names of internationally infamous serial killers from the early 1900s, like Belle Guinness, Henri Landru and Earl Nelson are barely recognized today. In the United States, between the years 1900 and 2010, there were more than twenty-three hundred of them.

Carl "Coral" Eugene Watts, a black man from Michigan, confessed to the murders of 12 women and hinted that he killed more than 80; yet, he was never well known to the public. The most publicized serial killers in America are white males, possibly because "the establishment," including the press, consists mainly of whites. Yet, serial killers span all racial and ethnic groups. Since 1900, approx. 52% of U.S. serial killers have been white, 41% black and the remainder a mix of different ethnicities (Aamodt, 2015). Women make up 8.9% of all serial killers (Ibid).

Serial killers strike fear into the hearts of the public partly because of their ability to blend in. The most famous one of all, nineteenth century London murderer Jack-the-Ripper, became a household name not just because of his gruesome murders, but because people realized that he must be walking around, looking like an ordinary fellow. He could be *anyone*.

Serial killers are far from ordinary, but are experts at hiding their true selves. A person might recognize that their new neighbor has strong opinions or makes off-color remarks once in a while, but might not believe that he is capable of murder.

PART 1:
BECOMING A KILLER

LEARNING TO BE NORMAL

Whenever a serial killer is identified, the popular impression is that "no one could have known." Neighbors often describe the killer as shy and polite, and even the killer's parents say there were no indications. In reality, the childhoods of serial killers are rife with examples of strange and concerning behaviors.

Jeffrey Dahmer, who would later become known as the "Milwaukee Cannibal," had an uncomfortable family life. Dahmer's parents fought frequently prior to their divorce, and his sickly, anxiety-ridden mother attempted suicide by drug overdose. By the age of 14 Dahmer was already a borderline alcoholic, smuggling alcohol to school and drinking gin in class. By 18, he was being arrested for disorderly conduct once or twice a year, according to father Lionel Dahmer and stepmother Sheri Dahmer, including once where he pulled out a handgun in a bar. They also became aware that he had built a satanic altar. Despite all this, they maintain there was "no hint that there was a darker side to his life" (King, 2004).

Aileen Wuornos was born in Rochester, Michigan in 1956. Her parents filed for divorce while she was still in the womb. Wuornos' father, a convicted sex offender, died in prison without ever having met her. By the time she reached grade school Wuornos was known for her odd behavior, most notably her explosive temper tantrums. Since she felt no particular moral concerns regarding sex, she began having sex with her brother. By the age of 11, she was prostituting herself to neighborhood boys for spare change and cigarettes. At 20, Wuornos moved to Florida. Her appearance was respectable enough to attract the attentions of the 69-year-old president of the local yacht club. Their wedding was announced with pride in the society pages, but lasted only nine weeks. During their brief marriage, Wuornos physically assaulted her elderly husband with his own cane.

Michael Swango, who in later life became a medical doctor who poisoned his coworkers and patients, grew up with a strict military father who was an alcoholic. While still a child, Swango's father taught him to march and do military drills. When his father wanted to introduce his three sons to houseguests, he would have them march into the living room and stand at attention. Once introduced, he would dismiss them and watch them march out. Starting in Grade 6, Michael Swango developed a passion for scrap booking that would last throughout his life. Specifically, he created scrapbooks from newspaper and magazine clippings of crime stories, disasters, and fatal car accidents. Swango's mother, always supportive of him, helped him cut out and arrange the articles. When Swango's father died due to complications arising from his alcoholism, the family discovered he had also kept a scrapbook of violent death, just like his son. Michael's mother gave the scrapbook to him as a memento. Michael is said to have responded, "I guess my dad wasn't such a bad guy after all" (Stewart, 1999).

As a child, Dennis Rader strangled cats and dogs for amusement in his hometown of Wichita, Kansas. Always fawned over by his mother, he claims that he slept in her bed until an age when he began to appreciate her smell and the feeling of her underclothes. When he was 10 or 11, he masturbated into his mother's underwear. When she found the stains, she whipped him with a belt. Rader said that although the punishment hurt, "Sparky liked it." Sparky was the name Rader had given to his penis. As an adult, Rader married a bookkeeper and together they had two children. Their marriage lasted 34 years, until Rader's arrest for serial murder.

The childhood personalities of serial killers are anything but normal. Over time, however, these future killers *learn*. They learn to conceal the thoughts and actions that make them outcasts. They learn to appear normal. They still reveal their true personalities, but only in brief glimpses and outbursts that are easily dismissed.

"OOOh god i HATE my life, i want to die really bad right now - let's see what i have that's good: A nice family, a good house, food, a couple good friends, & possessions. What's bad: no girls (friends or girlfriends), no other friends except a few, nobody accepting me even though i want to be accepted, me doing badly & being intimidated in any & all sports, me looking wierd & acting shy - BIG problem, me getting bad grades, having no ambition of life, thats the big shit."

Columbine High School shooter Dylan Klebold's personal journal entry for April 15, 1997, highlighting differences between mass murderers and serial killers. Mass murderers want to fit in, but can't. Serial killers also hate society, but are accepted either by mainstream society, or at least by a subculture group.

NATURE VERSUS NURTURE

People want to believe that the propensity for serial killing is like a disease, and that if we could discover the cause we could cure it. Combinations of genes certainly make people prone to aggression, impulsivity, addiction, and psychological disorders. But bad genes alone do not create serial killers. There is no gene for murder.

It's likely that many factors contribute to a "serial killer personality." One clear factor is a stressful childhood involving harsh parenting, alcoholism and abuse. Another is brain damage. The frontal lobe area of the brain is of particular interest since this area is responsible for higher functioning, including feelings of remorse, regret, and morality. Other factors are social, such as being raised in an environment that encourages violence and cruelty.

Criminal partners Perry Smith and Richard Hickock, who were the subject of Truman Capote's classic novel, *In Cold Blood*, provide an excellent example of how different environmental factors may result in murderous criminality. Smith had a promiscuous, alcoholic mother who was regularly beaten by his father. A troubled boy, Smith was sent to detention homes where he wet his bed regularly and was ridiculed by his peers. Richard Hickock, in contrast, described his home life as "normal," his parents as hardworking, and remembered that they had only one serious argument during their entire marriage. After high school, Hickock became involved in criminal activities such as burglary, but was not known as violent or antisocial. The following year he was involved in a car accident and suffered severe head injuries, after which his crimes became more frequent and more violent.

Years after the accident, Hickock claimed that a piece of glass worked its way out of his head, coming out of the corner of his eye. Those who knew Hickock said that the accident altered his personality drastically, rendering him distant and unfeeling.

Unfortunately, there are many ways to negatively affect the human brain, all of which have a profound impact on behavior. There are direct, physical ways, such as head trauma and concussions, disease, infection, seizure damage, cancer and blood clots. Then there are the cognitive ways. One can repeatedly and unpredictably scream at a child, causing their stress hormone levels to soar, forever damaging their ability to deal with everyday situations. One can teach a developing child that the world is unfair and that no one can be trusted, thereby damaging the neural connections that relate to human interaction. One can scramble a child's definition of "love" by telling the child that you love them as you are beating them. All of these situations and more are found in the lives of serial killers.

> "I do not think you can be born and live this way. I think some traumatic events that occur early in life direct a person's development. What is traumatic for one individual is not necessarily for another."
>
> "Torso Killer" Richard Cottingham (Fezzani, 2015).

In an early FBI study of serial killers (Ressler et al, 1985) it was found that half of the murderer's families had criminal histories, and more than half had psychiatric problems. Seventy percent of the families had histories of alcohol abuse, and a third had histories of drug abuse. The researchers were stuck by the "high degree of instability in home life and by the poor quality of attachment among family members." They serial killer's families as "emotionally deficient."

Though the evidence suggests that a "serial killer personality" is due to a combination of factors, serial killers themselves rarely give credence to any explanation except a genetic one. They believe in survival of the fittest, and consider themselves the fittest.

INFANCY

Doctor: What are you trying to do to your brother [when you stick pins in him]?
Beth: Kill him.
Doctor: Why do you want your brother to die?
Beth: 'Cause I was hurt so bad, and I don't want to be around people.

Beth Thomas, age 6. Beth was neglected, starved, and sexually abused prior to being adopted by another family at 19 months of age (Magid, 1990). Beth received extensive self-worth improvement therapy. She has not violently offended as an adult.

In order to properly understand childhood development – or the absence of it – we must get away from the common understanding of the term "abuse" and broaden it substantially.

In their first days of life, babies are completely dependent upon their parents: they're unable to feed themselves, unable to turn over, unable to escape their own excrement. They will never be this vulnerable again.

Parents of neglected children tend to interpret every milestone in their child's life as negative. A mother who herself feels neglected or unloved is *grateful* that her baby cannot live without her. She does nothing to encourage its development. While a healthy mother may look upon her baby's first steps as an achievement, a maladjusted mother may view her baby's first steps as an attempt at abandonment.

> "No baby will play peek-a-boo halfway through his first year if he's apathetic or failing to thrive. If he can't play peek-a-boo, things are probably not going well."
>
> Diane Campbell, M.D., (Lankford, 2002).

Anyone who has played with a smiling, giggling baby knows how much they enjoy face-to-face interaction. Such interactions help develop their vision, motor skills, coordination, hearing, and even social skills (babies mimic facial expressions). A baby who does not receive an adequate amount of eye contact, cuddling and play is an abused child, as it has been deprived of the conditions that would help it grow into a confident, trusting adult. A baby whose cries go unheeded is an abused child. A baby who is yelled at or struck is an abused child. A baby whose parents are not in control of their own lives, due to drugs or alcohol, is an abused child.

Abuse is the absence of security. And the earlier it starts, the worse the consequences. As adults, serial killers often express the view that at least one of their parents did not share joy with them, but merely raised them out of obligation.

> "For children to master developmental tasks...they need opportunities, encouragement, and acknowledgement from their caregivers. If this stimulation is lacking during children's early years, the weak neuronal pathways that had been developed in expectation of these experiences may wither and die..."
>
> U.S. Dept. of Health and Human Services (2009).

CHILDHOOD – ONE INCIDENT AT A TIME

When the author was a teenager, my friend's father was once giving us a ride to their home. Out of nowhere, he began lecturing us on the perils of drinking and driving. He told us that it was dangerous, and that if we did it we could be killed. He told us that even if we didn't die, we could hit an innocent person and end up in jail. My friend and I looked at each other: *What is this all about? Why now?*

The answer came seconds later, when my friend's father reached underneath his seat, pulled out a bottle of whiskey, and took a long swig. He had made his speech to say, *never do what I am about to do.* We were less than ten minutes away from his home, but he clearly couldn't wait that long to have a drink. My friend looked deeply ashamed.

When neighbors talk about the home life of a serial killer, they often describe the family as perfectly normal, nothing unusual, nothing amiss. What people don't realize is that it only takes a few "special" moments to change a child's life forever.

Ted Bundy was intelligent, charismatic, and infamous for killing at least 30 women and girls between 1974 and 1978. One of the defining moments in Bundy's life was when he confirmed that his "sister" was actually his mother. Worried about the stigma of being a young, unwed mother in the late 1940s, Bundy's mother had allowed her parents to raise him as their son – telling family, friends, and even Ted himself that they were his parents. Bundy's real mother pretended to be his big sister. Bundy always suspected the ruse, but didn't confirm it until he tracked down his original birth certificate in Vermont in 1969 (Rule, 1980). Bundy harbored a lifelong resentment toward his mother for lying to him for so many years.

As a child, future Air Force Colonel Russell Williams appeared to be a normal, good-looking boy in a comfortable upper-middle-class family. The life of this family, however, was not idyllic. Unhappy with their marriage, Russell's father and mother literally swapped spouses with another local family, the Sovkas. Dave Williams (Russell's father) married Marilyn Sovka, while Christine Williams (Russell's mother) married Jerry Sovka. Soon, Christine changed her surname to Sovka and started using her middle name – Nonie – as her given name. Imagine the confusion in a child's mind when your father is no longer around, your mother is suddenly living with your neighbor, and family friends are referring to your mother as "Nonie Sovka" when, until recently, she was "Christine Williams." The incident taught Russell that a person is just a façade – a false construction that can be changed at will. Russell was just 6 years old at the time.

One event among many that changed Robert Pickton's fate was the death of his pet calf. Twelve-year-old Pickton, whose family owned a farm in rural Canada, played with the calf every day, slept beside it, and said that he wanted to keep it as a friend for the rest of his life (odd in itself). His parents, presumably, gave no indications that they had more practical plans for the animal. One day Pickton came home from school and couldn't find his beloved pet. When he asked his parents if they'd seen it, they cruelly suggested that he "look in the barn." There he found the calf hanging upside down, cleaned out and butchered. Pickton was so upset that he didn't speak to his family for days. The incident gave him a fatalistic view of life that has remained with him: "We're here for the time that we're here for," he often says.

"Scarborough Rapist" Paul Bernardo's mother was a recluse who rarely left the basement of their home. Paul's father regularly molested his daughter (Paul's sister), and would later molest his granddaughter as they watched cartoons together. On Paul Bernardo's 16th birthday, his mother informed him that he was a bastard and had been fathered by another man, showing him a photo of a businessman to prove it. By the time he was 26, Bernardo had become a voyeur and rapist. With the assistance of his attractive girlfriend, Karla Homolka, he would soon become a killer as well. Together, the trendy-looking pair became known as the "Ken and Barbie" killers.

> "If a child lives in a threatening, chaotic world, the child's brain may be hyperalert for danger because survival may depend on it...The result may be a child who has difficulty functioning when presented with a world of kindness, nurturing, and stimulation."
>
> U.S. Dept. of Health and Human Services (2009).

Experiencing childhood trauma doesn't necessarily mean that a person will become a killer. Childhood trauma does, however, lead to confusion and emotional anger for which coping mechanisms must be found. Children who grow up to be healthy individuals tend to look outward, seeking friendships, joining groups, and taking up sports to channel their aggression. With luck they have teachers, relatives and friends who can put them on the right path. Children who grow up to be serial killers tend to channel their energies inward, into the world of fantasy; in this world they are powerful and controlling, seeking revenge upon those who would hurt them. These are not healthy fantasies of escape to a beautiful world, but fantasies where they are the supreme masters of the existing one.

"One big fucking problem Is people telling me what to fuckin do, Think, say, act, and everything else. I'll do what you say IF I feel like it. But people (I.E. parents, cops, God, teachers) telling me what to do think, say, act, and everything else just makes me not want to fucking do it! That's why my fucking name is REB [Rebel]!!! no one is worthy of shit unless I say they are, I feel like GOD and I wish I was, having everyone being OFFICIALLY lower than me. I already know that I am higher than almost anyone in the fucking welt in terms of universal Intelligence."

Personal journal entry of Columbine High School mass murderer Eric Harris, dated April 12, 1998. Unpopular in school, Harris was bullied constantly. He often used German words like "welt" (world) in his writings, and declared his admiration for Hitler and the Nazis. Like serial killers, mass murderers harbor hidden rage, and compensate for their feelings of inferiority and exclusion with bravado. They construct vivid fantasies highlighting their personal power and importance.

CHILDHOOD INDICATORS – THE HOMICIDAL TRIAD THEORY

The Homicidal Triad was first reported by psychiatrist John M. Macdonald in a 1963 article in the *Journal of Psychiatry*. The Homicidal Triad is so named because it lists three warning signs said to predict extremely violent behavior: fire starting, cruelty to animals or peers, and enuresis (regular bedwetting beyond the age of 5). The cruelty and fire starting are said to reveal children who are desperately trying to be the masters of their environment, while the bedwetting proves they are not. What Macdonald probably didn't recognize is that although the Triad predicts future violence, these same behaviors are also telltale signs of child abuse and neglect.

There is currently an odd movement to dismiss the Homicidal Triad as fiction, saying that it has little empirical support, that it isn't linked with sociopathic behavior, and that in regard to bedwetting "it's not even clear that kids who wet the bed are particularly distressed by their condition" (Dewar, 2013). In my opinion, this outright dismissal is bizarre. First, I've never heard of any child who wasn't mortified about wetting the bed. Secondly, cruelty to animals and fire starting are *already* antisocial behaviors. Thirdly, and most importantly, serial killers themselves say that engaging in such acts made them realize they were embarking upon a dark and dangerous path.

FIRE STARTING

After American serial killer Israel Keyes burglarized a home in Texas in 2012, he doused the contents with gasoline, opened all the windows for ventilation, and set it ablaze. He then drove to the parking lot of a church overlooking the property, pulled out a pair of binoculars, and lost track of the time as he watched the structure burn to the ground. He was impressed by how much excitement the fire caused.

John Douglas of the FBI's Investigative Support Unit famously reported that killer David Berkowitz, the "Son of Sam," lit more than two *thousand* fires in the Brooklyn-Queens area, documenting them all in a meticulous diary (Douglas, 1995).

With its ever-changing wisps of smoke and orange-red flickering hues, many people find fire fascinating. For those who lack self-esteem and desire attention, fire has an even greater attraction – it is power.

A large fire can cause fire fighters to come running, mobilize tough police officers and ambulance drivers, and set a whole neighbourhood to panic. Fire is the only way a single, unarmed individual can make an entire building come crashing down or an entire forest disappear.

"Yes, when my desire for injuring people awoke, the love of setting fire to things awoke as well. The sight of the flames delighted me, but above all it was the excitement of the attempts to extinguish the fire and the agitation of those who saw their property being destroyed."

Killer Peter Kürten, explaining his fascination with fire to a packed courtroom (Phoebus Publishing, 1976).

Juvenile fire-starters make up about half of all arson arrests (Zipper & Wilcox, 2005), but the true number could be much higher, since neighbors and law enforcement officers are often reluctant to press charges against children.

So-called "playing with matches" is a normal childhood activity. About one-third of children start fires with no intention of hurting anyone or destroying anything. It's only when fires are started to damage or cause panic that concern is warranted.

CRUELTY

The torture of animals or other children figures prominently in the childhoods of serial killers. Already, their lack of empathy and desire to lash out against personal pain and perceived injustice are apparent.

At age 13, British "Railway Killers" John Duffy and David Mulcahy began torturing animals, starting with a hedgehog in the school playground that Mulcahy beat to death with a piece of wood before stomping on its head. At 17, Duffy and Mulcahy were convicted of causing bodily harm for shooting at passers-by with an air rifle. After finishing school, the pair carried out burglaries and arson before moving on to rape and murder (Clough et al, 2001).

At the age of 14, Israel Keyes took his sister's cat, tied it to a tree, and shot it in the stomach with a .22 caliber revolver he had earlier stolen. He laughed as he watched the cat run around the tree in circles, trying to escape its pain. A friend who was with Keyes at the time was so traumatized by the scene that he vomited.

Further examples of serial killers who tortured animals as children are endless. They include German Friedrich "Fritz" Haarman, who at the age of 9 found pleasure in stabbing sheep, goats and other farm animals. Prior to his conviction for murder, Haarman received seventeen sentences (about 20 years in prison) for theft and arson. They include Joseph Methany, who threw gasoline on cats and then set them on fire, watching them run away in distress (2012, Earley). They include Ed

Kemper, who killed pets and also started fires as a child, calling his urges to do so "little zapples."

When a child coldly takes the life of another animal, especially a pet, it indicates that the child has developed the emotional numbness frequently found in dangerous criminals.

> "I had several bad things happen to me at an early age which started me on the path of hurting others before they hurt me. It all started with me hurting insects then animals then I turned my frustrations to other kids."
>
> Killer Joseph Methany (Earley, 2012).

BEDWETTING

Of the three components of the Homicidal Triad, bedwetting is the most benign, since it causes no physical harm. A child's terror of bedwetting comes primarily from the family's negative reaction to it. Since serial killer's families tend to be unsupportive, it's not surprising that their reactions to bedwetting can be extreme.

At the tender age of 3, California "Hillside Stranger" Kenneth Bianchi's adoptive mother took him to see a physician because she thought it was unusual that he was still wetting the bed (the physician noted, "mother needs help.") By the age of 7, Bianchi began experiencing daytime "urinary dribbling," and by the age of 9 was having "involuntary urinations." As a solution, Bianchi's mother forced him to wear women's sanitary napkins in his underwear.

"Green River" killer Gary Ridgway was still wetting the bed as a teenager. After each incident, his attractive mother would belittle him: "Only babies wet the bed. Aren't you going to grow up?" Then, she would take him to the bathtub and thoroughly wash his penis and testicles clean for him, often making him erect in the process. According to Ridgway, they repeated this ritual at least three times a week and sometimes every day. To say that Ridgway had mixed feelings about these incidents is an understatement. Although attracted to his mother, at the same time he entertained thoughts of "mutilating her, killing her," and "burning down the house with her inside" (Malong, 2003).

Ridgway displayed all three activities from the homicidal triad as a child. Aside from wetting the bed, he also killed birds and cats, including his sister's cat. At the age of 8 he set fire to his neighbor's garage. At 16, Ridgway stabbed a six-year-old boy with a pocketknife. When the little boy looked down upon his bleeding torso and asked Ridgway why he had done it, Ridgway replied, "I always wanted to know what it felt like to kill somebody." After the stabbing, Ridgway ran home and hid in his basement.

This author had a hometown acquaintance who displayed at least two traits of the homicidal triad as a child (I'm not sure about the fire-starting). His mother humiliatingly reported to any visitor that he still wet his bed. In his early teens, he began killing neighbourhood cats by shoving them into garbage bags and throwing them off a local bridge, delighting as they screamed in terror on the way down. As far as I know, he didn't become a killer. He did, however, spend a significant amount of time in prison for breaking and entering, burglary, and violent domestic abuse.

A child who exhibits the traits of the Homicidal Triad will not necessarily become a serial killer, or even necessarily a violent adult; it is, however, an indication the child is in serious need of counselling and guidance to avoid going there.

INDICATORS OF
CHILD ABUSE & NEGLECT

from the U.S. Department of Health and Human Services
(Crosson-Tower, 2003)

- **Cruelty to peers and animals (especially pets)**
- **Fire starting**
- **Enuresis (bed or pant wetting) beyond age appropriateness**
- Destructiveness without guilt
- Cowers or demonstrates fear of adults
- Self-destructiveness (ex. cutting or scratching oneself)
- Substance abuse
- More sexual knowledge than is age appropriate
- Seductive behavior
- Talk of being "damaged" or sore
- Defiant attitude
- Emotional withdrawal
- Reports regularly caring for younger siblings
- Appears tired and listless due to lack of structure around bedtimes
- Poor hygiene

THE TEEN YEARS

The teen years are a confusing time for even well adjusted youths. Normal kids display many of the same characteristics and habits as potentially dangerous ones: defensiveness of personal space and belongings; underperformance in school; alcohol and drug experimentation; sexual experimentation; and, an interest in the occult/horror genre.

For any teen, it's not necessarily the actions/activities themselves that are of grave concern, but the degree to which they're exhibited. Though many youths experiment with drugs or alcohol, most do not become teenage alcoholics like Jeffrey Dahmer or Israel Keyes. Though many teens experiment sexually, most do not become prostitutes or sleep with siblings like Aileen Wuornos, nor combine their sexual activities with assault like Charles Manson.

Due to the stress of their dark thoughts, future killers may develop symptoms such as facial tics and stuttering (which worsen with stress), as well as depression and ulcers. They may also self-medicate with drugs and alcohol. Potential killers exhibit the traits of teen angst more powerfully and darkly than most. Moreover, such activities are not passing phases, but intensify over time.

Special mention needs to be made of devil worship/Satanism, since so many serial killers claim to have an interest in, or have been influenced by, a belief in the power of evil.

In his early 20s, Israel Keyes was having difficulty coming to terms with his dark personality, especially since his entire family was deeply religious. He recognized he was different from others. He knew he had unspeakable urges.

Initially, he tried to "blame it on Satan and religious things," but ultimately accepted that his dark personality was simply who he was (Goeden, 2013).

> "Remember: suicide kicks and fasting is awesome. Bones rule! Death Rules! Death Kicks. I love death. Kill the fucking world."
>
> Future killer Karla Homolka's inscription in classmate Lyn Getney's high school yearbook (Williams, 2004).

As a high school student, Karla Homolka (future wife of killer Paul Bernardo) wore dark clothes and black eye makeup, read books about the occult and Satanism, conducted séances, and regularly joked about suicide. Yet disarmingly, Homolka was also was a fan of cute cartoon characters and stuffed animals. She would later use teddy bear stationary to write letters from prison.

Serial killers do not become murderers because they are Satanists. Rather, they tend to become Satanists because they recognize that their innermost thoughts are not aligned with the concept of goodness. They notice that their sexual interest in physical pain and gore is abnormal, and against the basic tenets of mainstream religions. Realizing that their interests more closely align with the world of Satanism and the occult, they turn toward these beliefs.

> "I felt so hopelessly evil and perverted that I actually derived a sort of pleasure from watching that tape."
>
> Jeffrey Dahmer, explaining why he always watched the horror movie, *The Exorcist III*, before committing murder (*Inside Edition*, Feb 8, 1993).

Walking into the room of a teenager obsessed with dark imagery and death is a memorable experience. Whereas most teenagers decorate with images of their favorite actors, friends, or music bands, the rooms of disturbed youth look appropriately disturbed: dark imagery of horror movies, death metal posters, mangled toys, and crude phrases scrawled on the walls. Some decorate with actual pictures of death and destruction.

Most teenagers who are interested in horror films and the occult are completely normal. In fact, horror films are *marketed* to teenagers since they're so popular within that demographic. The vast majority of teens will pass through their occult phase without incident, the same way they passed through their former interests in dinosaurs or unicorns. For others, the occult becomes a consuming passion and a lifestyle that demands additional investigation.

"Scarification, blood, piercings, criminal psychology, hatchets, fire, ducktape, moonlight, wicca, safety pins, thunderstorms, wooky noises, kinkyshit."

Items listed as "likes" on the vampirefreaks.com profile of 12-year-old Jasmine Richardson, who killed her entire family with the help of her boyfriend the same year.

PART 2:
ADULT CHARACTERISTICS

SEXUALITY

A good way to illustrate serial killer sexuality is through the life of "Hillside Strangler" Angelo Buono. Buono's former roommate, Artie Ford, noted that Buono had peculiar habits: he would play with himself while watching high school students across the street using binoculars; he bragged about "banging" his stepdaughter and about letting his sons do the same; he had sex with his son Peter; and, he dated an assortment of fatherless or confused teenage girls, stating that he liked young girls' pussies because they "smell real good" (O'Brien, 1985). When he got one of his young admirers pregnant, he arranged an abortion for her. At 40, Buono was invited to dinner at the home of his 15-year-old girlfriend, who lived with her parents. The girl's parents (previously unaware of Buono's age) objected strongly to their relationship, but Buono continued to see her anyway. Buono sometimes slept with his son's girlfriends, or watched pornographic movies with them. Later, Buono's sexual preferences would include killing women by strangulation, forced methane gas inhalation, and lethal injection.

As dangerous narcissists, serial killers have no moral objections to anything sexual and they don't care what "society" thinks about it. If an adult serial killer wants to date a 12-year-old and finds one willing to date, he will do so. If he wants to have a series of extramarital affairs, he will. If he wants to strangle a girl or boy for his own pleasure, he'll do that also. It's all about freedom. And unlike Angelo Buono, most killers keep their sexual habits a well-guarded secret.

> "Sex to me is like going to the toilet. Whether it's a girl or not, it doesn't matter. I don't play that girl-guy shit. I'm not hung up in that game."
>
> Charles Manson, 2013, age 79 (Hedegaard, 2013).

Serial killers are sometimes described as bi-sexual (ex. Karla Homolka, John Wayne Gacy) or homosexual (Jeffrey Dahmer) but the more accurate description is "anysexual." To serial killers, human beings are merely objects.

Since serial killers view their victims as collections of parts, they are able to do things to them that regular people consider revolting. For a sexually motivated serial killer, a slippery vagina and a slippery intestine may hold similarly stimulating properties. It doesn't matter if a partner is male or female, is a friend or relative, is alive, or is even in one piece.

In an example of dehumanization, killer Dennis Rader strangled to death a petite and beautiful woman, Nancy Fox, then ignored her body while he masturbated into her nightgown. Jeffrey Dahmer found stimulation from wearing his victim's glistening intestines around his neck as fashion accessories. Lacking functional human understanding or emotions, killers use the objects of their desire with a cold efficiency that is difficult for normal people to understand.

In their "'regular" relationships with lovers and spouses, serial killers tend to either be nearly sexless, or to engage in behaviors that mimic their extracurricular activities, minus the killing.

Karla Homolka was Paul Bernardo's girlfriend and later accomplice in murder. At first, they had a vigorous and satisfying sex life. After they began killing, however, Bernardo was no longer satisfied with the relatively safe sadomasochistic play they had previously enjoyed, and became violent even with Homolka. She left Bernardo after he beat her in the back of the head so violently that her eyes nearly popped out of their sockets, leaving her with "panda bear" bruising around her eyes.

"Hillside Strangler" Angelo Buono, during his marriage to his second wife, Mary Catherine Castillo, regularly called her a "cunt," an expression he also used for his mother. He would tie up Castillo, rape her violently, and tell her that she was a "dead piece of ass." Buono also beat her in front of the children, arguably *preferring* to do so. Castillo filed for divorce, citing extreme cruelty. After their divorce Buono continued his ways unabated, forcing his girlfriends to have rough fellatio with him by shoving himself down their throats and holding their heads until they passed out from asphyxiation.

When police interviewed "Green River Killer" Gary Ridgway's second wife, they asked her about their sex life. She indicated that Ridgway not only wanted sex constantly (up to 3 times per day), but that he preferred to have sex outdoors. She took the police on a tour of all the places that she and Ridgway had engaged in outdoor sex, showing them various fields, forests and side-roads. The officers immediately recognized that she was (unwittingly) taking them on a tour of sites where Ridgway had dumped the bodies of prostitutes he had murdered.

For sex crime investigators, a history of fraud, petty theft, nuisance crimes, solicitation, indecent exposure and spousal abuse are all signs that the subject is a potential match.

RAPE-MURDER ESCALATION

"Mobile serial predators like Bernardo are exceptionally dangerous. They are hard to recognize and detect and they create a unique challenge to law enforcement. They change their presenting criminal patterns like chameleons and they escalate, sometimes from stalking to rape, sometimes from children to elderly victims to young adults, sometimes from rape to murder."

From the Bernardo Investigation Review (Campbell, 1996). When Paul Bernardo was still unidentified and known as the "Scarborough rapist," FBI agent Gregg McCrary predicted that his behavior would escalate to murder.

By the time 26-year-old Paul Bernardo met teenage girlfriend and accomplice Karla Homolka, he had already moved from voyeurism to serial rape. The pair soon graduated to murder, their first victim being Karla's younger sister, Tammy Lyn. With knowledge of sedatives gained from her work at a veterinary clinic, Homolka helped her boyfriend drug Tammy Lyn until she became unconscious. Together they had their way with her, videotaping the experience so they could relive the moment. Unexpectedly, the unconscious Tammy Lyn choked on her own vomit and died.

For Bernardo and Homolka, a compliant or even unconscious victim was now insufficient to fulfill their sadistic sexual desires. Bernardo forced their next victim, 14-year-old Leslie Mahaffy, into his car at knifepoint with Homolka's help.

At home, Bernardo and Homolka raped and tortured the girl for 24 hours before they finally strangled her to death with an electrical cord. They cut her body into parts with a circular saw, encased the parts in concrete, and dumped them into a nearby lake.

Similar to the ongoing debate as to whether the use of soft drugs like alcohol and marijuana are gateways to the use of harder drugs like cocaine, there is a debate in law enforcement as to whether "nuisance" crimes like voyeurism and personal property theft (ex. underwear theft) lead to more serious sexual crimes. Though not every criminal's behavior escalates, there is sufficient evidence to believe that nuisance crimes should be taken very seriously.

After their capture, rapists-turned-murderers have often revealed how their violent progression unfolds. Sometimes, as in the case of Karla Homolka and Paul Bernardo, the transition from rape to murder is semi-accidental, the result of a longstanding fantasy gone wrong. In other cases, the transition is planned and intentional.

In December of 1985, future "Railway Killer" John Duffy was attending magistrate's court, appearing on a charge of assault against his wife. Duffy was shocked to see a woman he had earlier raped, Allison Day, sitting in the same courtroom. She even made eye contact with him. Although she didn't recognize Duffy, he immediately decided he would kill his next victim. As a precaution, he also corrected his mistake, killing Allison Day just twenty-seven days after his court appearance (Canter, 1993).

For California's "Hillside Strangler," Angelo Buono, the escalation from rape to murder occurred mentally, prior to committing a sexual crime. While still in the fantasy stages, Buono studied the life of then-infamous rapist Caryl Chessman, known as the "Red Light Bandit." Chessman robbed and sexually molested his female victims while posing as a police officer, with a red light attached to his car. Chessman's *modus operandi* gave Buono the idea of impersonating a police officer to obtain his victims, which he later used successfully. However, Chessman did not kill his victims, a choice that eventually led to his identification and conviction. Buono decided that when the time came, he would kill his victims (O'Brien, 1985).

"His career began with simple break-ins, but he gave off indicators of his pathology when he stole women's undergarments and urinated and defecated in the homes he'd entered. Eventually, his fantasies of violent sexual crime escalated to murder."

Robert Keppel, regarding "Lipstick murderer" William Heirens (Keppel, 1997).

The fear of being identified and arrested, along with the desire for power and the fulfillment of sadistic fantasies, leads rapists to become murderers. Rapists need to control their victims completely, demonstrating their mastery and power over them. A victim who fights back, screaming and kicking, reminds a rapist that he is *not* in control, and not getting the compliance that he "deserves." If a rapist has a seduction fantasy, a screaming and fighting victim certainly destroys that fantasy. Even after the act is completed, a living victim will always remain a threat, both physically and as a person who can identify her assailant. As put succinctly by Hicks & Sales (2006), "killing the victim reinforces the offender's power by eliminating the threat the victim poses."

WHY SERIAL KILLERS KILL:
DRIVE REDUCTION, HOMEOSTATIS &
PHYSIOLOGICAL AROUSAL

> "I thought about this a lot. Was this a thing to get the thrill of killing and the sex was just an extra bonus, or was the sex the main thing and the killing was just a necessity afterwards? I'm not sure. It could be either one of these. It could be a variation of both of these."
>
> "Hillside Strangler" Kenneth Bianchi (O'Brien, 1985).

A principal explanation for human motivation is drive-reduction theory, which proposes that a bodily need (ex. sex, hunger, thirst) creates a tension or imbalance in the body that must be corrected. Once this imbalance is corrected, the body goes back to a homeostatic or balanced state. For instance, a lack of energy in the body creates the drive to eat, known as hunger, which is fulfilled by consuming food. In this case, drive-reduction theory is intuitive. Other examples, however, are less straightforward.

Non-smokers, when they smoke cigarettes, feel a rush of excitement and mental alertness caused by chemicals such as nicotine. However, something interesting occurs as a person becomes a regular smoker. Each time a person smokes a cigarette, the body recognizes that it is in a state of imbalance and works toward correcting it. Each time a person inhales nicotine, the body combats this overload of chemicals by limiting its own production of similar chemicals. Over time, the body produces less and less of its own neurochemicals, so that a smoker *must* have a cigarette for the body to reach a balanced state: this is addiction.

The childhoods of serial killers are fraught with stressful situations. If a child is subjected to frequent stress, the body combats this stress by reducing – or possibly damaging – its ability to produce cortisol and other stress-related neurochemicals, so that when stressful situations occur the body is closer to a balanced level and therefore more equipped to handle them. The lack of caring seen in rapists and killers could be a survival response from living in emotionally charged environments.

Killer Dennis Rader called it "factor X." David Gore called it his "URGES" (always in capitals). Ted Bundy referred to it as a buildup of "destructive energy." Jeffrey Dahmer referred to it as "compulsions." Whatever the name, serial killers describe a pressure that builds within them until the point where they can't ignore it. Only killing releases the intolerable buildup of frustration and tension, bringing them temporarily back into balance.

"These [evil] thoughts are very powerful, very destructive, and they do not leave. They're not the kind of thoughts you can just shake your head and they're gone. They do not leave."

Jeffrey Dahmer (Masters, 1993)

INTIMATE DEATH & FIREARMS

Erotic asphyxia, or sexual strangulation, occurs when the carotid arteries to the brain are partially blocked, causing a feeling of lightheadedness and giddiness that enhances sexual pleasure. Carried too far, erotic asphyxia results in loss of consciousness and death. Sexual self-strangulation (autoerotic asphyxia) has caused the deaths of notables including INXS singer Michael Hutchence, Reverend Gary Aldridge, and actor David Carradine.

Serial killers believe that, by strangling their victims, they are giving them sexual pleasure immediately prior to causing their deaths. From a serial killer's point of view, death by strangulation is powerful and personal.

Stabbing and bludgeoning are two other preferred killing methods for serial killers. Like strangulation, both require close personal contact with a victim. Killers talk about "pushing the knife" into a body in a way that clearly has sexual connotations. For sexual killers the entire experience – the knife penetrating the flesh, the warm sticky blood – is a sexual act described in sexual terms. Killers who prefer bludgeoning, like Ted Bundy, tend to be necrophiles whose goal is to render their victims safely unconscious or dead as quickly as possible, foregoing the pre-mortem stimulation that occurs with strangulation or stabbing.

Necrophilia, or interest in the dead, is often a fetish for killers even before they commit murder. Jeffrey Dahmer, for instance, found pleasure in collecting road-kill for "morbid curiosity" while still a child (FBI, 1992). In other cases, however, necrophilia develops as a consequence of personal killing methods like strangulation.

When a victim is strangled, she may expire before the killer achieves sexual satisfaction. If this happens, the killer may continue to have sexual intercourse with the victim while the body is still warm, marking the beginnings of necrophilia. Kenneth Bianchi did exactly this with victim Jane King: he brought her in and out of consciousness several times by strangulation, accidentally killed her before he achieved orgasm, then "finished" after she was dead.

> "Why did I use my bare hands? To feel life slipping away and then release your grip and bring them back. Ah, that is a feeling...that is a feeling. So powerful, so real."
>
> Arthur Shawcross (Earley, 2012)

Some law enforcement circles maintain the erroneous belief that serial killers don't use firearms. Although serial killers *prefer* intimate methods of killing, one should never assume that a murder wasn't perpetrated by a serial killer just because a firearm was used. A firearm is the most efficient (and least risky) way to kill a person. As "practical" people, serial killers employ firearms in approximately 42% of all murders (Aamodt, 2015). Strangulation, stabbing and firearms – or some combination of the three – together account for approximately 93% of all serial killer murders. Bludgeoning makes up most of the remainder (Ibid). Female serial killers are an exception: possibly due to their slighter strength and stature, they prefer to kill by poisoning (Scott, 2005).

SERIAL KILLER INTELLIGENCE

"Mr. Bundy is undoubtedly one of the top undergraduate students in our department. Indeed, I would place him in the top 1% of undergraduate students with whom I have interacted... He is exceedingly bright, personable, highly motivated, and conscientious."

Professor Ronald E. Smith, in his recommendation letter for Ted Bundy, later found to be a serial killer (Rule, 2013). Smith's letter also noted that Bundy "has become intensely interested in studying psychological variables which influence jury decisions."

Serial killers are known for their genius IQs. They evade police for long periods of time (sometimes forever), hide their true personalities from friends and neighbors, and are successful predators. Surely these qualities require genius?

The Intelligence Quotient score, or IQ score, is the most popular measurement of academic intelligence in human beings. The mean IQ score is 100, with a range of 85-115 considered normal.

Though genetics probably determines the IQ range a person may possess, environment determines the rest. A child who is raised in a nurturing, interactive environment might end up with an adult IQ of 110, while the same child raised in an abusive environment might end up with an IQ of only 90. Since criminal's homes tend not to be nurturing ones, their IQ scores tend to be limited to the lower end of their potential.

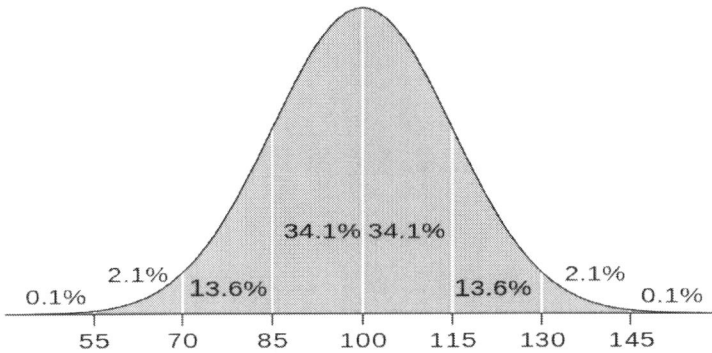

Normalized distribution of IQ with mean of 100 and standard
deviation 15
Dmcq (2013), from Wikimedia Commons

Ted Bundy and Richard Ramirez, among other serial killers,
were known for their intelligence despite any learning
disabilities (such as dyslexia) they may have had. Yet, there
are also numerous examples of serial killers whose IQs are
average or below average.

Some of the most prolific serial killers, including
Robert Pickton, Gary Ridgway, and Fred West were known
amongst co-workers and friends as somewhat dim-witted, and
after their arrests no one has suggested otherwise. Dennis
Rader evaded capture for 31 years, yet his brother-in-law
described him as an "ordinary, inarticulate doofus" (Wenzl,
2015).

> "I failed grade 2 twice and I failed grade 3. I never
> stopped for lunch. I never stopped for recess. Because
> I kept studying 'cause I'm getting behind again."
>
> Serial killer Robert Pickton, from his audio diary
> (Nielsen, 2011).

The impression that serial killers have genius IQs probably stems from several factors. First, serial killers in the movies are often presented as masterminds, since these make more compelling characters. Secondly, law enforcement officers likely find it comforting to believe that the killers they spend months or years pursuing are geniuses. Thirdly, normal people *want* to believe that serial killers are as different as possible from themselves. When I asked a group of friends to guess the average IQ of a serial killer, answers ranged from 120 to 125 – well above average. Finally, serial killers themselves believe they are superior to others, and intelligence is a component of superiority.

> "Intelligence: very high, but of course I haven't had an official 'test' in years and I am rating myself so make of that what you will. I do have an extreme intolerance for 'stupid' and a general contempt for much of the human race."
>
> Comment by a reader of a psychopathy discussion website, May 26, 2011.

The serial killer database (Aamodt, 2015) has recorded a wide range of IQs for killers, from 54 to 186. Some serial killers do have genius IQs, and no doubt every killer who reads this page will think this is true of himself. Nonetheless, the bland reality is that the average IQ of a serial killer is 94.8 (Ibid), which is completely normal, slightly below the mean, and about the same as the general prison population.

> "I wasn't really good at math, or anything like that. But I did graduate with a C+ average. It's not bad."
>
> Serial killer Cody Legebokoff, in an interview with Cpl. Paul Dadwal (Nov. 29, 2010).

PART 3:
THE NARCISSISTIC CONNECTION

YOU CAN'T SPOT A NARCISSIST (RIGHT AWAY)

"... I realize that I'm different. Because I just don't care what I do to you, as long as it gets done and I'm content. It's like a natural instinct that you know, I have to hide this from people, or else I won't survive."

Anonymous comment on a sociopathy discussion website, Sept 19th, 2010.

The word "narcissist" is derived from the ancient Greek myth of *Narcissus*, a brave hunter renowned for his physical beauty. As might be expected, this brave hunter with a great body was popular with the ladies. However, Narcissus treated his admirers badly, heartlessly rejecting their declarations of love and devotion. The goddess of revenge, *Nemesis*, decided to punish Narcissus by luring him to a pool of water where he gazed down upon his own reflection, instantly falling in love. Narcissus died without ever finding a love as great as the love he had for himself.

Normal people go through stages – typically as young children and again as teenagers – when they believe they are more capable, more worldly, and more right than they really are. It's in these stages that we're actually unsure of ourselves, working to establish an identity. In time, we become comfortable knowing we aren't perfect.

Some people, however, never get past their insecure, self-obsessed stage. They rationalize their weaknesses and selfish actions instead of working to improve them. They don't care if they hurt or manipulate others. The world revolves around them and their needs. This is narcissism.

Most narcissists are neither serial killers nor criminals. However, all serial killers are narcissists. Indeed, there is no act more selfish than taking away someone's life due to anger or indifference, or for a few moments of perverted sexual pleasure.

It's important for law enforcement officers to recognize the habits and philosophies of narcissists, because these same characteristics are found in serial killers.

"He was absolutely...considerate and romantic and all of the things anybody could hope for - dream for. He bought me beautiful things. We went fun places. He was happiest when we were together."

Barbara Pedren, wife of serial killer Richard Kuklinsky, describing their first days together (*The Iceman Tapes: Conversations with a Killer*, HBO, 1992).

Most people think they can "spot" a narcissist, and so will never be fooled by one. Most people are wrong. A narcissist will flirt with you, laugh at your jokes, and be refreshingly modest. A love letter from a narcissist will be the most beautiful and adoring one you will ever receive. They will tell you about the deep personal connections they feel with their friends. A narcissist will tell you how their personal beliefs enrich their soul. A narcissist will be a great conversationalist, funny, and attractive. Most men and women who fall in love with a narcissist believe they have truly hit the jackpot.

In time, you'll start noticing things. A narcissist's reactions to emotional situations aren't quite normal. If anyone gives them well-meaning suggestions or advice, they'll complain bitterly, even if the advice is good. They'll do inconsiderate things without realizing it, almost as if they are trying to be hurtful. They will talk their way out of difficult situations, giving *possible* – though not necessarily *believable* – explanations for what they've said or done. In an argument they'll change the context of the conversation, giving inconvenient words new meanings. Your intuition will tell you that something is wrong, but since you care about them you will ignore it.

Much later, you'll learn that the beautiful love letter you received was also sent to other people. You'll discover that the friend with whom they feel a deep personal connection is someone they hardly know. You'll realize you know almost nothing about them, even though they know so much about you. You will catch them in lies. Even so, you'll refuse to believe that someone who cares about you could be using you.

The devil does not show up with horns and a spiked tail. The devil shows up as the most perfect person you've ever met: kind, polite, sharing your views and believing in you. For narcissists, life is a game and you are a pawn.

DEFINITION OF NARCISSISM

> "He undoubtedly had a number of personality disorders - probably narcissistic, borderline, and sociopathic."
>
> Anne Rule, regarding her friend, serial killer Ted Bundy (Rule, 2008).

People with cold or limited emotions are often confused as to what they are. In their attempts to understand themselves, they read descriptions of narcissists, malignant narcissists, psychopaths, sociopaths, and those with Asperger's syndrome or borderline personality traits, and find things in common with all of them.

Few people outside the field of psychology realize how controversial the categorization of mental disorders can be. The official classification of personality disorders is messy, confused and political – with strong overlap between the various disorders.

Although narcissistic qualities have been recognized since the beginning of time, the modern use of the term "narcissist" was introduced to the world by Dr. Sigmund Freud at a meeting of the Vienna Psycho-Analytical Society on Nov. 10, 1909. Yet, Narcissistic Personality Disorder (NPD) wasn't widely recognized as a disorder until 1980 with its inclusion in the Diagnostic and Statistical Manual of mental disorders, Version III (the DSM-III). Then, many of the criteria describing the disorder were changed for the subsequent edition. When the DSM-V was published in 2013, the disorder was dropped from the official list altogether (*The New York Times* magazine joked that narcissists would be upset to find out they'd been ignored). However, due to demand from psychologists who found the diagnosis useful, Narcissistic Personality Disorder was officially reinstated, and remains so at the time of printing.

The important thing to remember is that while the names and definitions of disorders may change, the behaviors of the people they're attempting to describe do not. Narcissists lie, manipulate, and have grandiose beliefs, whether one calls them sociopaths, psychopaths, narcissists or something else.

In everyday use, the word "narcissistic" is a substitute for the word "selfish." We all know people who are selfish: who spend too much time in front of the mirror, act rudely, show off, and are cool and indifferent to the needs of others. Although these people have narcissistic qualities, most of them reveal their true (selfish) personalities to the people around them. The most dangerous narcissists are the ones who disguise their true selves.

The term narcissist, as used in this book, refers to a person who holds two sets of psychological phenomenon. First, the narcissist has most of the traits of Narcissistic Personality Disorder:

- **A lack of empathy; a grandiose sense of self-importance**
- **Fantasies of unlimited success, power, beauty and love**
- **A belief that he or she is special and unique, and can only be truly understood by high-status people**
- **The need for excessive and constant admiration**
- **A sense of entitlement; exploitive behavior (i.e. "using people")**

- **Envy of others or a belief that others are envious of him or her**
- **Arrogant behaviors and attitudes.**

Secondly, their narcissistic qualities must be anti-social enough to require the construction of a socially acceptable personality known as the *projected self.* Such people are unable to reveal their true personalities and thoughts, because their true personalities and thoughts are too unacceptable to be revealed. The construction of a projected self – a false personality to show to the world – is what makes a narcissist so convincing, and so dangerous.

Some readers may be surprised that the term used in this book is narcissism, as opposed to the terms more commonly associated with serial killers – psychopathy and sociopathy.

Antisocial personality disorder, or "sociopathy," is a term used by the American Psychological Association. The word "psychopathy" is an older term for the same illness that was re-popularized by Dr. Robert Hare, who has spent years promoting the term for use with his best selling diagnostic tools and lectures. To some researchers, psychopathy is supposed be caused primarily by genetics, while sociopathy is supposed to be caused primarily by upbringing; but as yet, no one has come up with a method to differentiate between the two, if such a distinction even exists. Psychologists continually try to invent differences between the sociopath and psychopath depending on which term they favor, and everyone seems to have their own pet theories. Nonetheless, the two terms are just different words to describe the same people and the same behaviors.

Serial killers display traits from many of the official personality disorders, but no single disorder is a perfect match. To eliminate the confusion (and avoid the politics), I've created a term specifically for this book – *dangerous narcissism* – that encompasses their major traits.

"A person suffering from psychopathic personality, whose behavior is aggressively antisocial."

The definition of "Sociopath" from the American English Dictionary (2015). Antisocial personality disorder is a term for sociopathy. Just one example of the incredible confusion that exists with personality disorders.

Serial Killers and Personality Disorder Overlap

	Serial Killers	Antisocial Personality Disorder (Sociopathy)	Narcissistic Personality Disorder (Narcissism)	Borderline Personality Disorder (BPD)	Psychopathy
Failure to conform to social norms / laws	yes	x			x
Childhood violence or severe mistreatment of others	yes	x			x
Criminal behavior	yes	x			x
Deceitfulness / lying / conning	yes	x			x
Use of false personalities / aliases	yes	x		x	x
Impulsivity / decision-making based on gratification	yes	x		x	x
Sensation seeking / high relationship intensity	yes	x	x	x	x
Sense of superiority / self-importance / grandiosity	yes	x	x		x
Promiscuous sexual behavior	yes	x	x	x	x
Irritability/ hostility/ anger	yes	x		x	x
Exploitative / parasitic / manipulative behavior	yes	x	x		x
Lack of remorse / regret / empathy	yes	x	x		x
Hypersensitivity / unstable emotional responses	yes	x		x	x
Glibness/ superficial charm/ seductiveness	yes	x	x		x
Desire for admiration	yes		x		
Fear of abandonment	yes			x	
Fear of losing control	yes			x	
Dissociation, out-of-body experiences	yes			x	
Prone to depression / negativity	yes			x	

x indicates that the trait is *explicitly* listed in the official criteria. Traits that are not explicitly listed may still be present.

DEVELOPMENT OF NARCISSISM – CHILDHOOD

We know that dysfunctional parenting, parental drug and alcohol abuse and similar factors have a negative effect on a child's development. Yet, we also know that many children grow up in such environments and become neither narcissistic nor antisocial. The relationship between a dysfunctional childhood and narcissism is unclear. However, if you ask narcissists directly, they seem to know which factors held special significance for their world.

As an only child raised during China's strict one-child policy era, one woman told me that she could "do no wrong" as a child. Her parents sometimes scolded her and threatened to punish her, but they never followed through with it. Most of the time, she ignored them and did as she pleased. When it appeared that her parents would actually make good on their threats, she needed only to cry or tell them that she loved them and their threats would melt away. In other words, her parents inadvertently *taught* her how to be manipulative. As she grew older, she realized that although she doesn't enjoy the same level of immunity outside the home, lying and manipulation still go a long way toward getting what she desires.

Another woman, when asked about the source of her narcissism, immediately told me about her relationship with her mother. When the woman was a girl, her mother had often compared her to other children: "How come so-and-so gets better grades than you? Why is your eyesight so bad compared to other children? You're costing us a lot of money." She remembers that her mother always seemed bitter. As an adult, the woman's relationship with her mother is decidedly complicated: "My mother," she says, "represents everything I despise."

Everyone wants to be held in high esteem. When someone of authority (teacher, mother, priest etc.) repeatedly tells a person that they are unworthy or unwanted, the most convenient psychological defense is to dismiss that authority figure or the entire group they represent: "I don't care what they say. They can't tell me what to do. I'm better than they are!"

One way to escape a stressful world is through fantasy: the fantasy of self-perfection, and the disregard of people who would seek to harm you.

"I had a lot of bad things happen to me when I was a very young and I learned to block it out over the years, but in reality, all that did was make me hollow inside. In some ways, that's a good thing, for when you no longer have a conscience or the ability to care or have emotions and feelings, then no one can hurt you anymore."

Serial killer Joseph Metheny (Earley, 2012).

THE PROJECTED SELF –
CONSTRUCTING A PERFECT
PERSONALITY

Narcissists have a dilemma: *How can I do whatever I please, when this may involve things that are unacceptable or illegal?* A narcissist can't tell his wife that he is going to cheat on her as often as possible, taking advantage of every opportunity that comes his way. He can't tell his neighbors that he wants to have sex with their underage daughters. Narcissists know that if people find out who they really are, they will be ostracized.

A narcissist's best defense is to have such a lovely, charming disposition that his true personality will never be suspected; and, if suspected, that he'll always be given the benefit of the doubt. As a bonus, this great personality will receive the constant praise and admiration that the narcissist craves.

"When the police came out here [looking for evidence] in March 2000, I told them that they had to be after another John Robinson. It couldn't be mine. He was so personable and friendly. He was very energetic and knowledgeable. A happy person. He would always talk to me and he was always smiling."

Loretta Mattingly, owner of a storage locker business in Raymore, Missouri (Douglas, 2003). The man she was naively defending was using her lockers to store the personal belongings and body parts of his victims.

Knowing full well they take advantage of others, narcissists take great care to appear to be good members of society and "avoid detection." They may recycle their garbage, attend church, dress fashionably, give to charity, attend school events, and anything else they feel will be looked upon admirably. In some communities a perfect persona may involve driving a sports car and wearing a suit; in others, wearing a cowboy hat and driving a pickup truck. Yet, all the while, their true belief is that society's rules are worthless, that no one can tell them what to do, and that their own needs always come first – even if that involves hurting others.

Narcissists don't believe they are part of society, but separate and distinct from it. Society is the machine that tries to control them. Society is "them."

"Don't say that I am a wretch! But if I am, it's your fault - yes, *you* as the representative of society!"

Joseph "French Ripper" Vacher to Judge De Coston, 1898 (Starr, 2010).

"Yes, I will be a candidate for rehabilitation, but not for what I have done, but what the system has done to me."

Serial killer Ted Bundy to Judge Hanson, 1976 (Kloepfer, 1981).

Although a projected self is initially constructed to hide inadequacies, over time it becomes stronger as the person utilizing it starts accepting that their projected self is real. Narcissists develop a grandiose sense of self-worth in part because their personalities are composed of characteristics they believe people will admire. Who wouldn't feel grandiose after constructing a "perfect" personality?

In stronger cases, a person may view their projected self as an actual character, dissociated from their true self. A narcissistic friend of mine serves as a good example of this out-of-body existence. Whenever she visited my apartment in the evening, she would insist upon having the blinds open on the kitchen window. She'd sit at the table, talking with me while looking out the window. At first, I thought she was doing this to see the beautiful city view. Eventually, I figured out what she was doing. She was using her reflection in the glass to watch herself have a conversation with me. She was watching the movement of her mouth, adjusting her posture, adjusting her hair and her accessories. She was using our conversations to improve and develop her projected self.

Serial killers are often described as living "compartmentalized" lives, or as having split personalities. A killer may be described as being a murderer on one hand but a loving father and church member in another. Compartmentalization helps one understand how a serial killer lives, but it's not entirely accurate. Being a good father or church member, as in the example above, is not a separate personality or lifestyle, but part of an overall strategy of existence as a successful user of people.

"I did not care about anything or anybody. If I could inflict pain, I inflicted it to the max. I wanted others to hurt the way I hurt. But the thing was that although I had all the rage, it wasn't like I just went off. I internalized it and vented it out very cool and methodically. For instance, if you were to meet me back then you would think I was the nicest guy cause that's what I wanted people to see. That way, they would not put their guard up and I could strike."

Serial killer David Gore (Earley, 2012).

TRAITS OF THE NARCISSIST

SUPERIORITY & RESISTANCE TO CHANGE

> "Deep inside I know that I am a selfish, self-centred, immoral person. I fear that people (except those whom I feel safe to expose the true me) will find out; but also I know so far these dark traits have served my self-interest."
>
> Email to author, Feb 26, 2008.

An insurmountable problem in the treatment of narcissists is that they have no desire to change. A narcissistic male may use his cunning to move up quickly in his career, looking down upon those who follow the rules. A narcissistic female may enjoy dozens of affairs during the course of her marriage, looking down upon the foolish women who limit themselves to only their husbands. Narcissists believe that their cold personality traits give them an edge over their "weak and emotional" counterparts.

Since they feel they're able to fake emotions when required, narcissists believe there is no downside to their condition – this despite a lifetime of lost friendships, abandoned relationships, and depression-inducing disconnection from others. It's rather like asking a vampire if he wants to be cured, when the vampire believes that the person asking is his prey. When dealing with people, even family members and friends, narcissists are always looking for weaknesses that can be exploited. They sincerely believe that, since they are incapable of change, others should accept being lied to and used.

Since they view themselves as "the next step in evolution" and intra-species predators, some use derogatory language that reflects their image of regular people as their prey: "the genetically-inferior," "the mediocre," "average people," "normals," and "empaths." They may refer to their victims as being "cute," like pets.

Narcissists are deeply confused as to how normal people function. They believe that people must be bags filled with emotions, bursting at the seams, ready to explode. They can't imagine what it's like to feel emotions spontaneously, without having to "decide" which emotions to express at any given moment. In their view, regular people must be too emotional to be effective in risky situations where immediate action is required – this despite the fact that police officers, special forces troops, firefighters etc. prove them wrong every day. Normal people in such jobs develop a professional steadiness in panic situations, yet retain the ability to empathize with others. One nurse described it as "distance with empathy." Just like with narcissists, this calmness in the face of stress takes its physical toll in the form of stress disorders, alcoholism, ulcers, and other health issues.

> "Now people call that [sense of superiority] Narcissism, as if *knowing* I'm a better person somehow needs a pathology connected to it. If I am superior with using logic and knowing how people tick, and have an objective view on most things, does that make me mental? NO! That makes me clear headed. That makes me superior. That makes the best person at what I do. I'm not mentally challenged, I was born with a superior genetic predisposition, and any naysayer's opinion otherwise means fuck all to me."
>
> Comment by a reader of a website discussing psychopathy, April 2011.

If a narcissist actually does seek treatment, one can pinpoint the moment of recovery: the patient will begin denying statements that were said just moments earlier, changing the context and meanings of statements to suit them most favorably, and trying to charm the counselor they hired. In other words, their "improvement" is the full reinstatement of narcissistic qualities.

FEAR OF ABANDONMENT & ISLANDS OF STABILITY

"It [killing them] was the only way I knew of to keep them there and keep them with me. It gave me a sense of total control and increased the thrill I guess...there was no hatred involved at all."

Jeffrey Dahmer, explaining why he killed his victims (FBI, Aug 13 1992). Dahmer tried to create zombies out of his victims by drilling holes into their heads and injecting them with acid. When that plan failed, he kept trophies and body parts instead. Like all narcissists, Dahmer feared abandonment.

Since narcissists are exploitative and put their own needs far above the needs of others, their fear of abandonment is a valid one. Narcissists don't seem to realize that their selfish actions have a cumulative negative effect on their relationships. If a narcissist is caught cheating on his spouse but is forgiven, he may not realize that the relationship was weakened by the action, and that it will never entirely be forgotten. Narcissists often find that their longest, closest relationships suddenly fail due to accumulated grievances.

To avoid being alone, and to maximize the amount of affection and compliments (narcissistic supply) they receive, narcissists employ a *backburner approach* to relationships, sometimes referred to as "cycling." In this approach, the narcissist cultivates several relationships simultaneously, so the loss of a single one will not be felt too severely. The relationship that is currently providing the greatest amount of narcissistic supply will be given the most attention, while others will be delegated to the backburner. A narcissist will also cultivate a number of opposite-sex friendships to draw on and develop, if necessary.

All of a narcissist's relationships will move forward or backward in importance over time, but they'll never *end* in the traditional sense. A relationship that supposedly ended in turmoil years earlier may be reinstated with the first sign that the person is willing to provide the narcissist with additional affection. Like drug addicts, narcissists don't hold grudges against their suppliers.

"...it was possible to believe that his domestic stability and the love of his family had anchored him in such a way that he could be relatively normal at home and a monster in other places. It was possible to believe that he could go out and do horrendous things knowing that he could always return to those who perceived him as a basically good and productive man."

Former FBI agent John Douglas, regarding killer John Robinson (Douglas & Singular, 2003)

Although most of their relationships are imbalanced (in favor of the narcissist) and fleeting, a narcissist will also maintain one or two *islands of stability* for support. These are people who stick by the narcissist despite knowing of their lies, manipulations, and infidelities. If the narcissist loses one of these resources (for instance by death or divorce) it is devastating. Despite their contempt for human emotions, narcissists react to the loss of an *island of stability* with rage, self-defeat, and breakdown. Losing an "island" is a common reason for a narcissist to seek psychological counseling.

ADMIRATION & EMOTION MANAGEMENT

"I've often found that in carrying on an act of normalcy, I can get carried away with trying to blend in and become a new person altogether. Although I've no problem with that aspect of the ruse, it can often leave an isatiable feeling of emptiness in knowing that you're not really connecting with the people that surround you but essentially taking in what they say, processing it like a computer, and just using logic and experience to match up and emulate appropriate responses."

Anonymous comment on a sociopathy discussion website (2015).

Narcissists appear to be complete human beings but are actually hollow shells. Always putting on a false front, they never really connect with the people they're interacting with. Without a constant source of narcissistic supply, they quickly deflate into melancholy and depression.

Narcissists learn that the best way to *receive* compliments and affection is to *give* compliments and affection, often to extreme levels. Reading the basic correspondence of a narcissist is like reading a romance novel. Even with friends, narcissists gush with over-the-top emotionality: "We can spend quality time together." "I am honored to be your friend." "Our time together was too short." Opposite-sex friends often interpret this level of affection as meaning that the narcissist is in love: another reason why they have numerous affairs.

Though narcissists fear the vulnerability of being in love, they crave the excitement and admiration that romantic relationships involve. Therefore, while in relationships they attempt to keep their partners at an emotional disadvantage.

If a narcissist finds that his level of attachment is becoming too high (or if he is becoming bored), he will reduce his dependency by seeking affairs, acting distant, spending less time with his partner, taking holidays alone and other acts until he feels the relationship is once again balanced in his favor. Narcissists actively manage their emotional attachment levels.

FRAUD

Dr. Kenneth Bianchi held a Master of Science degree from Columbia University. Though he was certified as a sex therapist, he worked primarily as a weight-reduction counselor in North Hollywood, charging lower fees than his colleagues. His tower office proudly displayed his Honorary Doctorate from the National Psychiatric Association of America, and his Certificate of Achievement Award from a hospital in New York. Despite his credentials, Dr. Bianchi had only had a few clients. This is probably a good thing, since "Dr. Bianchi" did not have a Master of Science degree, was not trained as a counselor, was not a doctor, and had never worked at a hospital. His entire identity as a professional was fabricated with fake diplomas and rote memorization of terms. He was also a serial killer known as the "Hillside Strangler."

Since narcissists construct false personalities, the next logical step is to construct entire identities. These identities are invariably of people more likeable and successful that the individuals creating them.

When discovered and confronted about a false identity or character traits, narcissists will rationalize their deception by saying that they're merely displaying the qualities that they *will* have in the near future: "I *will* become an art dealer." "I *will* work with children's charities." "I *will* become a movie talent scout—some day." They pretend to be people they have not yet become, and likely never will be. Pretending to literally "be someone" is a cover for immoral and/or criminal activities, allows them to manipulate others more successfully, and provides them with the admiration they so desperately crave. For the average person and the law, such deception is simply known as fraud.

SHAME & REGRET

> "Yes, because I got caught."
>
> Killer Dennis Rader, in a prison questionnaire, asking whether he felt shame or embarrassment (Wenzel, 2015).

Narcissists do not regret their misdeeds. If discovered, they feel only anger and embarrassment. Moreover, they believe that the person who discovered their secrets is responsible for their trouble, completely failing to recognize that if they had not committed misdeeds there would have been nothing to discover.

Narcissists have difficulty understanding logical connections between their acts and the consequences. For instance, a serial killer may rape and murder for years without incident. Then one day, the killer is arrested, tells the truth (ex.

a confession) and is punished. From the killer's perspective, the punishment occurred as a result of telling the truth, rather than as a result of his crimes. After being discovered, narcissists often express the belief that they are "being punished for telling the truth," which they find deeply unfair.

As dangerous narcissists, serial killers fully understand that their antisocial activities are morally wrong and/or illegal. They nevertheless feel justified in committing them, and have difficulty understanding their accountability.

"We would commiserate with guys who would bemoan the fact that their lives were ruined, tears streaming down their faces - ruined, in their minds, not because of what they did but because they were caught. That taught us a lot, too."

Former FBI agent John Douglas, regarding insights from his time researching serial killers (Douglas and Olshaker, 1999).

PSYCHIATRISTS & MANIPULATION

> "...even the newest and most naive prisoner soon learns the particular jargon and poses that will get him a good report from his shrink."
>
> Former Manson Family member Charles "Tex" Watson (Watson and Hoekstra, 1978).

Law enforcement agents hold a famous disdain for psychiatrists and other mental health professionals, since these professionals so often fall prey to the manipulations of dangerous criminals. To be fair, psychiatrists typically work with patients who have a genuine desire to improve their mental state and have no reason to deceive them. Narcissists are unique patients because they intend to deceive and are resistant to change. Incarcerated narcissists simply tell psychiatrists whatever they want to hear; that is, they "fake it to make it." Psychiatrists have been known to support killer's phony insanity defenses, and give clean bills of health to individuals with high probabilities of recidivism.

In a famous case, David "Son of Sam" Berkowitz claimed he was ordered to kill people by demons that gave him instructions through a talking dog. Psychiatrist Daniel Schwartz interviewed Berkowitz, believed his story and argued for an insanity defense. To Dr. Schwartz's surprise, Berkowitz entered a guilty plea in court, ignoring all of their previous discussions. The psychiatrist later received a letter from Berkowitz explaining why: "I'm a faker. I made the 'demon' story all up from the beginning." Berkowitz added that since he had no idea what his real motivations were, he "decided that the demons, as a cause, would be appropriate."

It's impossible for narcissists to feel genuine regret. Narcissists may perform regret, but immediately work on methods to be more successful with their future deceptions. If anything, psychotherapy and counseling (discussing feelings with others) only serve as empathy-faking-improvement courses.

"A model inmate...a non-violent person...does not present a threat to society...is a devoted family man...has taught his children a strong value system."

From the *1990 Report of Clinical and Medical Evaluation* of John R. Robinson (McClintick, 2013). After his release from prison Robinson immediately resumed killing.

GREGARIOUS YET ALONE

"Being around people is difficult, because I have to wear a mask all the time. It's actually very tiring. I guess that's because I couldn't care less about what people think."

Narcissist in conversation with author, Dec. 4th, 2013.

Although they seem outgoing, most narcissists spend a great deal of time alone. Alone, they don't have to face the scrutiny of others. They don't have to engage in the challenging task of wearing false personalities and of guarding every move.

Narcissists don't share their personal thoughts often, because many of their thoughts are un-sharable. Moreover, they get confused as to which thoughts are sharable and which are not. Occasionally, they make comments they *believe* are normal and acceptable, but which others find shocking. One woman, for example, told me that she's never played a game with her daughter: no peek-a-boo, no teatime or dollhouses, no hide-and-seek, ever. Her daughter was 11 years old. When I asked her why, she looked at me as though it were a stupid question. "Because I don't want to," she said. "I'm not interested in those games." Seeing my surprise, she asked me why she should be expected to play games she has no interest in. "Because," I explained, "you wouldn't be doing it for yourself, you'd be doing it to see the joy that your daughter gets." The concept that a person would do anything strictly for the benefit of someone else was clearly a confusing idea. Having heard my explanation, she'll no doubt incorporate this concept into her projected self, since she knows it will garner a positive reaction from others. The next time someone asks her if she played games with her daughter, she'll likely say, "yes."

"Inside I was screaming, but I couldn't do or say anything!"

A woman describing the frustration she felt when her co-workers decided they should eat lunch at a famous New York sandwich shop, when she wanted to eat noodles instead. For narcissists, even the most trivial compromise is an excruciating experience.
(Conversation with author, December 2013).

As part of their masks, narcissists have to pretend to care about the opinions of others. They have to pretend to care about birthdays and anniversaries (other than their own). Worst of all, they are forced to *compromise* to maintain normal human relationships. Narcissists despise compromise. By definition, compromise means that no one gets precisely what they want. Narcissists want to get their own way, all of the time, no matter how mundane the issue. Since group decisions inevitably involve compromise, narcissists find time in groups highly frustrating.

When the desire for human companionship hits, narcissists prefer spending time with a few select people (often lovers or family members) with whom they can reveal a greater percentage of their true personalities without serious repercussions. They will engage in conversations about art, business, culture, etc. willingly, since they find these topics interesting and safe. They'll discuss the injustices of government, or the faults of society. But, always paranoid about being "discovered," they'll avoid revealing anything they think could be used against them.

Experience tells narcissists that while sharing *some* of their thoughts will bring others closer, sharing *most* of their thoughts will push others away.

"None of us knew he had a brother. He had talents none of us even knew about, like his music. Neither of them [Russell or his wife] really opened up about everyday things, and looking at things in hindsight, every answer - everything - was a guarded response."

George White, describing his neighbor, killer Russell Williams (Appleby, 2011).

GIVING AND RECEIVING ADVICE

For a narcissist, receiving unsolicited advice from well-meaning parents or friends can be humiliating. Since narcissists don't fully understand the concepts of love and affection, they think anyone who gives advice must be doing so to display their superiority. One woman, for example, told me she was angry because a man had given her advice after her father passed away. Although the man's own father had passed away a few years earlier and he had successfully made it through the grieving process, she didn't think this entitled him to give her advice. Narcissists don't consider that people give advice because they care, since that doesn't make sense to them.

> "He always thought other people were pretending to be nice to other people, and then he realized at some point only he was pretending."
>
> Federal Prosecutor Frank Russo, regarding killer Israel Keyes (DeMarban, 2012).

Although narcissists despise getting unsolicited advice or being told what to do, they nonetheless liberally dispense advice to others. In fact, it's hard to *stop* them from stating their strong opinions, even in completely unsuitable or inappropriate situations. In a polite cocktail party situation, for instance, a narcissist may debate his points vigorously; then, when others back off due to etiquette, believe he won the debate due to his superior moral position.

Narcissists generally avoid giving advice to individuals in 1st person ("I think that you should...") but instead share stories or philosophical beliefs. By stating their opinions as philosophies, they can give advice to others while assuring themselves they aren't. Killer Charles Manson famously took advice giving to the next level: his followers lovingly referred to his never-ending speeches as "sermons."

If a narcissist is put in the uncomfortable position of receiving advice that he thinks is valuable, he has a predicament. If he takes the advice, this means he is changing based on the suggestions of another person – a loss of independence and superiority that is unacceptable. He must therefore convince himself that he's doing it because it's his own desire: "I'm not doing it because you told me I should. I'm doing it because it's my choice."

LYING & MANIPULATION

> "You can convince anybody of anything if you just push it on them all the time. They may not believe 100 percent, but they will still draw opinions from it, especially if they have no other information to draw their opinions from."
>
> Charles Manson (Bugliosi & Gentry, 1974).

Although lying is psychologically uncomfortable – even for the narcissist – it's a necessity. Narcissists believe they lie because there's no other option ("*I couldn't tell you the truth!*"). They don't consider avoiding the unacceptable behaviors they lie about, since this would limit their freedom, and any limitations on personal freedom are unthinkable. Of course, lying is also an expression of subconscious anger. When a person looks into the eyes of a loved one and sincerely says, "I'm sorry, I'll never do that again," without any intention of keeping their promise, it's an aggressive act.

Narcissists spend extraordinary amounts of time perfecting the art of lying. They carefully study body language and facial expressions. They try to "read" people in public places. Some spend hours in front of the mirror, practicing facial expressions. Like the comedian who practices punch lines or the diplomat who practices important speeches, narcissists ceaselessly work on their manipulative abilities.

Narcissists are excellent manipulators not only because of the time and effort they put into this craft, but also because they use strategies others don't take advantage of, even though they could. For instance, the average person isn't likely to say, "I love you so much!" to someone they don't love: if they did, they'd feel uncomfortable. Our conscience prevents us from using and deceiving others, especially those closest to us. Narcissists are successful manipulators in part because they lack the ability to limit their deceptiveness – and can't understand why anyone would even want to.

Though narcissists have a well-earned reputation as successful manipulators, they nonetheless grossly overestimate their abilities – sometimes referred to as "magical thinking." *Magical thinking* is when narcissists imagine themselves having godlike powers of control. Imagine two friends deciding where to go for dinner. A friend asks the narcissist, "Would you like to go for sushi tonight?" The narcissist responds, "How about Italian food instead?" If the friend agrees, the narcissist considers this a victory because he has successfully manipulated his friend into doing what he wants. If a narcissist throws seeds on the ground and pigeons come flocking, this is successful manipulation of the pigeons. If a dog comes running toward a narcissist with its tail wagging, this is proof of his magnetic leadership abilities. Narcissists see every moment as an opportunity to manipulate, and see evidence of their superiority everywhere.

SHALLOW RELATIONSHIPS

"I just can't seem to connect with people. Sure I can hold doors open for women and smile and be charming, but when it comes to basic relationships I just don't have it. There is something wrong with me."

Serial killer Ted Bundy (Kloepfer, 1981).

There is perhaps no greater "opportunity" to use and betray someone than while in an intimate personal relationship. Narcissists put great effort into training their lover(s) to accept their selfish behaviors. A narcissistic man may try to convince his wife that asking, "Where are you going?" is an intrusion into his privacy. He may try to convince his wife that if he fails to show up to meet her, no explanation or apology is required since people in love shouldn't have to follow business protocol. Though narcissists know they're being manipulative, they feel entitled to their demands and react angrily if they're not met. They train their partners unceasingly, revisiting arguments over and over until they are accepted.

After years of persuasion a narcissist's partner may accept when he leaves the house without explanation, spends time on his computer in a locked room, spends quality time with opposite-sex "friends," and take vacations and extended business trips without consideration or input. Narcissists don't want free-spirited, independent partners. They want trained doormats.

"I never questioned him. And you just knew, *don't do it, don't ask.* If he got up a 2 o'clock in the morning, or during dinner, and put on his shoes and walked out the door, you said, 'Bye!' You didn't say, 'Where are you going?' or 'Why are you going?' And it was just understood that that's the way it was."

Barbara Kuklinsky, wife of serial killer Richard Kuklinsky (HBO, 2002).

SADISTIC TRUTH

When confronted with undeniable evidence of their misdeeds and forced to tell the truth, narcissists may respond with *sadistic truth.* Sadistic truth is when the truth is used as a weapon to make the listener as uncomfortable as possible.

Narcissists are capable of feeling moral guilt, even though they stifle it effectively. When forced to tell the truth (often only after being presented with overwhelming evidence) they will use the opportunity to purge themselves of any accumulated moral guilt, giving details and descriptions far beyond what's necessary or expected. A woman who is found cheating on her husband, for instance, will tell him not only the basics of the affair, but will add details such as how often they met, how much she enjoyed being with him, and what a nice guy he was. Narcissists use the truth to hurt: *If you're forcing me to expose myself, I'm going to make this as painful for you as possible. I'm going to defeat you.*

When people close to narcissists discover how they've been betrayed, they often respond emotionally, crying and breaking down. Narcissists see this as further proof of their superiority. Narcissists hope that if their confessions are distressing enough, their partners will be so traumatized that they won't pry into personal matters in the future.

Once purged of their moral guilt – and having established their superior position – a narcissist will promise to "never do it again." Narcissists understand betrayal, but feel it's always justified.

THINGS THAT NARCISSIST'S
LOVERS COMMONLY SAY

My lover/husband/wife:

- is very kind
- is a good person
- does things for me
- we have a great sex life / non-existent sex life (one of the two)
- is charming
- keeps to himself/herself / is a loner / is private
- is a spiritual person / religious / believes in God
- lies often
- changes the context of stories / changes the meanings of words / invents new endings to past arguments
- doesn't tell me everything / is secretive
- is hard to get close to
- can be arrogant
- lacks conscience / lacks a sense of morality
- don't like being told what to do / gets upset easily
- is calm when alone / has difficulty with crowds
- can get depressed
- is not someone I know as well as I should

FEELINGS AND EMOTIONS

> "Nothing haunts me. No murders haunt me. Nothing.
> I don't think about it... If I think about it, it would wind
> up hurting me. So I don't think about it."
>
> Mafia hitman Richard Kuklinsky (HBO, 2002).

INTERPRETING EMOTIONS: THE TWO-FACTOR THEORY

First proposed by pioneering psychologist William James in 1890, the two-factor theory of emotion states that human beings understand emotions through two factors: physiological reactions (such as a fast heartbeat or clammy skin), and the mental interpretation of those reactions. That is, the brain searches for an emotional label for the physiological reactions being felt, based on the situation and environment.

In a famous study about emotions conducted in Canada in 1974 (Dutton & Aron), an attractive female researcher stopped random men and asked them to fill out a questionnaire. For half of the questionnaires, she situated herself in the middle of a long suspension bridge that swayed precariously over a 230-foot drop to a canyon below. For the other half of the surveys, she situated herself on a sturdy wooden bridge over the same canyon. After each survey was finished, she offered the men a slip of paper with her phone number on it in case they wanted to talk further. The result was that men who she questioned on the suspension bridge were four times more likely to call her, and their surveys contained more sexually suggestive responses. Why?

The hypothesis is that the men on the seemingly dangerous suspension bridge felt fear while the men on the sturdy bridge didn't, and that the men on the suspension bridge interpreted their fear as attraction to the female giving the questionnaire: *my heart is beating fast and my palms are sweaty. This woman must be really attractive.*

Everyone *interprets* emotions, and sometimes we're wrong. A woman whose lover tells her that they're breaking up may scream at him, telling him that he's terrible and that she wanted to break up anyway. She may be *angry*. But it isn't really anger she's feeling, it's shock, and she'll feel the sadness that results from the breakup soon afterward.

Narcissists have difficulty seeing or interpreting emotions in themselves as well as others. They confuse self-loathing with boredom, anger with excitement, contempt with determination. They deny feeling emotions, even as their faces are contorted into situationally-appropriate expressions.

Narcissists genuinely feel and express emotions more often than they realize or acknowledge. Partially this is because even when they're experiencing emotions they're unable to recognize they are. And, because when they do recognize they're experiencing emotions, they often act to suppress them.

HYPEREMOTIONALITY & SUPPRESSION

"Even psychopaths have emotions if you dig deep enough. But then again, maybe they don't."

Richard "Night Stalker" Ramirez, in an interview with *Inside Edition* (Feb 8 1993).

Narcissists are often thought of as emotionless and incapable of feeling, but in fact they exist on two polar extremes of behavior. On one hand, narcissists can be hyperemotional. Raised in stressful or neglectful environments, they become hypersensitive, always "walking on eggshells." At the same time, however, coping mechanisms allow them to shut these emotions down.

Narcissists put conscious effort toward nullifying their hyperemotionality, but this goal is never entirely reached. Narcissists continue to be hyperemotional for things that affect them personally, and the attempt to suppress these emotions only heightens them. They are, however, highly successful in suppressing emotions for things that don't affect them directly. When faced with all but the most stressful situations they can shut their emotions down as if turning off a light switch.

In one memorable event, a narcissistic woman I know received bad news and immediately curled into a ball, sobbing uncontrollably. Then she started talking herself out of it: "There's no point in crying about this. It's already done. There's nothing I can do about it." The tears dried up, and she began discussing plans for lunch. The total elapsed time from bursting into tears to complete recovery was probably less than three minutes. The following day, she denied it had occurred at all: "What do you mean, I was crying and upset? I have no idea what you're talking about."

Killer "Karla [Homolka] had a strange, uncanny capacity to distance herself from the immediate moment - to step outside of herself, as it were, and objectively regard any predicament in which she found herself from a distance" (Williams, 2003).

Since narcissists can be overwhelmed by emotions, friends and neighbors might be mislead into believing they are sensitive and thoughtful. Narcissists may cry while looking at the beauty of autumn leaves, or reading poetry. They may grieve bitterly at the loss of family members, or personal divorces. They may become deeply upset if small things don't go as planned. Anything experienced at a personal, individual level is felt deeply. Beyond this individual experience, however, narcissists have difficulty experiencing the majority of emotions to their full extent.

"Gary" (not real name), a successful salesperson, nicely illustrates the narcissist's seemingly incompatible hyper- and hypo-emotionality. When Gary picked up his 11-year-old daughter from school one day, she informed him that a classmate had fondled her during a game of hide-and-seek. The boy had lifted up the girl's shirt and touched her. She was deeply upset by this betrayal of friendship, and wept as she told the story to her father.

"I knew that I should be supportive," Gary told me, "but I couldn't be. Her crying was really annoying! She should either shut up and get over it, or do something about it. Crying doesn't solve anything." Gary thought about why the young boy might have chosen *his* daughter to molest. "What if," he asked himself with horror, "it's because she looked weak?"

Even with his own daughter, Gary was entirely unable to empathize. About a year after this incident, Gary's father passed away. He spent months in depression, crying at even the smallest reminder of his father.

> "I wake up every day knowing I'm not psychopathic. I care about people. I cried during 9/11. I cried during Columbine."
>
> Serial rapist and killer Paul Bernardo, in an interview at Kingston Penitentiary (Makin, 2006).

Although narcissists are unable to experience the full range of human emotions, they can nonetheless be quite good at performing them. To fit in, they rely heavily on cues and mimicry. Simple emotional situations are relatively easy to understand. If a person is crying, they know the person is sad. If a person is laughing, they know the person is happy. In more complex cases, narcissists use mental checklists to understand what a person is feeling: *This person is touching his chin, looking up and giggling to himself. He must be thinking of a good memory.*

Because they rely on cues and don't actually experience the emotions, narcissists often misread complex emotional situations, and their interactions with people may be wildly off base. Disgust, for instance, may be confused with anger or even flirtation. Fear may be confused with boredom or mental disability (a "blank look"). Strangely, narcissists are excellent at recognizing sarcasm, perhaps because it involves acting.

If you ask a narcissist about his feelings, his definition of love etc., he has a problem: how can he explain these feelings when he doesn't feel them? To explain emotions, narcissists rely heavily on quotations from books, movies and poetry rather than their own words. To the receiver this may seem wonderful and romantic, but the purpose is purely practical.

> "What occurs mechanically when one does not align one's selfish interests correctly with those of another. A self-reflecting/mental autopsy procedure, initiated after an outcome isn't what was wanted."
>
> "An object that can communicate with you, telling you about its characteristics, and revealing its weaknesses."
>
> Woman in conversation with the author (Dec 22, 2014), describing her definition of the words "disappointment," and "person."

Since they're unable to feel most emotions at normal levels, narcissists crave intense emotionality. Some want intense, passionate love affairs and intense sex, including sadomasochism. Others want constant stimulation in the way of travel, business challenges and life changes. Dangerous narcissists may engage in fighting, theft, murder, and other forms of suffering.

In a vain attempt to "feel," serial killers go to bizarre extremes. Richard Kuklinsky, a former mafia hitman, sometimes tied up his victims and set hungry rats upon them, recording the events with a video camera. He would later watch the videos at home. "It used to make me nervous for some reason," Kuklinsky said, "but I did it because it gave me a feeling of some kind, and I was trying to find out what it was that was giving me some type of feeling" (HBO, 2002). Kuklinsky's attempts to feel genuine human emotions were never successful. To this day, he doesn't understand *why* he felt uncomfortable watching the videos.

Symptoms of Borderline Personality Disorder are reached when narcissists lose emotional touch with the world to the extent that they begin to doubt their own existence. People who reach this level may self-mutilate or engage in extreme sadomasochistic behaviors to remind themselves they are real and alive.

"I had started having sex, but sex didn't feel enough and emotions didn't feel enough. And in a moment of wanting to find something honest, I grabbed a knife and cut him, he cut me back and we had this exchange of something. Then covered in blood and my heart racing, thinking there was danger, I felt more honest than whatever the sex was supposed to be. So I went through a period that when I felt trapped I would cut myself. I have a lot of scars."

Actress Angelina Jolie, describing her sex life at age 14 (Express Newspapers, 2010). The following year, she enrolled in a funeral director's course. Jolie was diagnosed with Borderline Personality Disorder. As an adult, Jolie volunteered as a United Nations representative for sexual violence and wartime rape. Some people work within their psychological framework more successfully than others.

EMOTIONAL FRUSTRATION

"I didn't have what you'd call feelings back then: happiness, sadness, fear, or even any warning system. I'd see other people reacting to various situations, letting their emotions show, and it was like watching aliens from another planet. I thought *they* were the crazy ones."

John Miank, partner of serial killer Robert C. Browne (Hess & Seay, 2008).

Since narcissists don't fully understand human emotions, it's not surprising that they can find them frustrating. Narcissists find complex emotional situations unbearable when adequate cues are not available, or when a person is not behaving according to expectations.

When a serial killer murders on a whim, it's often due to emotional frustration. It occurs when the killer is put in a situation where their inability to feel (and their pride in their callousness) causes them to look with disgust upon the highly emotional person before him.

Dangerous narcissists describe their anger as like being the passenger of a speeding vehicle that doesn't have a steering wheel or brakes: they feel their frustration level building, they know that the results will be disastrous, but without emotional understanding they are powerless to intervene. On the surface their anger cannot be seen – until the very moment of lashing out.

"She kept begging and pleading and pleading and begging, and I got sick of listening to it. So I stabbed her."

Susan Atkins, follower of Charles Manson, regarding the murder of Sharon Tate (UPI, Feb 1971). Atkins stabbed her pregnant victim sixteen times.

"I had this pistol in my hand. He just was annoying me to no end with his babbling. And he was going on and on and on. And I fired."

Richard Kuklinsky, describing shooting a man who owed him $1600 (HBO, 1991).

Serial Killer Emotions

Reduced Ability to Feel or Understand	Ability to Feel or Understand
Empathy	Shame
Remorse	Humiliation
Regret	Rage / Anger
Compassion	Sorrow / Depression
Pity	Arrogance / Superiority
Love	Lust / Obsessive Love
Fear	Exhilaration
Disappointment	Rejection
Disgust (Revulsion)	Disgust (Contempt)
Embarrassment	Envy
	Fondness
	Contentment
	Satisfaction
	Paranoia
	Confusion
	Ridiculousness / Absurdity

Serial killers are often described as "emotionless," which is not correct. Rather, the range of emotions they are able to feel is limited. In some cases, the range of emotions they *allow* themselves to feel is limited. Shame and Humiliation are not felt when serial killers break the rules of society, but when it's implied they are inferior.

PART 4:
NARCISSISTIC PHILOSOPHY & WORLDVIEW

"With his dysfunctional background and psychological makeup, Coleman seemed to have no conscience, no concern for the rights, feelings, or pain of others. Somebody like this would perceive that nothing was given to him and nobody cared, and also he was entitled to take whatever he wanted and didn't have to care what anybody thought."

John Douglas, FBI, regarding murderer-rapist Alton Coleman (Douglas & Olshaker, 1999).

Glaucon, the philosopher Plato's older brother and a contemporary of Socrates, had one of the most cynical views of human nature and justice in the ancient world. Glaucon argued that people are naturally selfish, and that it's a benefit to be able to harm others as long as one doesn't suffer any negative consequences as a result. However, it's terrible to be the person harmed, especially if there is no recourse. Overall, Glaucon concluded that although there is advantage to be gained in harming others, there is an even greater disadvantage in being harmed.

In response to the realization that the ability to harm others is not as beneficial as freedom from harm, humans have developed systems of morals and laws, roughly stating that any person causing harm to another will be punished by a harmful action imposed on them by society. For instance, a man who commits murder will either be killed or have his freedom taken from him. A man who commits adultery may be divorced by his spouse, sued for support, and lose custody of his children. Many employers now have codes of ethics so that even if an employee does not do something *illegal*, he may still be fired for doing something *unethical*. In a system of justice, the personal benefits of harming others are lost. Justice is a social compromise that attempts to achieve maximum benefit for all.

Of course, narcissists despise compromise and rules. Their goal is to take advantage of Glaucon's ideal: to do whatever they like, without suffering the consequences. They don't necessarily *intend* to hurt others, but if they harm others in the course of getting what they want, then so be it.

For the record, in contrast to Glaucon, Socrates argued that being a just and moral person will, in the long run, make one happier and more successful than someone who merely obeys the rules.

In the United States, the M'Naghten rule states that a person is legally insane if unaware that society views their actions as wrong. Interestingly, this means that while narcissists are not actually insane, they pretend they are, and try to convince themselves they are. By pretending that the rules of society don't apply to them, narcissists *act* insane without actually *being* insane.

> "Why should we call someone insane simply because he or she chooses not to conform to our standards of civilized behavior?"
>
> Judge Ronald M. George (O'Brien, 1985).

Throughout childhood, narcissists hear they must follow the rules and be good people. They experience pressure to express themselves (ex. cry at funerals), and to display emotions they don't have. They quickly learn that in order to be accepted, they must fake emotions and lie. A major source of resentment for narcissists is that "society" made them become liars and fakers, but then punishes them for being liars and fakers. Seeing others overreact to emotional events only solidifies their belief that being detached and calculating is a superior way of being.

Narcissists are correct in believing that decisions made solely using emotions are bad ones. When a person sells their stocks in the panic of a market crash, or gives money to a drug addict who insists he will use it for food, this is the folly of using only emotions as a decision-making tool. On the other hand, narcissists are wrong in believing that decisions made using without emotions are superior. When a dictator kills millions of people from the ethnic minority that wishes to depose him, or when a corporation President decides to increase profits by canceling the railway safety repairs, this is the folly of emotionless decision-making. The best decisions involve a combination of emotions and logic.

At some point, narcissists all seem to reach the same conclusion: human beings make rules; human beings are flawed; therefore rules are flawed and don't need to be followed. Although this "revelation" is common amongst narcissists, they nonetheless believe that it is groundbreaking, that they are among a select group of people who know it, and that this makes them special.

At its simplest, narcissistic philosophy says that because society's rules change and are in hindsight often immoral, individuals should develop their own standards of morality, and decide for themselves which rules they would like to follow and which they can ignore. At least on a conscious level, narcissists believe they have high standards of morality. In reality, when people who are incapable of empathy embrace moral relativism, the results are often disastrous.

Although the argument that moral values change is a valid one, good morality is not the narcissist's real concern anyway. The narcissist's true purpose is to come up with excuses that allow them to do whatever they please in the name of "freedom." *Society's rules change and therefore I don't need to follow them* is merely one of dozens of potential justifications for self-serving behavior.

As their moral philosophy becomes established, some narcissists seek evidence of famous, important people who seem to be like them. Heroes of narcissists include Abraham Lincoln, Margaret Thatcher, Mahatma Gandhi, Napoleon Bonaparte and Adolf Hitler. At first, these persons may seem to have little in common. A closer look reveals that they share an important characteristic: they ignored the opinions of society and did what *they* thought was the right thing to do. They bent the rules, mislead others, or lied to obtain their objectives. Obviously, in some cases this worked out better than others.

Of course, most narcissists aren't trying to free slaves or champion equal rights. Their objectives more often include mundane acts like committing adultery, committing fraud, and in more violent cases rape and murder. That they use their feelings of moral superiority to justify these acts only exacerbates the problem.

"I don't take well to other people's laws. I don't like to be told what to do. I don't like being programmed. I don't like being pushed around. I feel that people spend their whole lives like that, and they're not really free."

Killer John Hughes (KMBC Kansas City, aired March 2nd, 2010). He apparently did not recognize the irony that he was giving his interview from prison.

90

THE INFLUENCE OF BOOKS
AND THE MEDIA

Just prior to his execution, serial killer Ted Bundy gave a famous interview with Christian evangelical leader James Dobson (1989), blaming pornography for his murders. In the interview, he said that finding discarded pornography and "true crime" books in the trash fueled his fantasies, leading to his murderous life.

People often say that they were influenced by a book or movie, as if it changed their way of thinking. In fact, people's beliefs are shaped mostly by their personal experiences and the beliefs of those closest to them. Books, movies, and other media usually serve as reinforcement for what a person already believes.

Normal human beings actively seek reinforcement for their existing beliefs to reduce the anxiety caused by internal conflicts. Famous books such as *Mein Kampf* by Adolf Hitler, *The Communist Manifesto* by Karl Marx, and *The Origin of Species* by Charles Darwin were popular and influential not because of their originality, but because the ideas they contained were already gaining acceptance at the time the books were published. These books gave the public the confidence they needed to state their beliefs openly.

Like everyone else, narcissists seek reinforcement for their existing beliefs. Ayn Rand books, such as *The Virtue of Selfishness* and *Atlas Shrugged* are commonly adored. Other popular books include *Crime and Punishment* by Dostoevsky, *Sperm Wars* by Robin Baker and *The Selfish Gene* by Richard Dawkins – the latter of which states, "I shall argue that a predominant quality to be expected in a successful gene is ruthless selfishness" (1976). Any book that presents a cold, biological case for individual superiority, or that says that we can determine our own morality without the input of society will find favor with a narcissistic audience. Upon reading this type of material, narcissists experience a profound sense of belonging: *I've always known I was different, but now I know I'm superior. I don't have to feel wrong about being selfish! I should embrace it.*

Serial killers, unsurprisingly, enjoy reading about other serial killers. "Nightstalker" Richard Ramirez, for example, was said to be a walking encyclopedia of serial killer history. Serial killers also enjoy true crime and medical books, sadomasochistic pornography, and violent or gory movies.

Dahmer: ...as far as pornography? No, no that doesn't cause anybody to do this.
FBI: No, but you were so engrossed in pornography...
Dahmer: It just fueled the fantasies. But I don't think it [avoiding pornography] would have stopped it, from happening.

Jeffrey Dahmer (FBI, 1992).

Ted Bundy was correct in saying that the combination of pornography and violence can be dangerous. Sex is an incredibly powerful reinforcer. Many countries, including the United States, Canada and England have restrictions on material that combines sex and violence. Yet, even Ted Bundy noted that within him lies the final responsibility: "I'm not blaming pornography. I'm not saying it caused me to go out and do certain things. I take full responsibility for all the things that I've done."

SERIAL KILLER'S BOOKSHELVES

Jeffrey Dahmer: *Tales from the Crypt, Grey's Anatomy*
Karla Homolka: *Brainchild, The Bell Jar, The Compendium of Pharmaceuticals and Specialties 22nd Edition*
Paul Bernardo: *American Psycho*
Kenneth Bianchi: *Dracula, Psychoanalysis & Behavior Therapy, Handbook of Criminal Psychology*
Michael Swango: *Crime and Punishment, A Poor Man's James Bond, The Modern Witch's Spell Book*
Rose West: *The Prince of Tides, The Shell Seeker*
Joel Rifkin: *The Search for the Green River Killer*
Gary Ridgway: *Rules of Prey*

Serial killers tend to read practical information related to anatomy or killing, fiction related to evil or killing, and philosophy regarding questions of morality, ethics, and self-determination.

CASE STUDY: CHARLES MANSON & NARCISSISTIC PHILOSOPHY

In 1969, people were mesmerized by an odd little man: a philosopher, poet, and hippie cult leader with a long criminal history known as Charles Manson. Manson was arrested after members of his "Family" hippie group killed a number of people in gruesome fashion, including Sharon Tate, an actress and the wife of famous movie director Roman Polanski. Though Manson denied being their leader, his member's dedication to him was obvious. They seemed to have identical personalities, and to parrot everything Manson said or did. People wondered how this strange man could have such an incredible influence.

> "Not just Watson but nearly every other member of the Family had dropped out [of society] before meeting Manson. Nearly all of them had within them a deep seated hostility toward society and everything it stood for which pre-existed their meeting Manson."
>
> (Bugliosi & Gentry, 1974)

In fact, Manson's influence is easy to explain, since he used methods similar to every other successful cult leader. First, Manson ensured that new Family members came from broken homes and troubled pasts. Confused teens, in particular, were attracted to his "no one can tell you what to do," utopian ideas. Secondly, like any good cult leader, Manson told his members whatever they wanted to hear. As Manson himself put it, he was merely "a mirror" or "reflection" of them. Thirdly, he systematically erased whatever morals and societal views remained in his members. He told them they had been "programmed" by their parents and society, and needed to abandon their existing beliefs to experience true freedom. He encouraged the women to have lesbian and group sex. He had them take LSD regularly. He told Family members that their egos were "dead" and their old selves didn't matter anymore. He reminded them that they belonged together, and warned them that "anyone who broke the bond would have his throat cut" (Watson & Hoekstra, 1978). He moved the group from the city to a ranch, physically isolating them from outside influences.

> "He [Manson] realized that once my own life meant nothing, no one else's life would mean anything either."
>
> Former Family member Tex Watson (Watson & Hoekstra, 1978)

Since everyone likes to believe they're doing good even when they're not, Manson constructed a philosophy that supported his members in their transition to his anti-social ideas. When he sent them dumpster diving for food, he told them they were taking advantage of society's wasteful ways. When he had them steal gasoline and cars, he told them he was forcing others to share. He gave them a sense of closeness and purpose by telling them they were a unique group who alone knew that the war for the end of the world was coming. To prepare for war, he had them shoot pistols, ride dune buggies in the desert, and break & enter homes without detection. He called his predicted world racial war "Helter Skelter," after the popular Beatle's song.

On the following pages is a synopsis of Ayn Rand's novel, *Atlas Shrugged* (a popular title with narcissists) published in 1957, compared to the *Helter Skelter* story that Charles Manson repeatedly shared with his Family cult members over a decade later. Both *Atlas Shrugged* and *Helter Skelter* involve common working fantasies of narcissists: for a cataclysmic event to free them from society's rules and regulations; to feel included by finding a group of like-minded people; and, to be fully recognized as superior by the society whose opinions they claim not to care about.

In these fantasies, the narcissist doesn't have to change to be accepted by society. The entire world changes to accept the narcissist.

SYNOPSIS OF AYN RAND'S NOVEL, *ATLAS SHRUGGED*

There exists a group of heroes in the world - elite artists, professionals and industrialists. These are people who don't care what society thinks, and who ignore existing rules and morals. They are people of action who invent and create for the purpose of making money. They live their lives however they want. In their selfish efforts to make money, they invariably do good things for society.

Since they appear selfish, they are shunned. The world is trying to change them and make them conform to society's rules. To fight back, the heroes leave their jobs and families without notice to meet in a secret valley hidden in the mountains. There they live in peace, inventing and creating. Without them the world quickly falls apart: patients die on operating tables; bridges collapse; transportation stops.

After the world self-destructs, society will recognize how important the heroes are, and invite them back. The heroes will emerge from their hidden valley to rule the world.

SYNOPSIS OF CHARLES MANSON'S
HELTER SKELTER

There exists a group of heroes in the world - the Manson Family members. They don't care what society thinks, and ignore existing rules and morals. They don't care about money. In their efforts to live in peace, they work in harmony with nature and each other.

Since they appear rebellious and unlawful, they are shunned. The world is trying to change them and make them conform to society's rules. During a worldwide rebellion known as "Helter Skelter" (where black people will fight white people for control of the earth), the Family members will retreat to an as-yet-undiscovered bottomless pit of paradise, hidden deep in the earth under Death Valley, USA. Outside, the "Helter Skelter" battle will rage, causing the destruction of the world as we know it.

Black people will be victorious in the battle, but once they control the world will be unable to successfully govern it due to their lack of creativity. The Family members will then emerge from the bottomless pit to rule the world.

The "narcissist's utopia" fantasy is grounded on the belief that although narcissists are parasitic and manipulative with normal people, they wouldn't be this way with each other. Their backstabbing and lies would cease, and they would work together to achieve personal perfection. Unfortunately for narcissists, there is no evidence to suggest any of this would be the case.

> "As much as I'd like to meet other sociopaths, I don't think we'd make a good society. Far from it. I'm parasitic by nature, living off others rather than being productive save from fits of obsessive interest that usually end with incomplete projects. In a society of sociopaths, however, I would do horribly. Besides the fact that a parasitic existence would be hard in a society where everyone expected that from everyone else, the continual dominance games and petty crime would quickly become exhausting."
>
> Comment by a reader of a sociopathy discussion website (2009, February 05)

SUMMARY OF NARCISSISTIC PHILOSOPHY

- I can decide for myself what is right or wrong: society can't tell me what to do.
- No one has the right to judge me.
- No one has the right to tell me how to live.
- No one has the right to give me unsolicited advice.
- I am free to state my strong opinions about anyone and anything. This is not the same as judging.
- Truth is subjective. Your truth may not be the same as mine.
- Emotions are a weakness that should be carefully controlled; they have little or no value.
- I am superior to most people.
- My friends are superior people who are worthy of being my friends.
- People use words like "love" and "friendship" too easily. I have few friends because I select only the best.
- If my friends give me unsolicited advice, judge me, or develop flaws they should be abandoned.
- I don't care about what other people think.
- If I care about what a person thinks but then they judge me, I no longer care about what they think.
- My survival depends upon society not discovering my true personality.

PART 5:
LAW ENFORCEMENT TERMINOLOGY

SERIAL KILLER CLASSIFICATIONS

In the late 1700s, Carl Linneaus and his fellow scientists thought they arrived at something magical when they invented modern binomial nomenclature. The system they created neatly places each living thing into a category with which it can be compared to others. A common housecat, for example, is *Felis silvestrus catus*. Human beings, classified as *Homo sapiens sapiens*, held a place of honor as the "most evolved."

At first a useful tool, the classification system's flaws became apparent as new species were discovered. A duckbill platypus is technically a mammal – it has hair and the female produces milk – yet it also lays eggs, which mammals aren't supposed to do. Under the world's oceans the problem was even worse: is a sponge an animal or a plant? The number of exceptions and subcategories kept growing and growing.

Although taxonomy is still used today, scientists aren't slaves to it as they once were. They've realized that although it's useful for making comparisons, not too much time should be spent trying to fit one of nature's square pegs into a round hole. Similarly, trying to fit a serial killer into a strict categorical box can be a waste of time. At its worst, it can lead law enforcement officers down the wrong path in their investigations. In other cases, excessive time spent classifying criminals may take resources away from more productive activities. Nevertheless, classification systems do have some value. They teach new officers how to observe and distinguish behaviors. And, the terms are necessary to learn as seasoned officers often use them.

ORGANIZED VS. DISORGANIZED

The FBI classifies serial killers as *organized nonsocial, disorganized asocial,* or *mixed* (Douglas & Munn, 1992). An organized serial killer is one who is able to keep some semblance of societal normality. The killer may have a vehicle, be married, hold a job, and perhaps be well dressed and approachable. In contrast, the disorganized serial killer may live with his parents, drive an old and beaten-up vehicle (if he drives at all), and live on the fringes of society (Ressler & Burgess, 1985). The organized serial killer will plan murders, while the disorganized killer will commit unplanned murders, often with elements of rage or confusion.

The problem with the *organized* and *disorganized* killer classification is that few people fit neatly within it, and the result – *mixed* – doesn't really help identify anyone. Robert Pickton, for instance, owned a farm and demolition business, traveled in a vehicle to pick up his victims, and had other characteristics of the *organized* killer. At the same time, he was accepted only within a narrow "skid row" group of friends and was infamous for his unkempt clothing and foul body odor – characteristics of a *disorganized* killer. Colonel Russell Williams was a married air force Colonel, which one would expect of an *organized* killer, yet he committed his crimes close to home and in a relatively unplanned manner – both signs of a *disorganized* offender.

In my view, a better way to classify serial killers is not by the *organized* and *disorganized* categorizations, but by separating their social personalities from their killing methods.

A *socially competent* killer is one who can participate in the community at large (not just a narrow subculture) without arousing suspicion or appearing to be an outcast. Ted Bundy, for instance, was able to work as a community volunteer and election official without arousing suspicion. A *socially incompetent* killer, in contrast, is one who would stand out in a negative manner. Joel Rifkin, for instance, was a loner, considered strange, and was unable to hold onto friendships or jobs.

A *disorganized killing method* is one where the killer does not plan killings, but engages them on a whim based primarily on opportunity. Robert Reldan, for instance, though socially competent and charming, killed in an unplanned and haphazard method, simply attacking whichever woman captured his attention as he was driving around the neighborhood. Robert Pickton (the pig farmer mentioned earlier), though socially incompetent, would drive to the Downtown Eastside of Vancouver, pick up his victims, bring them back to his farm, then kill them and dispose of them with prepared materials – a highly organized killing method. Similarly, Jeffrey Dahmer picked up local men at bars and invited them back to his home, where he had murder and disposal materials prepared – also an organized killing method.

In *Criminal Shadows* (1993), David Cantor tells the story of prostitute Lynette White, who was found viciously knifed to death with over 50 stab wounds, her head and neck partially severed. This vicious, seemingly random murder had all the hallmarks of a disorganized serial killer. In reality, Lynette had been stabbed by her ex-pimp, Stephen Miller, who was trying to take his share of her recent earnings as a prostitute. Since the incident took place with five other people present, Miller forced each person to take stabs at the body, hoping that their involvement would encourage their silence. Despite all logical attempts to re-create and understand criminal acts, there will always be bizarre cases such as this one, where the truth will be nothing that an investigator could logically surmise and where classifications won't help.

Far too much time can be spent trying to define and categorize a killer, with no real benefit to the investigation. Like scientific taxonomy, the categorization of serial killers should be viewed as a tool, useful for basic analysis and comparison, but not as an end in itself. Human beings are complex and rarely fit into neat categories.

> "Many law enforcement and psychiatry specialists have been stumped as to which category [convicted murderer] Russell Williams belongs, since the behaviors that he exhibited during the two sexual assaults and the subsequent two murders seemed to cross between distinctions" (Gibb, 2011).

MODUS OPERANDI (method of operating)

Imagine – if you can – being a killer. You've just raped and murdered a woman, and felt a rush of exhilaration from controlling your victim. Her blood is all over your hands and clothing. You have a knife in your hand with your fingerprints on it. You have a body in front of you, and you haven't thought about how you're going to dispose of it. Are you going to leave it here? Are you going to carry it to a hiding place, but risk being seen?

Kenneth Wooden (2011) noted that an 89-year-old pedophile was arrested in the U.S. on his way to the Philippines, with "$6000 in cash, sex toys, the names of little girls in that country, and a hundred pounds of chocolate." Like anyone else with a job or hobby, a criminal's methods will improve over time in the quest for efficiency and risk-reduction.

Experienced (or well-read) killers often prepare "rape-kits" or "murder-kits" consisting of items useful for their style of murder. A killer who left his first victim lying exposed in the forest may prepare for his next murder by bringing a shovel and lye. A killer who earlier risked being identified may bring a mask.

"BTK Killer" Dennis Rader provides an example of a killer who was extremely organized in his killing method, though his actual crimes rarely worked as smoothly as planned. Rader would trail potential victims for weeks or even months, following them to and from work, peeping into windows and strolling alleyways, looking for hiding places and escape routes while keeping detailed notes and photographs. Because he spied on multiple women at a time and often didn't know their names, Rader assigned each woman a project name to help him keep track. For instance, "Project Dogside" was his name for secretary Dolores Davis, who lived near a dog kennel. Rader's job as a city by-law enforcement officer provided a convenient cover for his snooping activities. Rader even planned exact dates to kill his victims to coincide with convenient alibis. In one case he went to a Boy Scout campout with his son, but told everyone he had a headache so was going to retire to his tent early. He snuck away in the darkness, killed his victim, and returned to his tent before dawn.

After Rader experienced difficulty strangling almost the entire Otero family (Rader's hands became numb in the process), he prepared for future strangulations by squeezing rubber balls to strengthen his hands. When Rader tied victims, he intentionally changed the details in an attempt to deceive law enforcement, using ropes during one assault but nylon stockings in the next. Feeling invincible, Rader gave himself the nickname BTK (Bind them, Torture them, Kill them) and informed police via a letter that he'd begin *limiting* his methods to fit this nickname, as if the whole thing were a game. Tauntingly, Rader wrote, "Since sex criminals do not change their M.O. or by nature cannot do so, I will not change mine." Though Rader confused *modus operandi* and *signature* (more on this later) his letter is a reminder that methods are dynamic, and that just because one victim is killed by a slightly different method than another, this doesn't rule out a single killer.

In some cases, a serial killer's murder rate will increase until he reaches a *manic curve*. The manic curve is the point where a murderer kills at a rate higher than his disposal method can efficiently control. It's in this stage of mental exhaustion that police describe killers (and they sometimes describe themselves) as "hoping to get caught," as their consciences overwhelm them and they realize their actions are unsustainable. Jeffrey Dahmer, for instance, devised an efficient small-scale method for disposing of bodies within his apartment, cutting them to pieces in his bathtub and storing them in the freezer before dissolving the pieces in barrels of hydrochloric acid. As the bodies broke down, he would flush the flesh down the toilet and put the bone fragments in the trash. However, as his compulsions worsened, he started killing people too frequently for his disposal method to handle. When he was apprehended, police found several of his victims in various stages of "completion." If Dahmer had devised more industrial methods for disposing of his victims, he likely wouldn't have been apprehended until much later.

FBI: This ritual you had with your victims, how long of a period of time did this go on with just one victim until you were totally satisfied?
Dahmer: It's, for a very long time it was just once every two months. Near the end it was once every week.
FBI: Once a week?
Dahmer: Yeah, just got completely out of control.
FBI: Now as the skeletons started filling up in your apartment there, were you concerned about detection? Or about the police?
Dahmer: Not until a point where it got to the point where I couldn't even fit them in the freezer...

Jeffrey Dahmer (Aug 13 1992).

The number of active serial killers in the world is probably underestimated. If a person is caught shoplifting, it's unlikely that this was their first attempt at theft. A person who is caught selling drugs has likely done it many times before. An average child sex offender has 144 victims (Wooden, 2011). And yet, when someone commits murder, it's often assumed that this was their first time. As with other crimes, law enforcement officers would be wise to assume that an apprehended killer has killed before.

Experienced rapists/killers should exhibit less change in their methods than inexperienced ones. An evolving *modus operandi* suggests a relatively inexperienced killer, or one who has recently experienced a significant life change. When experienced killers change their methods, it's recognizable because they'll swap one effective method for another equally effective one.

EXAMPLES OF RAPE/MURDER KITS

Ted Bundy: Crowbar, ice pick, rope, handcuffs, ski mask, nylon stockings, gloves, flashlight, wire, garbage bags.

Ivan Millet: Hunting knife, electrical tape, cable ties, rope.

Dennis Rader: Handgun, handcuffs, masking tape, rope, leather belt.

Russell Williams: Rope, duct tape, black mask, sexual lubricant, heavy aluminum flashlight, camera.

Israel Keyes: Handgun with silencer, duct tape, cable ties, blindfolds, gloves, headlamp, shovel.

Lawrence Bittaker: Sledgehammer, ice pick, pliers, wire hanger, camera.

Rape/Murder kits have been found in duffel bags, briefcases, and even bowling bags. Occasionally, murder kit items are found in plain view in a killer's vehicle.

M.O., SIGNATURE and DENIAL

Modus Operandi is Latin for "method of operating." *Signature*, in contrast, is composed of activities that aren't essential to the perpetration of the crime, but represent the psychological needs of the offender (Douglas & Munn, 1992). The FBI considers the distinction between M.O. and signature an important one. While M.O. can vary greatly, the theory goes, signature remains static.

An easy example of signature comes from the 1991 movie, *Silence of the Lambs*. Although the killer, *Buffalo Bill*, modifies his murder and disposal methods, he would always insert a rare moth into the throat of a victim and remove a portion of her skin. The insertion of the moth and removal of skin are Buffalo Bill's signature acts, representing his psychological need.

In some real life examples, the distinction between *modus operandi* and signature is just as clear as in the Buffalo Bill example. Consider a killer who always inserts an object into his victim's vagina. The insertion of an object is consistent, yet not a necessary part of the murder, and is therefore considered a signature act. But what about less obvious cases?

Consider a murderer who transports his victim's bodies to the countryside to be dumped in the woods. Is the dumping of the body in the woods a method or a signature? As another example, consider finding victims who've been bludgeoned many times past the point of death, known as "overkill." All the bodies have plastic bags over their heads, placed there after death. A few days later, another victim is found in the same area with dozens of stab wounds. There's no bag on the victim's head. Does the new cause of death and lack of plastic bag necessarily mean that the killer is a different person?

Law enforcement officers and psychologists tend to disagree if a particular action is part of a signature, while new recruits have difficulty understanding the differences between M.O. and signature at all. If intelligent individuals have difficulty understanding a supposedly clear distinction, then that distinction may not be useful.

Rather than focus on M.O. and signature, it's simplest merely to consider what aspects of a murder are similar to each other and work backwards, the same way a crime linkage computer would. Is the location the same or similar? How about the methods of killing? Is there evidence of overkill? Do the victims share characteristics or habits? Focusing on the whole murder as a package, comparing it to others, and *looking for similarities* should result in fewer law enforcement dismissals ("We don't have a serial killer").

Law enforcement officers should recognize that when faced with evidence pointing toward the existence of a serial killer, they tend to use the psychological defense mechanism of *denial*. An active serial killer means boiler-room pressure, fear in the community, sleepless nights and false leads. No police force in the world is keen to admit that a serial killer is active in their backyard. Perhaps this is why police departments have been known to dismiss the presence of a serial killer long after the public has already figured it out.

AREA OF OPERATION

Criminals of all sorts generally conduct their crimes – especially their first crimes – on familiar territory. Crimes are surprisingly local. *Jack the Ripper* worked almost exclusively in the small Whitechapel area of London where he is presumed to have lived. Colonel Russell Williams worked primarily within a few *blocks* of his home.

When investigating the area of operation, remember that some barriers create psychological boundaries far stronger than a map would imply. A railroad track may seem to be an insignificant barrier as it's physically easy to cross. For a criminal, however, the "other side of the tracks" may be an unfamiliar world (hence the expression). Major roadways, rivers, and even overhead power lines may form psychological barriers that a criminal is uncomfortable crossing. Though not actually consisting of any physical barrier whatsoever, a poor working class area may be, in the criminal's mind, separate from a wealthier area only a few blocks away.

The downtown East Side of Vancouver, Canada, where killer Robert Pickton operated, is known for its homeless people and drug addicts. Located only a few blocks to the west is an upscale shopping area known for designer clothing stores and corporation headquarters. Yet, the drug addicts of the East Side seldom venture to this upscale area, as if blocked by an invisible wall. Presumably, an East Side heroin addict wandering into a designer clothing shop would experience the same discomfort as a designer clothing shopper wandering into an East Side drug deal.

In Britain, John Duffy and David Mulcahy were known as the "Railway Killers." Police knew that whoever was committing the murders must be familiar with the local rail lines, since every sexual assault and murder took place at or near a railway station. Investigators later discovered that Duffy had become familiar with the rail lines during his work as a carpenter for British Rail.

As with everything, there are exceptions to the "look locally first" rule. A killer who travels as part of his job might become familiar with many areas within a larger distance. And of course, killers can move or relocate just like anyone else, bringing new areas into play.

PART 6:
BEING A SERIAL KILLER

LIFESTYLE, JOB AND CAREER

> "Forget all about that macho shit and learn how to play guitar."
>
> John Cougar Mellencamp, from the song *Play Guitar*, 1983

People grossly underestimate the power of sexuality as a lifestyle-determining force. Maintaining sexual attractiveness is a primary reason why men and women go to the gym. It's why mothers teach their daughters to play piano and cook. It's why high school girls pretend to be stupid while in the presence of insecure teenage boys. It's why adult women follow fashion trends and buy expensive handbags. It's why gay men often live in gay areas, and straight men live in straight areas. It's why a man whose wife buys a membership to the gym, changes her wardrobe and begins studying a new language should make him exceptionally worried! Semi-consciously, sex determines whole career and lifestyle choices.

A professional woman who wants to cheat on her husband doesn't want a local 9-5 office job, since such a job would afford little opportunity for affairs. Her ideal career might involve frequent overnight travel, networking events or conferences, and working in a male-dominated industry – all of which facilitate affairs.

Pedophiles tend to seek positions of authority that keep them in close contact with children, including jobs as lifeguards, teachers, doctors, priests and Boy Scout leaders. Kenneth Wooden (2011) during his work as a fingerprint classifier for the state of New Jersey, discovered about a dozen child molesters, all of whom had applied for positions as school bus drivers.

"I apply to law school because my professional and community activities demand daily a knowledge of the law I do not have. Whether I am studying the behavior of criminal offenders, examining bills before the legislature, advocating court reform, or contemplating the creation of my own corporation, I immediately become conscious of my limited understanding of the law. My life style requires that I obtain a knowledge of the law and the ability to practice legal skills. I intend to be my own man...I apply to law school because this institution will give me the tools to become a more effective actor in the social role I have defined for myself."

Serial killer Ted Bundy's University of Utah admission's letter (Rule, 2000). In time, it became clear what Bundy meant when he said that his "life style" requires a knowledge of the law and an ability to practice legal skills. After his arrest for murder, Bundy represented himself in court. Note also that Bundy states that he is an actor in a social role. Dangerous narcissists live their lives as socially acceptable "characters" rather than genuine people.

Serial killers, of course, gravitate toward careers that are best for serial killers. A serial killer's world is dominated by perverse fantasies and the desire to act upon them. Any job that facilitates stalking prey or gaining proficiency as a killer is an ideal choice, though having antisocial personality traits tends to be a limiting factor.

Serial killers prefer jobs that involve low accountability to others (narcissists hate being told what to do), little or no team involvement, frequent travel, and where they set their own hours (for which every minute cannot be accounted for). In other words, a serial killer's ideal employment involves maximum personal freedom and minimum social responsibility.

If they attend post-secondary education, serial killers tend to take courses that give them the opportunity to "figure themselves out" or add to their practical skills, including psychology, criminology, pharmacology and crime scene investigation. Karla Homolka, as an example, obtained her Bachelor of Arts degree (majoring in psychology) while serving time for manslaughter. She also took one year of criminology before deciding she couldn't afford the tuition on a prisoner's salary.

"It gives me the opportunity to come out of the emergency room with a hard-on and tell some parents that their kid had just died."

Killer Michael Swango, explaining why he chose to become a doctor (Blundell, 2010).

Jobs where they can practice manipulating or controlling others – including sales, religious leadership, counseling, and political campaigning – are popular. Some killers find work that gives them exposure to the macabre, extreme emotion, or power over life and death. Popular jobs of socially competent killers include traveling salespeople, self-employed consultants, doctors, ambulance drivers, and firefighters. Only the most capable are successful in these fields, the majority being dismissed after relatively short periods of time.

Timothy Krajcir provides a textbook example of a socially competent serial killer's preferences and hobbies. He worked for the Southern Illinois University's ambulance service while majoring in administration of justice with a minor in psychology. He was also a player for the Carbondale City police softball team, and the Jackson County ambulance service team (Echols & Byers, 2010).

"...Perry likes to be his own Boss and if he is given a chance to work at a job he likes, tell him how you want it done...But dont get *tuff with him*...He is very *touchie*, his feeling is very easily hurt, and so are mine...A *White Colar* job is not for *Perry or me*..."

From "A History of My Boy's Life," by the father of mass murderer Perry Edward Smith (Capote, 1965). Narcissists despise being told what to do, since they feel this implies inferiority. As with Perry, many socially incompetent killers prefer self-employment and blue-collar work.

Common jobs of socially incompetent serial killers include positions as manual laborers and factory workers. They don't shy away from the so-called "3D jobs," which are those considered dirty, dangerous, and physically difficult. 3D jobs are not mentally taxing, which leaves them plenty of energy to use toward sexual fantasies and planning. Such jobs also make it easier to explain the inevitable scratches and bruises that result from their violent pastime. Many killers supplement their incomes with illegal activities such as burglary and fraud.

For serial killers, the quest for violent release is all consuming. Their careers must either support this quest, or at least allow them time to engage in it during their off-work hours.

PROFESSIONS AND HOBBIES OF KNOWN SERIAL KILLERS/RAPISTS

David Berkowitz: Army soldier, postal worker, street preacher
Kenneth Bianchi: land titles clerk, psychiatrist (faked credentials), security guard, ambulance driver, hospital supply person, County Sheriff's reserve officer
Ian Brady: brewery worker, chemical supply clerk
Ted Bundy: rape crisis center volunteer, criminal corrections consultant, Seattle Crime Commission assistant director, Republican Party volunteer, campus security officer
Angelo Buono: plasterer, fireplace builder, auto upholstery shop owner, pimp
Jeffrey Dahmer: Army medic, phlebotomist (blood plasma collecter), chocolate factory worker
Marc Detroux: electrician, male prostitute, mugger, drug dealer
Albert Fish: male prostitute, house painter
Wayne Adam Ford: Marine Corp chemical specialist, mechanic
Michel Fourniret: forest warden, school supervisor
John Wayne Gacy: mortuary attendant, building contractor, political precinct Captain, volunteer children's clown
Friedrich Haarman: apprentice locksmith, Army soldier, cigar factory worker, police informant
Robert Hansen: Army reserve soldier, bakery owner, big game hunter
Donald Harvey: Air Force soldier, male nursing aide, telephone operator, cardiac-catheterization technician, autopsy assistant
Gary Heidnik: Army medic, psychiatric nurse, church founder
Keith Jesperson: backhoe operator, welder, long-distance truck driver

Genene Jones (female): nurse
Israel Keyes: Army infantryman, construction company owner, bank robber
Sante Kimes (female): prostitute
Randy Kraft: gay club bartender, Air Force soldier, forklift operator, traveling IT consultant
Ivan Millet: construction worker, concrete factory worker, hunter
Dennis Nilsen: Army caterer, police officer, civil servant
Alexander Pichushkin: carpenter, supermarket shelf-stacker
Robert Pickton: pig farmer, demolition business owner, scrap metal dealer
Dennis Rader: Air Force soldier, camping gear factory worker, home security alarm installer, city compliance officer (dog catcher and by-law enforcement), church council president, boy scout leader
David Parker Ray: Army soldier, auto mechanic
Gary Ridgway: Navy sailor, truck painter
John Robinson: X-ray technician (faked credentials), systems analyst, self-employed medical consultant, life insurance salesman, self-employed financial consultant (charged by the S.E.C.), lawyer (fraudulent), self-employed venture capital consultant, scoutmaster, Sunday school teacher
Arthur Shawcross: Army supply clerk, butcher, cheese factory worker
Peter Sutcliffe: grave digger, truck driver
Michael Swango: Marine Corp soldier, ambulance paramedic, medical doctor
Vlado Taneski: crime reporter
Gary Taylor: machinist, welder
Jack Unterweger: author, crime reporter
Russell Williams: Air Force officer/base commander
Aileen Wuornos (female): prostitute
Robert Lee Yates: prison guard, Army pilot, National Guard soldier, aluminum smelter worker

HUNTING METHODS

Serial killers are predators who view other human beings as their prey. Like all hunters, they engage in stalking behaviors, plan traps and ruses, and continually improve their techniques.

From fairy tales and horror movies, people have become conditioned to believe that evil people look evil. But, while petty criminals may look evil (or at least unconventional), most serial killers wear socially acceptable masks that are difficult to penetrate. Serial killers are successful in part because they don't fit people's expectations of what a dangerous person looks like.

Like pick-up artists, killers put effort into looking like people their victims would spend time with and trust. They dress the same way, talk the same way, and pretend to share the same beliefs. And, just as a man in a pub pretends not to be too interested in a woman he likes, a dangerous predator pretends not to be too interested in his prey.

One of "BTK Killer" Dennis Rader's preferred hunting methods was to dress respectably in dress shoes, dress pants and a tweed sports jacket, carrying a leather briefcase that held his murder kit materials. He also carried fake business cards and a photograph of a little boy (his own). Rader would knock on the doors of women he had targeted, pretending to be a private investigator looking for a lost child. Once inside a home, he would lock the door behind him, pull out a gun, and announce that he had a "problem with sexual fantasies" (State vs. Dennis L. Rader, 2005). He would tell his victims that he was going to take photographs of them and have sex with them:

it will not be pleasant, but you will survive. Of course, Rader had no intention of letting his victims live.

Robert "the Charmer" Reldan was so smooth and clean cut that he had no trouble gaining access to women's homes. One day he was driving around when he spotted a woman who he immediately decided would be his next victim. He followed her back to her house, but realized he didn't have any plan to gain entry. On a whim, he took his own dry cleaning from the backseat, still wrapped in plastic, walked up to the woman's home as if he were a delivery person and rang the doorbell. When the woman opened the door to tell him he must have the wrong address, he forced himself in.

American killer Israel Keyes always broke into potential victim's homes through their attached garages, which tended to have lax security compared to the main residences. There, he would check a vehicle's registration to see the ages of the owner(s), search for toys or other signs of children (he was morally against murdering children), and examine the seats for dog hair. If everything checked out, he would break into the home.

Edward Kemper was able to freely pick up beautiful, hitchhiking students as often as he wanted, even after campus police warned students of the presence of a murderer, and despite his imposing size (Kemper was 6 ft 9 in tall). The girl's favorite topic of conversation was the local killer – "this guy that's going around doing this stuff." Kemper says the girls got into his car because they judged him not to be the killer (Hovath et al, 1984). Kemper made an art form of the non-verbal cues related to his game. He used his mother's car to pick up co-eds, since her University of California staff parking sticker gave him instant credibility. When pulling up in the car, he would ask the girls where they were going and then, after they responded, glance at his watch as if he were deciding if he had time to take them there. He *never* looked eager.

120

Serial killers often engage in what appears to be aimless driving. Paul Bernardo, for instance, drove an average of 650 kilometers (404 miles) per day for several days in a row while under police surveillance, for no discernable purpose (Campbell, 1996). While driving highways or neighborhoods, killers may be picking out potential victims, stalking, or scouting areas for future crimes. Serial killers enjoy driving because they equate driving with hunting. Israel Keyes, who logged thousands of miles in rented vehicles, called it "shopping."

Killers choose vehicles that are practical for either their work or hunting style, or both. For Ted Bundy, it was the small and innocent-looking Volkswagen Beatle; a model nicknamed "the love bug" for its popularity with peaceful hippies. The Beatle proved useful for Bundy, whose method for catching girls was to feign weakness (using crutches or wearing a cast), then ask a woman for help before knocking her out. In addition to being innocuous, Bundy stated that he liked the Beatle because it was able to hold large loads (i.e. bodies) despite its small size, and because it got good gas mileage.

Angelo Buono and Kenneth Bianchi, the "Hillside Stranglers," drove a 1972 dark-blue four-door Cadillac sedan (similar to unmarked police cars of the time) with a *County of Los Angeles* decal in the corner of the windshield. Bianchi and Buono cruised the streets of Los Angeles, luring unsuspecting girls into their car by posing as plainclothes cops, complete with fake badges.

For Gerald Gallego and Charlene Williams, the vehicle of choice was a white panel van. Williams (female) would lure girls to the van with the promise of free drugs. Once in the van, Gallego would rape and kill the girls while Williams watched. In male and female "partnerships" (ex. Ian Brady & Myra Hindley, Fred & Rosemary West, Alvin & Judith Neelley) it's typically the female who is in charge of obtaining female victims, since women tend to be less suspicious of other women.

Socially competent killers *tend* to hunt socially competent victims: housewives, students, and co-workers. That such victims can be successfully hunted implies that their murderers don't invite excessive attention; that is, they fit in. Socially incompetent killers *tend* to choose their victims from the "high-risk lifestyle" categories: drug-users, prostitutes and hitchhikers.

HITCHHIKERS & PROSTITUTES: "HIGH RISK" LIFESTYLES

> "I don't hitchhike myself, never have. And you know, when a girl hitchhikes, she's taking her life in her hands, man, she doesn't know who she's getting in the car with. It could be a guy escaped from a crazy house...I don't even do it."
>
> "Hillside Strangler" Angelo Buono, giving good advice about hitchhiking to investigator Bob Grogan (O'Brien, 1985).

When we were children, our parents and teachers did their best to teach us the basics of personal safety: don't talk to strangers; don't accept gifts from strangers; never get into a stranger's vehicle. Every eight-year-old knows to avoid what hitchhikers and prostitutes do on a routine basis. Simply stated, hitchhikers and prostitutes are popular with killers because they're considered easy prey.

Some people consider hitchhiking to be an expression of freedom. Bookstores sell hitchhiking guides in the travel section, and the whole image of hitchhiking is one of youthful, carefree hippie bliss. It's a pursuit where crime statistics and anecdotal evidence simply don't match.

"Put me down as absolutely against hitchhiking. I've written too many stories about female homicide victims who met their killers while they were hitchhiking."

Crime writer Ann Rule, stating her opinion to her friend, Ted Bundy (Rule, 1980). Bundy was employed by the City of Seattle's Crime Prevention Advisory Committee. At the time, Rule didn't know Bundy was a serial killer who murdered hitchhikers.

In a study done in the 1970s (a popular time for hitchhiking) it was found that female hitchhikers are seven to ten times more likely than men to be the victim of a crime, with nearly all of those crimes being sex-related (Pudinski, 1974). The drivers who sexually assaulted female hitchhikers had specifically gone hunting for them. Nonetheless, the same study found that the overall number of hitchhiking crimes was about the same as the level of crime in the general population – suggesting that hitchhiking is just as safe as walking down the street. This conclusion differs from the stated views of killers, who feel that hitchhikers are fair game due to their stupidity. High-profile serial killers who have targeted hitchhikers include Ted Bundy, Robert Pickton, Edward Kemper, Jeffrey Dahmer, Gary Ridgway and Joel Rifkin, among others.

> "Our favorite target was hitchhikers. We used to laugh and call them FREEBIES because there was basically no risk involved and they were easy to catch. I mean you have two men hunting for one and one jumps right in the car with you. How simple is that?"
>
> David Gore, regarding hitchhikers (Early, 2012). The same could be said for prostitutes.

For many killers, prostitutes are irresistible targets: they dress in a provocative manner; they represent everything that is "wrong" with women and motherhood; and, they are sexualized objects to be used at will. Prostitutes are vulnerable people who live on the fringes of society.

Street prostitutes are often homeless, runaways, or addicted to alcohol or drugs. When suffering from withdrawals, a prostitute's basic judgment may be deeply impaired. Since solicitation is illegal in most places, prostitutes also suffer from an "us vs. them" mentality against law enforcement. Prostitutes are unlikely to go to the police for help even if they're assaulted – something they refer to as a "bad date." When prostitutes are murdered, the community's reaction tends to be one of relative disinterest. The reputation of prostitutes as drug addicts and home-wreckers leads some private citizens to regard their murders as a public service. And, because prostitutes often use street names (as opposed to their real names), discovering their current whereabouts can be a difficult task. This may all sound unjust, but it is reality.

> **Honey**: ...he wouldn't use a condom, so, I tried to get out of his car, and he tried to stab me, and tried to lock me inside his car.
>
> **Bates**: And, how'd you get away?
>
> **Honey**: I, um, unlocked the damned door where he had me, like, trying to restrain me from getting out of the car. I unlocked it, I yanked it [the knife] away from him and I stabbed him in his arm with the knife, and I jumped out.
>
> **Bates**: Wow. Have you...do you very often have bad dates?
>
> **Honey**: Um, no. Not very often. Maybe...I at least have one, once a month, usually.
>
> "Honey," a street prostitute in Oklahoma City, as interviewed by Brian Bates, Jan 2013. Prostitutes are well aware of the dangers of their profession.

THE INTERNET AS A HUNTING TOOL

The Internet is a powerful tool for predators, with the most trustful, least suspecting users being the most vulnerable. Con artists are known for using social/dating websites and chat rooms to troll for victims. Sex offenders have used online classified ads, where women have advertised goods for sale, as a way to enter homes for sexual assaults. Users of social media websites have joyfully updated their profiles while on vacation, only to find their homes burglarized upon their return. A husband who posts information online about his next business trip unwittingly puts his wife and children in greater jeopardy.

Most people, as trusting individuals, don't stop to consider how their personal information can be used against them.

On the Internet, anyone can be important. A truck driver from Idaho can pose as a successful entrepreneur from New York. A bored, married housewife of 40 can be a single model of 25. And, as some pedophiles have discovered, a 30-year-old detective can pose as a 12-year-old schoolgirl whose parents have left for the weekend. More commonly, a person can be the same person they really are, minus all of their flaws and insecurities. Online, people can be however they want to be perceived.

Online interactions lack most of the cues we use to make effective judgments about people. Intonation and emphasis of words does not exist. Body language does not exist. Appearance can be rigged using edited photos, photos taken years earlier, or photos of another person altogether. There are no rules.

Serial killers find the Internet a ripe hunting ground. Having a limited sense of moral guilt, a killer can unabashedly write a future victim a love letter while his spouse is cooking dinner in the next room. He can make promises he has no intention of keeping. He can tell his victims exactly what they want to hear.

At 58, John Robinson was married and – according to his family – was a loving and caring father. While his daughter was growing up he had attended her flute recitals and refereed her school volleyball games. He was a neighborhood activist and a founding elder of the local Presbyterian Church (McClintick, 2013). He was also an ex-convict with a long history of fraud and embezzlement. As a free man, Robinson, aka "Slavemaster," used the Internet to lure women to his home in Kansas City with the promise of frequent BDSM (Bondage, Dominance, Sadomasochistic) sex and a kept-woman's salary.

Robinson hunted in BDSM chat rooms, posting comments about his desires for rough sex and providing potential lovers with photos of himself. In 1997, Robinson befriended college student and fellow BDSM enthusiast Izabela Lewicka, who was so intrigued with Robinson that she dropped out of college and moved to Kansas City to be with him, telling her parents that she landed a job there. Robinson greeted her with an engagement ring, a promise of marriage, and her own furnished apartment. Two years later Lewicka was dead, her body stuffed into a 55-gallon chemical drum. Robinson was so satisfied with the result that he continued hunting online until his arrest.

A testament to the power of the Internet to bring depraved people together is the almost unbelievable story of German-born Armin Meiwes. In 2001, Meiwes posted personal ads on several websites, asking for a "well-built man, aged 18 to 30, who would like to be eaten by me." Many masochists responded to the ad, most of who did not take the offer literally. One of the serious respondents was 43-year-old Bernd-Jurgen Brandes of Berlin, a man obsessed with self-mutilation.

In their online chats, Brandes let it be known that he would like to have his penis eaten. He also recommended that Meiwes use the ground powder of his kneecaps as fertilizer. Meiwes told Brandes that he would attack people on the street if he could, but that he "would rather only kill those who want to be killed" (Meiwes, 2008).

In March 2001, Brandes took the train to meet Meiwes at his cottage in Rotenburg, Germany. Brandes promptly asked Meiwes to bite off his penis, which Meiwes happily did. After three hours of heavy blood loss, Meiwes decided that his captive was taking too long to die, so he slashed Brandes' throat to finish him off. Meiwes spent the next several months eating Brandes' body parts, sometimes with his eggs at breakfast.

Meiwes was arrested and convicted for murder after placing another, similar ad. His life was made into the German film, *Kannibale von Rotenburg*.

> **Meiwes**: After you're dead, I'll take you out and expertly carve you up. Except for a pair of knees and some fleshy trash (skin, cartilage, tendons), there won't be much of you left.
> **Brandes**: There will be a good bit, like the knees, I hope you have a good hiding place for them.
> **Meiwes**: I'll dry out the knees and grind them up soon after.
> **Brandes**: Okay, they're good as fertilizer, I heard that once. I see you've thought about it. Good! Sounds like I'm the first.
>
> Online conversation between Armin Meiwes and his willing victim, Bernd-Jurgen Brandes, March 6, 2001.

The Internet is both a blessing and a curse for law enforcement. On one hand, the Internet has made grotesque sexual material more available than ever before, in websites and chatrooms that encourage and support deviant behavior. On the other hand, the web is also an excellent source of criminal evidence. When law enforcement has successfully infiltrated deviant-material websites, they have been able to arrest dozens of offenders at a time, often involving multinational cooperation.

TROPHY KEEPING

"As the numbers started to increase, as an ID, a photo...*OK, I know who that girl was.* A piece of jewelry...*OK, I know that it was from that girl.* So yeah, it [keeping personal items] would help keep the sequence, help me remember who was who and remember the events."

Killer Joel Rifkin, regarding trophy keeping (1993).

Athletes can't "save" the sporting events they've won, so event organizers fulfill the athlete's need for proof of their accomplishments by providing ribbons and medals. Businesses give awards and plaques to their best employees. Married people keep photos from their wedding day, but may also keep messages from past lovers who they have not quite gotten over. Big-game hunters display stuffed animal heads and antlers on their walls as memories of their successful hunts. Keeping souvenirs and trophies is a way to make intangible memories tangible.

In high school I had a friend who infamously kept a collection of used women's underwear under his bed, some of which were in cleaner condition than others. Why did he keep these dirty things? They were trophies. They were ways of reliving the moment, and as long as they had relevance, he couldn't bring himself to throw them away.

Serial killers commonly keep three categories of trophies: identification cards; personal items such as clothing and jewelry (which they often give to lovers); and, similar to big game hunters, they keep body parts.

When police arrived with their search warrant for room 213 of the Oxford Apartment building in Milwaukee, Wisconsin, they knew it wouldn't be pleasant. Police had already discovered gruesome trophies inside, placed there by former resident Jeffrey Lionel Dahmer. Their extended search revealed severed heads in the refrigerator, pairs of hands, hundreds of photos of posed and dismembered bodies, an assortment of silver-painted skulls with candles on top, and a 55-gallon drum filled with acid and body parts. It took days to document and remove the evidence. To prevent it from becoming a shrine for the unwell, the entire building was burned to the ground.

Barbara Sandre was the mistress of con artist and killer John Robinson. When Sandre moved into the apartment that Robinson had provided for her in Overland Park, Kansas, she was pleased. The apartment was furnished with unique items such as a Hungarian coffeemaker, an impressionist painting, a large number of books, and a bed with green-and-maroon cotton sheets. Robinson had filled the apartment with his trophy collection. Every time he visited, Robinson could look around and experience his past "victories" with the smug satisfaction of knowing that Sandre was unaware.

Not all serial killers keep trophies in an obvious manner. When police searched the home and grounds of Gary Ridgway in Washington State, they found nothing. They didn't find anything when they searched his former homes either. Ridgway *had* been taking trophies from his victims – mostly jewelry – but instead of keeping the items he had been bringing them to his workplace and leaving them laying around, where they would inevitably be claimed. Ridgway got the satisfaction of seeing his female coworkers proudly wearing the jewelry of women he had murdered.

Serial killers keep trophies for the same reasons as anyone else: reward and recognition, and a way to relive past glories. A trophy will be kept as long as the incident behind it remains a significant experience in that person's life.

> "It was my way of remembering their appearance - their physical beauty...if I couldn't keep them there with me whole, at least I felt that I could keep their skeletons."
>
> Jeffrey Dahmer (Inside Edition, 1993).

CANNIBALISM

Cannibalism is the ultimate objectification of the victim: the killer is not torturing the victim, he is "tenderizing meat;" he is not starving the victim, but "removing fat." Every sadistic action dehumanizes the victim a little more. The ingestion of a victim is the ultimate in trophy keeping. By ingesting the victim, the killer believes he is literally making the victim a component of his own body.

The idea that eating someone makes them a part of you isn't a new idea, and isn't limited to serial killers. In some tribal societies, eating the flesh of a recently deceased relative is believed to be a way of keeping the relative with you forever. In other cases, enemies are eaten to absorb their power. In 2014, for instance, a busload of residents in the town of Beni, northeast Congo, Africa, suspected a fellow passenger of being a member of an Islamic militant group that had recently terrorized their town. The crowd forced the man from the bus, stoned him to death, burned him, and ate him (Reuters, 2014). The flesh of a fallen enemy is not only regarded as a prize, but also believed to endow the victor with the strength of the person being eaten.

During his two trials in 2004 and 2006, German cannibal Armin Meiwes explained that he had always dreamt of having a younger brother, and that making another human being a part of him was a way of making that dream a reality. Meiwes said that each time he ate a piece of his victim, Bernd-Jurgen Brandes (who spoke English well), he felt his own English improved. The parallels to the beliefs of tribal societies are unmistakable.

"It was a way of making me feel that they were a part of me. At first it was just curiosity, but then it became compulsive."

Jeffrey Dahmer (Inside Edition, 1993), regarding eating his victim's hearts. Dahmer also stated that human flesh tastes similar to filet mignon (FBI, 1992).

TREATMENT OF THE BODY
& REVISITS

In a scene from the 2005 Stephen Spielberg movie *Munich,* three secret service agents, seeking revenge, go to the home of a beautiful woman who assassinated their friend. They shoot the woman, who is naked except for her housecoat, and watch with satisfaction as she slowly expires. She slumps into a chair with her housecoat open, exposing her naked body. One agent begins to close up the housecoat to cover her body. Another agent stops him and says, "Leave it." The first agent opens her housecoat to reveal her nakedness once again, knowing that whoever discovers the body will find her this way. Though semi-fictional, this scene accurately reflects the psychological underpinnings of a serial killer's treatment of a body.

John Douglas (former FBI), in his 1995 book *Mindhunter,* describes a young woman who killed her two-year-old son. When the boy's body was found, he was "in his snowsuit, wrapped in a blanket, then completely covered with a thick plastic bag." Despite the child being *dead,* his mother nonetheless took great care to protect his body and make him look comfortable.

Post-mortem behavior may indicate the level of respect the killer had for the victim, and his perceived relationship with the victim. Even if a body is heavily mutilated, if the body is subsequently covered by such things as a blanket, leaves or dirt, more respect is implied than if the body is left exposed. An exposed body implies little respect for either the body or the person who will find it. A body that's left with limbs sprawled randomly is probably less respected than a body that's placed in a restful position.

After killing 15-year-old prostitute Judith Miller, Angelo Buono and his partner Kenneth Bianchi dumped her body at the side of the road at 2388 Alta Terrace Drive in La Crescenta, California. The road is in a well-kept area with nice homes, frequented by local traffic. Why dump the body there? Buono chose this site because it was near the home of his ex-girlfriend, who he hoped would find the body. The horror that a body will cause for the person discovering it is one reason why serial killers find amusement in placing and posing bodies post-mortem. A posed body is a "middle finger" to society.

Many serial killers say the idea of cutting off limbs occurs to them when they first try to move a body and realize how heavy and unwieldy it is. Removal of the limbs is usually done to aid movement of a body, and may indicate that the murder took place indoors. Once removed, body parts can become part of trophy-keeping behaviors. Many serial killers keep hands, body fat, and severed breasts. Ted Bundy, Jeffrey Dahmer and Robert Pickton all kept heads.

Serial killers also dismember their victims for the practical reason that a body without a head and limbs is more difficult to identify as human, especially after a short period of decomposition. Robert Pickton, for instance, removed the hands, feet and heads of his victims, and then took the torsos (further cut up) to a commercial rendering plant for destruction. If Pickton had left the hands and feet intact, they would surely have been noticed by rendering plant staff.

Like all narcissists, serial killers have a mortal fear of being abandoned. Normal people think of killing someone as a way to be rid of them forever. Sexual serial killers, on the other hand, view killing someone as a way to *keep* them forever.

When killers make use of remote dumpsites, it's common for them to keep visiting a body for sexual gratification for days, even after the body becomes decomposed and maggot-infested. Ted Bundy spent hours at a time visiting his decomposing victims, grooming their hair (Bundy loved long hair) and having intercourse with their bodies until putrefaction and wild animal destruction rendered further intimacy impossible.

After serial killer Edward Kemper murdered 19-year-old Cynthia Schall, he buried her head in his backyard with her face turned toward his bedroom window. At night, Kemper would speak to her, "saying love things, the way you do to a girlfriend or wife" (Von Beroldingen, 1974).

Gary Ridgway told detectives he felt the bodies of his victims were his "property" until the moment they were discovered by the task force. Whenever the police discovered one of his caches of bodies, Ridgway felt they were stealing. Annoyed that the task force was finding and removing so many of his possessions, Ridgway dug up some of the bodies and moved them to more secure locations.

Though Ridgway found the idea of having sex with corpses repugnant, he couldn't stop doing it. He described sex with the dead as a sexual release that he didn't have to pay for (in comparison to living prostitutes), and added that he would do it until "the flies came" or until he found a new victim, whichever came first (Maleng, 2003). One can only imagine what Ridgway's wife thought when she discovered his habit.

Even after a body is discovered and removed, visiting the disposal site can be a gratifying for a killer through the memories of what occurred there. A killer may also visit the murder site (if different from the disposal site) and the cemetery of the deceased to regain a sense of superiority and for sexual gratification.

TESTING THE WATER

"You know that I'd like to do? I'd like to put dots all over somebody's body and take a knife, and then play connect the dots and then pour vinegar all over them."

Then-teenager Karla Homolka, commenting to a female classmate in the high school cafeteria. The classmate never forgot it (Williams, 2009).

Fred and Rosemary West. Angelo Buono and Kenneth Bianchi. John Duffy and David Mulcahy. Paul Bernardo and Karla Homolka. Many serial killers find a lover, friend or relative who becomes their partner in serial murder. The obvious question is, "How does a serial killer find someone willing to commit murder with them?" Serial killers are rare, and yet they have an uncanny ability to find each other. How can this happen?

One reason is simple enough: without the suggestive influence of the other, the single person may never have become a killer. Paul Bernardo, for instance, was a serial rapist (but not a murderer) prior to meeting girlfriend Karla Homolka. Homolka was a young woman who had never committed a sexual crime, yet had a known fixation with death and the macabre. It seems that Paul Bernardo's fascination with sex, combined with Karla Homolka's fascination with death, literally created a killer combination.

Testing the water is when criminals make twisted jokes or comments to trusted friends, hoping for a positive reaction that would indicate the friend's willingness to partake in a crime. Killer Joe Metheny, for example, was once drinking at a bar with a friend when he expressed his opinion that human flesh is tasty when barbecued. The friend laughed and called him "sick," at which point the topic was changed and the comment forgotten (at least until Metheny was convicted of murder). Had the friend not expressed disgust with the joke, but instead expressed interest and asked additional questions, he may well have become Metheny's new killing partner.

"Hillside Strangler" Angelo Buono, who would later partner with cousin Kenneth Bianchi, in known to have tested the water as early as age 14. Already harboring a strong hatred of women, Buono told a friend that he wanted to pick up a hitchhiker, rape her and "fuck her in the ass." Buono's friend, confused as to why anyone would want to do such a thing, asked his parents about it. They forbade him from ever seeing Buono again (O'Brien, 1985).

Serial killers test the water with co-workers and friends throughout their lives, hoping to find partners who will accept them in their entirety.

> "I'm not going to sit here and say that there perhaps wasn't something in the back of my mind as a fantasy sort of thing. It may have been just the chemistry between two people."
>
> "Hillside Strangler" Kenneth Bianchi, regarding his partner, cousin Angelo Buono (O'Brien, 1985).

With the advent of the Internet, finding a killing partner has become easier than ever before. Websites dedicated to the "vampire lifestyle," blood and gore, and serial killer admiration are commonplace. Gore websites display photos of horrifying death in a cavalier manner, and serve as forums for sick-minded people to encourage one another's beliefs. Billed as "uncensored news" websites to avoid legal ramifications, gore websites feature car-crash, crime scene and autopsy photos, supplied by disturbed community professionals such as ambulance drivers. One gore website I visited to research this book featured a photo of a headless corpse lying on a stretcher, with viewer comments like, "damn great photos...I want more more!!" and, "he still has a little bit of head not a complete decapitation oh well good enough I suppose." All six advertisements on the page were links to pornographic websites. There were also links to photos of dead children. This combination of sex and graphic violence can be a dangerous incentive for the unwell.

Some incarcerated serial killers, including (at the time of writing) David Mulcahy and Charles Manson, maintain official websites with the help of admirers, allowing them to promote their self-serving agendas. Typically, they try to convince others of their innocence, or convert new groupies to their personal philosophies. Manson's official website, for example, sells t-shirts and souvenirs, talks about the injustice of his conviction (the "lying-ass district attorney" sent me to jail with "filthy fuckin' lies"), discusses his love of nature and the environment, and showcases his supposedly deep philosophical poetry.

> " Air my Sun god, god Sun Air, Sweet love of life I am LOVE you Everywhere my air, IT's yours. Air Air, Everywhere there is a there."
>
> Sample of Charle's Manson's poetry, from www.mansondirect.com (Manson, Feb 2012).

PART 7:
BEING A SERIAL KILLER

CONSCIENCE MANAGEMENT:
BEING A GOOD PERSON

No one thinks they are a bad person. The woman who cheats on her husband believes that, aside from this one thing, she is a good person. The police officer who accepts bribes believes that, aside from this one thing, he is a good person. And the serial killer believes that, aside from this one thing, he is a good person also.

Killers may talk about being "terrible" or "evil," since this is what's expected of them; but they don't actually believe it and will revert back to describing themselves as "good people" minutes later. Nobody consciously thinks of themselves as sadistic and inhuman, because believing so would be too difficult to accept.

An example of the astonishing power of self-deception is former Columbian drug lord Pablo Escobar, once one of the wealthiest and most powerful dealers in the world. At the peak of his power in the 1980s, Escobar's group supplied upwards of 80% of the *global* cocaine trade. He controlled his market by forcing public officials and law enforcement officers to make one of two choices: accept a bribe and become complicit, or be killed on the spot ("silver or lead"). Escobar built massive estates with his wealth. One had a private zoo with elephants and zebras imported from Africa. He toured in private jets and built his own airstrips. He bolstered his image as a "man of the people" by building soccer stadiums, schools and housing – all paid for with drug money. When Columbian Presidential candidate Luis Carlos Galan publicly called out Escobar as a drug dealer, Escobar was deeply offended and hired a lawyer to sue Galan for defamation of character. Imagine: the biggest drug dealer in the world, hiring a lawyer to sue someone for calling him a drug dealer. When Escobar lost the case, he had Galan murdered instead.

Violent criminals have an almost limitless capacity for self-deception, and serial killers are no different. Serial killers not only believe they're good people, but typically believe they're *more* moral than others, since they are honest with themselves about their desires. They fail to believe that the average person does not wish to manipulate and harm others.

"I'm not really a bad person. I like to think of myself as a misunderstood person who just happened to make a lot of bad decisions. But those other good law abiding citizens out there don't see me like that. It's just a damned shame...but that's society for you. You kill and eat a couple of people and they never let you forget it."

Joseph Methany (Earley, 2012).

THE GINGERBREAD REACTION
& KILLER'S BLACKOUTS

> "This may sound rich coming from me, but the moment the girl became a corpse, I realized I had lost an important friend and even regretted killing her for a moment. What I truly wished was to eat her living flesh. Nobody believes me, but my ultimate intention was to eat her, not necessarily to kill her. To this day, I still think, *If only she had let me taste her, just a little bit...*"
>
> Japanese killer Issei Sagawa, describing his murder of a university classmate and friend (Kosuga, 2008)

I once arrived at a friend's house around Christmas time, and saw that he and his 4-year-old son had built a beautiful gingerbread house together. Later that evening, the boy wanted to eat some gingerbread. He begged his father excitedly for a piece. His father calmly broke off a small piece of the roof and handed it to the boy, who immediately burst into tears. The child hadn't realized that his desire for a piece of gingerbread would cause the destruction of the gingerbread house. Serial killers often react the same way to their treatment of victims. They wish to have their way with the "object" that is in front of them, and then react with shock and horror when they realize what they're done. One reaction to such severe mental trauma is blackouts, since these allow killers to psychologically skip the most uncomfortable part of their crimes.

It's difficult to say what's going on in the brain when a killer experiences a blackout. The first possibility is that the killer is experiencing a *petit-mal* seizure, and that once this happens some kind of dramatic event is inevitable – though not necessarily murder. A second possibility is that the trancelike state that appears to be a seizure is actually a physical reaction to the *decision* made by the killer to commit violence, and can be re-experienced during recollection of the event. This possibility was suggested to me by a retired corrections officer, who said that whenever she saw an inmate's eyes stare at someone with intensity and gloss over, she knew she had to act quickly to prevent a murderous act (Boutilier, 2014).

"The second occurrence was 1984, roughly. And I met this guy downtown, one of the Milwaukee bars. We went back to the hotel - just planning on getting drunk. I had put some sleeping pills in his drink, to render him unconscious. And, I was just going to spend the night with him. When I woke up in the morning, my forearms were bruised, and his chest was bruised and blood was coming out of his mouth. He was hanging over the side of the bed. I, uh, have no memory of beating him to death...but I must have."

Jeffrey Dahmer, in an interview with CNBC (1994), describing a killer's blackout.

Non-convulsive epilepsy, also known as "latent epilepsy" or "larval epilepsy" due to the stage of dormancy between episodes, was recognized in hospitals in France as far back as the late 1800s. The characteristics of non-convulsive epilepsy are changeable moods, exaggerated mental activity, spontaneous outbursts and mental instability. Feelings of dread, misfortune, or guilt generally predict an attack.

When attacks come, they're characterized by out-of-body sensations and a lack of conscious control. The hallmarks of this stage are rage and violence (sometimes including self-mutilation), followed by a loss of consciousness and deep sleep from which the sufferer awakes with no memory of the event.

The most famous early sufferer of non-convulsive epilepsy was painter Vincent Van Gogh. During one panic, Van Gogh cut off his own ear, gave it to a woman he admired as a present, and then went back to his room to sleep. He awoke with no recollection of the event (Naifeh, 2011). Today, we would recognize this description as a kind of *petit mal* seizure in which neurons fire randomly, scattering regular brain functions without producing convulsions.

"...she sat there without moving a muscle - for three hours; just staring, straight ahead. I couldn't take my eyes off of her. I was placing bets with myself on when she was going to move. She never even moved an arm, or shifted her legs or brushed a fly away; just stared straight ahead at nothing. It wasn't normal. It was the strangest thing I've ever seen. And it gave me the creeps."

Ernie England, describing his neighbor, Karla Homolka. Homolka had been sitting in a deck chair in her backyard (Williams, 2003).

Every serial killer who has blackouts experiences them in a slightly different manner. Some killers describe blackouts as "sudden sleepiness;" others describe it as being controlled by outside forces; and still others experience a panic with a period of partial or complete memory loss.

Arthur Shawcross described his blackouts as being similar to *petit mal* seizures, complete with visions. According to Shawcross' psychiatrist Dorothy Lewis, he would see bright white lights, and the next thing he knew he would wake up in his car with a body beside him. Killer Richard Cottingham described his blackouts as being a zone where he was guided independently, as if by remote control. Jerome Brudos described his blackouts as a kind of diabetic shock: "...I get this attack of low blood sugar, and I could walk off the roof of a building and not know what I was doing" (Douglas & Olshaker, 1995). Ted Bundy described it as being in a state of panic, then "breaking out of a fever," and finally waking up to the realization that he'd committed murder yet again.

As a child, Kenneth Bianchi suffered from facial tics and also daydreamed frequently. His mother called his daydreams "trancelike," and noted that his eyes would roll back into his head. She consulted a doctor who reached a diagnosis of *petit-mal* seizures, but was assured that her son would grow out of it (O'Brien, 1985). Killer John Wayne Gacy experienced seizures so frequently as a child that he was placed on anti-convulsive medication. Similarly, when Richard Ramirez was in grade school, friends said he would suddenly slump over in his desk until he fell to the floor.

> "I could often tell I was about to get what I needed from an offender when he would start talking about the crime and a look would come into his eyes as if he were in a trance, as if here were having an out-of-body experience. The crime - what he did to another person, the way he exerted power and control - was the most intense, stimulating, and memorable experience of his life."
>
> John Douglas, FBI profiler (Douglas & Olshaker, 1999).

As an adult, rapist and murderer Russell Williams entered a trancelike state while in front of hundreds of guests during his speech at a flight-school graduation dinner. According to a guest who was present at the event, Williams suddenly stopped speaking, then "just stood there looking at everybody with a grin on his face. Not a word was said, everybody was just stone quiet, and conversation that was going on while he was talking just totally stopped" (Gibb, 2011).

Some law enforcement officers doubt the existence of blackouts, and contend that they're merely excuses serial killers use to "conveniently forget" details of their crimes. Such doubt is surprising, since law enforcement officers experience the same seizure-like states and blackouts when *they* are put into life-and-death situations. In a study of Officer-Involved Shootings (OIS), for example, it was found that many officers experienced their shootouts in slow-motion or with altered sensory states such as heightened clarity of vision, tunnel vision, and intensified sounds or silence (Artwohl, 2002). Officers reported being "on autopilot," with no real awareness of what they were doing, while 40% had a kind of out-of-body experience. One officer said that during a shootout he was surprised to see beer cans floating through the air past his face, with the word *Federal* written on them. He later realized that the "beer cans" were actually the shell casings being ejected by the officer firing next to him. Almost half of the officers (46%) reported memory loss.

"I told the SWAT team that the suspect was firing at me from down a long dark hallway about 40 feet long. When I went back to the scene the next day, I was shocked to discover that he had actually been only about 5 feet in front of me in an open room. There was no dark hallway." (Artwohl, 2002).

While blackouts are common for serial killers, they're not an excuse to forget the facts during an interrogation or in a courtroom. A killer may not always remember the murder itself, but will certainly remember the events leading up to it and following it, often with remarkable clarity and detail even years after the event.

Despite their efforts to distance themselves from their murders, their subconscious minds know the truth. Killers frequently use drugs and alcohol in their attempts to cope with the resulting stress, and ulcers are commonplace.

CARING ABOUT VICTIMS

In his book, *Criminal Shadows* (1993), criminal profiler David Canter wrote about a serial rapist in the U.K. who, after raping a victim at knifepoint, gave her directions to find her way home as if he genuinely cared about her well-being. Why do serial killers and rapists believe that during sexual assaults, they are developing relationships with their victims?

At first glance, one can dismiss the criminal's notion of "relationship building" as sheer fantasy, or as stemming from an inability to understand real relationships. But it is more than that. Rapists and killers may feel they're bonding in part from the actions of their victims, who instinctively use appeasement language and submissiveness as survival techniques.

Upon realizing they're overpowered and that resistance will only result in further harm, many victims switch immediately to compliance and relationship building. Saying to a rapist, "I know you would never hurt me," implies that the perpetrator is too kind to commit murder, as is simultaneously a positive suggestion.

Stockholm Syndrome, a complex form of denial and attachment, occurs when frightened and confused victims actively seek to bond with their abusers. Victims want to bond with their abusers as quickly as possible, because they believe this will prevent their abusers from harming them further (sometimes it works). In the process, victims may convince *themselves* they have bonded as well.

After having received many "compliments" from victims, a rapist or murderer may come to believe that he is forming genuine bonds with them, and that the bonding was not merely born out of fear.

Killer Russell Williams told one victim during an assault that she was "pretty and sweet," allowed her to check on her baby, and asked her a host of personal questions, such as how long she had lived in town and how old her baby was. With a second victim, he loosened her blindfold after she said it was too tight, got her a Tylenol when she complained of a headache (she had a headache because he had beaten her in the head) and even massaged her temples. As the woman's ordeal was coming to an end, she actually reminded Williams to wipe his fingerprints off the Tylenol bottle. Williams could be forgiven for imagining that the assault was "not that bad," and that the victim had his interests in mind.

> "I got to know them, and they me. They came to understand what was expected of them and almost always willingly complied. I learned everything about their lives, and they rarely lied to me...the ironic thing was that most of my ladies actually came to like me."
>
> "Torso Killer" Richard Cottingham, describing his rape victims (Fezzani, 2015).

In some cases, if a victim does not use appeasement language, a criminal may force the victim to supply it. In the FBI profile of then-rapist Paul Bernardo (Document D115; Nov 17, 1998) it notes that he forced his victims to say, "Tell me you hate your boyfriend and love me," and "Tell me that you love me, tell me that it feels good," all while holding his victims at knifepoint. The FBI profile called these statements "ego-gratifying." Forced statements serve the dual purpose of gratifying the offender's ego, while also easing his conscience. Though Bernardo was committing forced rapes, he still got to hear words that made it seem as though his victims were willing participants.

In Sedgwick County Court (June 27, 2005), Dennis Rader explained that when he was tying up the Otero family, whose home Rader had broken into, Mr. Otero complained of pain due to a cracked rib from a recent car accident. Rader placed a thick coat underneath Mr. Otero for cushioning, put a pillow underneath his head, and loosened his bonds. "I re-loosened the bonds a couple of times," Rader explained, and "tried to make Mr. Otero as comfortable as I could." Once Mr. Otero was comfortable, Rader strangled him to death.

For normal people, such erratic behavior is difficult to understand. How can a person be kind and caring one moment and brutal the next? One must remember that for a serial killer, such distinctions are meaningless. Tying up a man is an action. Putting a pillow underneath his head is an action. Killing him is an action. It's all part of making the fantasy go as smoothly as possible.

"If I could eliminate those fantasies, those overwhelming fantasies, starting when I was 15 or 16 – short-circuited them, not think about them, not entertaining them – then that probably would've stopped everything."

Jeffrey Dahmer (FBI, 1992).

DEFENSE MECHANISMS

DENIAL

> "My parents might have made some mistakes that they weren't really aware of."
>
> Columbine High School mass murderer Eric Harris, in a home video filmed on March 15, 1999 (Evidence Item #265). Though Harris doesn't give any specific examples of his parent's mistakes, one is obvious: according to Harris, his parents took away a box he had labeled *explosives*, in which they found pipe bombs. Not only did his parents fail to alert the police, but after removing the pipe bombs they gave the box back to Harris, still filled with clock parts and fuses. This is denial.

A question that always arises once a serial killer is exposed and convicted is, "How on earth didn't his spouse/family/friends know about this? Surely they must have known."

In high school I had a friend (we'll call him "Jim") who, in a moment of idiocy, decided to drive around in his highly recognizable truck, shooting out car windows with an air rifle. Jim's father heard rumors that his son had committed the crime. A few day's later, while I was at their house, Jim's father confronted his son about the accusations. Jim denied everything. Jim's father left the house for several minutes, then reappeared holding a packet of air gun pellets. "I found these behind the seat of the truck," he explained. But then Jim's father shocked us both. "Someone must have planted these in your truck," he said. "From now on, you'll have to lock your truck in the garage at night." Faced with reports from citizens who said they saw his son shooting out car windows, knowing his son owned an air rifle, and now having evidence of air rifle ammunition in the vehicle, Jim's father did the only thing he could: apply psychological denial. His son was still a good son, and he was still a good father. The incident was not discussed again.

Ted Bundy's girlfriend, Elizabeth Kloepfer (aka Meg Anders), was well aware of the description of a killer on the loose in her hometown of Seattle, Washington: a man with brown hair, drives a Volkswagen Beatle, introduces himself as "Ted," and feigns injury with a cast or crutches. She also knew that her boyfriend fit the description.

Several times, Kloepfer had confronted Bundy about his odd behavior and his similarities to the purported killer. She once saw Bundy retrieving a crowbar from under a radiator in their hallway, and noticed the pockets of his jacket bulging. When she reached into his pocket to see what was there, she pulled out a surgical glove. She couldn't remember how he had explained it, only that it seemed weird. When she found plaster of paris and crutches in his room, he said he'd stolen the plaster from a medical supply centre, and that the crutches belonged to his landlord.

When they first met, Bundy had swept Kloepfer off her feet with admiration and romance. He took her for fancy meals and to expensive hotels. He made her breakfast while she slept. He wrote her poetry. He wasn't jealous about her daughter from a previous marriage; he read bedtime stories to her and made her laugh. For her daughter's birthday, Bundy baked a cake and decorated it himself. Of course, life wasn't perfect.

Kloepfer often fought with Bundy about his infidelity, his shoplifting, and his lies.

If Kloepfer admitted to herself that Bundy could be the killer, she stood to lose a great deal. She would lose the handsome man who regularly told her that he loved her. She would lose the time and effort she had invested into their relationship. She would have to confront the demons of her own situation: *Why has a killer chosen me as a girlfriend? What's wrong with me?* Kloepfer finally gave Bundy's name to police after a friend insisted she do so, only to discover that three other people had already submitted his name. She soon got back together with Bundy, scolding herself for ever having doubted him. Bundy was later convicted of murder and sentenced to death.

> "...if there was the slightest chance that he was innocent, I couldn't and wouldn't let go."
>
> Elizabeth Kloepfer, girlfriend of Ted Bundy (Kloepfer, 1981).

Amy Voell, girlfriend of killer Cody Legebokoff, stated in court that during their relationship she visited him at his apartment three or four times a week, often staying the night. Voell testified that she had noticed the blood stains in her boyfriend's apartment, including a "bloody hand print" on the wall near the entrance, a "big blood stain" on the carpet leading to the bedroom, another one on the living room curtains, and yet another on the sofa. Legebokoff had told her that the hand print was from a night he had been drunk and injured his foot. The curtain stain was from a nosebleed. Voell apparently didn't ask about the other stains. She also didn't ask why he hadn't cleaned up the stains, nor did she ask about the logger's pickaxe leaning against the wall in his bedroom.   Instead, they discussed marriage.

In serial killer investigations, the powerful psychological defense mechanism of *denial* is everywhere. It's found when police officers refuse to accept that a serial killer is operating in their jurisdiction, despite the consistency of the missing persons. It's found when a mother refuses to believe her daughter is dead, insisting that the officers standing in her doorway must be mistaken. Denial is found in the killer, who refuses to accept that he is not a superior being who can do as he pleases. And, denial is found in the lovers, family and friends of the killer. Denial is the conscious rejection of any fact that is too painful or earth shattering to be dealt with at the present time.

There are many elements that make denial a formidable psychological force, guilt being primary among them. A social worker once told me that she could always spot abused children by how loving they are toward their parents. Visiting a typical family, a social worker will chat with the parents while the children play nearby, ignoring the adults and their boring talk. Abused children, in contrast, will often sit on a parent's lap, hugging them and telling the social worker how much they love daddy or mommy. They know what their parents have done, and are afraid they'll be taken away. Sigmund Freud's name for this is *reaction formation*: the tendency for anxiety-ridden people to act strongly in the direction opposite to their true feelings.

When confronted with facts showing that her lover could be a killer, a woman may become more attached to him than ever before. She will defend him. She will work tirelessly toward his exoneration. She will refuse to believe she has been duped.

When reality begins to overwhelm denial, killers will attempt to re-build feelings of guilt in those closest to them in order to keep *reaction formation* flowing. In a process called *gaslighting*, for instance, killers make the people closest to them doubt their intuition, even suggesting they should feel guilty for not believing ridiculous explanations. A killer might say to a loved one, "If you keep doubting me, how can our relationship grow?" Killers attempt to make the act of doubting itself something to feel guilty about.

On Feb. 25, 2005, an FBI agent knocked on the door of Kerri Rawson, the daughter of Dennis Rader. The agent told her that her father was a suspect in multiple murders, and that they needed a sample of her DNA for comparison. Kerri was furious at the agent: *How dare he accuse my father!* Yet, just after the agent left, she took down a photo of her father that had been hanging in the hallway and stuck it in a closet (Wenzl, 2015). At some level, she knew.

Ann Rule, a former police officer who was Ted Bundy's friend (and later biographer), refused to believe that her friend Ted could be a serial killer, even after his arrest. One night, she dreamed that she was cuddling a baby she knew to be Ted. Suddenly, the baby revealed sharp teeth and bit her hand. When she woke up, her period of psychological denial was over.

Remember that a narcissist's lies are effective not because they are necessarily *believable*, but because they are *possible*. Only a hint of doubt is necessary for loved ones to maintain their beliefs. But while self-doubt and guilt make an unlikely explanation acceptable on a *conscious* level, that same explanation will never suffice at a *subconscious* one. As denial fades, the truth is laid bare.

No discussion about denial would be complete without addressing the elephant in the room: *hybristophilia*. Some women are attracted to men who lie, cheat and murder. Some women *know*. They stay not because they are abused, and not because they're in denial. They stay because they enjoy the thrill of being with a dangerous man who "needs them."

Ted Bundy, during his incarceration, is said to have received hundreds of love letters. Similarly, prosecutors at the trial of Richard Ramirez were appalled to see a crowd of female teenage groupies filling the courtroom, giggling with joy whenever Ramirez made eye contact with them.

"This is the term I've been searching all along and I finally found it. I've been saying right from the start that I believed that my infatuation with Luka began as a psychlogical protection mechanism of some sort. That the thought that someone like Luka could commit such a gruesome crime, and the implications that has that literally ANYONE I see anywhere could also be a killer, have caused me such anxiety that my mind subconsciously surpressed any negative emotions towards Luka by covering it up with "warm fuzzy" feelings. Like a psychological self-medication against extreme anxiety."

"Lexa Mancini," a girl who ran a Luka Magnotta fan website from July-Dec 2012, describing *reaction formation*. Magnotta, whose real name was Eric Newman, was a male stripper, gay porn actor and prostitute incarcerated for dismembering a student and mailing the body parts to local schools and government officials.

A woman who is in love with a serial killer is little different from a woman who is in love with an arms dealer or gangster. She may know that her husband is not entirely above board, but is willing to "not ask questions" in order to enjoy the benefits (or at least the fantasy) and the thrill of the relationship. In some cases, a woman will become complicit with her lover's crimes, even taking the lead.

Other women have difficulty reconciling the murderous facts surrounding a criminal with the mild-mannered, polite person staring them in the face. They find the criminal's relative normalcy terrifying, and they hide their fears with affection. Women in such relationships are looking for someone to nurture. They believe that a killer is a misunderstood person who can change with just the right combination of love and affection – *their* love and affection. They are wrong.

> "...young women, older women, married women, all seemed to go crazy over the cons who were working at the [mental] hospitals. I assume the aura, or adventure, danger, the chance for a little excitement drove them. I know all the inmates, ugly or handsome, back or white, had their hands full. It was amazing to me."
>
> Serial killer Timothy Krajcir (Echols & Byers, 2010).

Though less common, men can also become attracted to killers. Jodi Arias was a shapely, intelligent young woman who made world headlines after she was arrested for murder. She had killed her ex-boyfriend by shooting him in the head, slicing his throat, and stabbing him at least 27 times. In prison, Arias said she received a proposal for marriage almost every week, often from already-married men who found her combination of sweetness and viciousness exciting. She eventually accepted one of the offers and was married in a prison ceremony.

RATIONALIZATIONS

> "What's violent about pulling your finger across the trigger? There's no violence. It's just a person there and you move your finger and they're gone. What's violent about that?"
>
> Charles Manson, Age 76, describing shooting a person (Hedegaard, 2013).

Rationalizations occur when people invent explanations for negative actions that don't fit their self-image. A woman who considers herself a good mother will rationalize why she gets drunk in front of her daughter. A woman who considers herself a good wife will rationalize why she has affairs. A man who considers himself a good father will rationalize why he beats his children. In an interrogation, it's important for law enforcement officers to accept a subject's rationalizations. As an interviewer, if you are condescending or judgmental, the subject has no incentive to continue. If you *encourage* rationalizations that redirect blame away from the speaker, you're more likely to hear details that the speaker would find impossible to discuss otherwise.

Accepting and even encouraging rationalizations is difficult. It's not easy to accept the rationalizations of a killer who sincerely believes that his victims "deserved it." It's difficult to accept the rationalizations of a killer's spouse when she insists he's a wonderful man. But, although rationalizations let the speaker temporarily avoid responsibility, they also encourage the truth. One may take consolation in the fact that when people rationalize, it's because they've failed their own expectations of themselves.

"My, my intent was to decrease suffering in people I saw throughout my career. I didn't intend for these patients, for these people to suffer, to go through unusual things, you know. I know codes [patient emergencies] aren't pretty, but believed that my actions would not cause them pain and suffering. That I would just cause them to pass away and not to suffer or linger..."

Nurse Charles Cullen, in an interview with police, Sept 12, 2004. Cullen repeatedly claimed to have been mercy-killing his patients to end their suffering. In fact, he had been injecting insulin into prepared IV bags he knew would be distributed to patients randomly. He would then watch the hospital's computer monitor, as if it were a video game, to see which patients his death-laced bags would "hit." When a patient went into insulin shock and began convulsing, Cullen was often first on the scene for the vain attempt to save the patient, looking like a concerned hero. To their credit, the police interviewers accepted Cullen's rationalizations without berating him, and encouraged him to continue speaking.

3RD PERSON NARRATIVES

"Well, those people, they don't know Robert. They don't know me."

Musician R. Kelly, from a 2008 interview with BET, responding to the question, "Some people think that you like underage girls. What do you say to that?"

"I" is one of the most common words in the English language, showing our innate self-centeredness. And yet, something interesting happens when people explain things about themselves that are overwhelmingly negative or demeaning: they stop using "I." Sometimes they use their own name to refer to themselves, as if the speaker were a different person: "Bob made a mistake." Sometimes they refer to themselves as "he" or "she" ("He did something terrible"). Sometimes they eliminate a pronoun altogether: "It was a terrible thing that happened." Avoiding first person voice ("I") is a way for one's mind to take mercy on itself.

"I feel guilty about what happened."
"I feel guilty about what I did."

Subtle differences in phrasing show whether or not a person is ready to accept responsibility for their actions.

A young lady I once knew wrote down her entire life story in an attempt to make sense of her complicated youth. At the beginning of the story, when she was describing her relatively carefree childhood, she exclusively used "I." When her story reached the point where she began experimenting with drugs and ran away from home, she suddenly began using her own name: "Suzy was confused and didn't know what to do." At the moment in the narrative when she decided to take action and improve her life, she immediately switched back to "I." Until I pointed it out, she hadn't been aware she had done this. It was a subconscious choice.

Serial killer's lives are filled with abuse and violence. Avoiding "I" enables them to distance themselves from the action and reduce their psychological discomfort.

> "He stayed off the streets and vowed he'd never do it again and recognized the horror of what he had done and certainly was frightened by what he saw happening. It took him over three months to get over it. In the next incident, he was over it in a month."
>
> Ted Bundy, in a prison interview with journalists Stephen Michaud and Hugh Aunesworth, describing his first murder and the *gingerbread reaction.* The "he" Bundy is referring to is himself (CNBC, Nov 25, 2012).

BENIGN LANGUAGE

In a famous scene from the 1987 movie, *Full Metal Jacket*, Lieutenant Lockhart is addressing a room full of Marine Corps press agents during the Vietnam War. Lockhart informs the group that central command has given them a new directive: "In place of 'search and destroy,'" he says, "substitute the phrase 'sweep and clear.' Got it?" The Marine press corps clearly understood the ability of benign language to sterilize a mentally uncomfortable image.

Serial killers use benign language to minimize their deeds, applying neutral or even pleasant euphemisms to their violent actions. Rapists like to use the term "party" to refer to rape and assault: "I partied with her." Child molesters prefer the term, "spend time together." Charles Cullen, a nurse responsible for killing patients, called his botched murder attempts "attempts" (minus the word "murder"), and his successful murders "completions." He almost never used words like "kill," or "murder."

Whatever the expressions employed, the purpose of benign language is to ease the conscience of the speaker, and direct their attention away from the harsh truths of their existence.

Bates: How do you refer to yourself? I mean, do you call yourself a prostitute, or...
Honey: Uh, no, I call myself a professional entertainer.

"Honey," a street prostitute in Oklahoma city, as interviewed by Brian Bates, Jan 2013

BLAMING OTHERS – FALSE CONSENSUS & PSYCHOLOGICAL PROJECTION

> "Frankly, I can't fathom why everyone doesn't feel this urge to eat, to consume, other people. Don't you ever feel like this?"
>
> Japanese killer Issei Sawawa, to reporter Tomokazu Kosuga (Kosuga, 2008).

False consensus is a cognitive bias whereby a person overestimates the extent to which the beliefs and opinions of others are similar to their own. A cocaine addict, for instance, may believe that many people secretly use cocaine, or would want to. A rapist may believe that everyone wants to commit rape. A serial killer may sincerely believe that anyone who tried killing someone would like it. People want to be unique, but not in negative ways. For their negative traits, people seek inclusion and consensus. They convince themselves that other people think like them and support them.

> "And I'm telling you [the reason is], because the cops let me keep killin' 'em Nick, don't you get it?!"
>
> Aileen Wuornos, angrily explaining to interviewer Nick Broomfield that the reason she killed seven men is because, by not capturing her earlier, the police implied it was acceptable: an example of false consensus (1992).

Psychological *projection*, first described by Sigmund Freud, is when one's own psychological deficiencies are projected onto others. A person who is worried about being weak, for example, may overcompensate by wearing "tough" clothing and bullying others, casting other people as the weak ones. A rapist or murderer who is unable to control his own sexual impulses will commonly label his victims "whores" and "sluts" or refer to them as "wanting it," thereby minimizing his inability to control himself. He might blame society for having too many rules. He might blame the victim for not fighting back hard enough. He will blame anyone but himself and his own weaknesses.

Officer: So what are you thinking as you're sitting there, thinking, 'Jeez, I just killed this lady?' What are you thinking? What's going through your head?
Gary Ridgway: You made me do it, you bitch, you whore, you worthless piece of garbage.

Inside the Mind of Serial Killer Gary Ridgway, CNN interview, aired Feb. 18, 2004

LIE AVOIDANCE – OMISSIONS, PARTIAL TRUTHS & REDEFINITIONS

On a subconscious level, even criminals feel uncomfortable lying, especially to friends and family members. To reduce their mental discomfort, they rely on psychological defense mechanisms specifically related to lying. These defense mechanisms are successful in part because they help criminals convince themselves they aren't lying at all.

Omission is telling part of the truth, without revealing all of the truth. A criminal might say, "I had lunch with her," when the truthful answer would be, "I had lunch with her, then went sightseeing with her, and then spent the night with her." Criminals prefer partial truths because they can tell themselves that they "didn't lie," which eases their conscience.

> "Do you solemnly swear that you will tell the truth, the whole truth, and nothing but the truth...?"
>
> The sworn testimony oath of the United States was designed to make omissions/partial truths the crime of perjury.

When asked a specific question, criminals will often redefine the question into the narrowest possible meaning. For example, if asked, "Are you having an affair with that woman?" a criminal may instantly redefine *affair* as "having a loving relationship while married." Using this new definition, and knowing that he is not in love, he can now answer "no" with full conviction. If asked a nonspecific question such as, "Have you seen Karen recently?" a criminal might mentally redefine *recently* as "the last 5 minutes," at which point he can confidently answer "no."

Police officer: Why did you have a baseball bat in the backseat of your car?
Suspect: I didn't. That wasn't my bat.

To avoid having subjects redefine important questions, it's useful to switch between general questions and specific ones: "Tell me about your relationship with her." "How often have you met her in private?" "Did you ever have sex with her?" When asking questions about time or place, be specific: "When have you seen her in the last 7 days?" "Did you see her last Thursday?"

Narcissists adore lie avoidance strategies, as evidenced by multitudes of interviews. To get as much of the story as possible, officers must be prepared to pepper suspects with multiple questions from multiple angles, and to ask frequent follow-up questions

---

AM640/John Oakly: Have you ever used crack?
Mayor Robert Ford: Johnny listen, I'm not a drug addict. I'm not an alcoholic...I can assure you Johnny, I do not use drugs.

Toronto mayor Robert Ford, responding to allegations that he smoked crack cocaine while in office. Ford instantly redefines "ever used crack" as "be addicted to drugs" in order to answer in the negative. A video later surfaced showing Ford smoking from a crack pipe. Aired May 30th 2013, AM640 Radio

---

WANTING TO BE CAUGHT

"Thank God! I've been stopped!"

Killer Albert DeSalvo's response to a phone call at home from police, asking him if he'd mind dropping by headquarters to answer some questions (DeNevi & Campbell, 2004).

The FBI currently rejects the idea that serial killers desire to be caught (Morton & Hilts et al, 2005), despite the persistence of the idea and the wealth of anecdotal evidence behind it. Killers leave clues at crime scenes, insert themselves into investigations, and taunt police and the media with cryptic letters and other completely unnecessary communications. Why would they do such things unless they want to be caught? On the other hand, if serial killers want to be caught, why do groups of trained law enforcement officers require weeks or even years to apprehend them, if ever? There are likely two separate but overlapping factors at work: narcissistic arrogance, and subconscious moral backlash.

Most of us have flawed images of ourselves and who we are. We downplay our flaws. We criticize those who show imperfect or immoral behavior, even if we do the same things ourselves. No one's image of himself is completely accurate.

Cognitive Dissonance Theory is the idea that people experience stress when faced with inconsistencies between their beliefs and their actions. The more inconsistent a person's beliefs and actions are, the more stress a person feels. In an attempt to reduce this stress, people tend to change their beliefs (the easy thing to do), rather than change their actions (the difficult thing to do).

An addicted smoker who knows that smoking causes cancer has two options: he can quit smoking, or he can convince himself that smoking isn't harmful. Either option reduces stress at a conscience level, but only the first option (quitting) removes stress at both a conscious *and* a subconscious level. Even if the smoker convinces himself that smoking is not harmful, his subconscious knows better.

In a powerful example of cognitive dissonance, psychologist Edmund Bergler (1958) observed that gamblers *want* to lose money. Gambling allows a person to avoid all sorts of pressures since it's an excellent excuse for failure. A man who doesn't particularly care about success, but who suffers years of relentless pressure to succeed from his wife and family, can turn to gambling and instantly be absolved of responsibility. It's no longer his lack of ability, lack of planning, inflexibility or any other personal flaw that accounts for his lack of success – it's his gambling. Although it seems like any person should want to quit gambling and succeed, in this case gambling reduces the stress caused by his family's desires (high success), versus his desire to live a simple life. He will therefore continue gambling.

In a similar vein, people may remember the housing bubble years of 2005-2008 in the United States. It was an era of prosperity, when housing pricing increased dramatically along with wages and incomes. Faced with an income and/or net worth higher than anything they ever expected, Americans went shopping. Instead of saving their newfound wealth, people renovated their homes with marble countertops and swimming pools and bought expensive new vehicles. Many of them would later lose these homes and vehicles to bankruptcy. Their fiscal irresponsibility was the result of the incongruence between their image of themselves (poor or middle-class), and their new condition (wealthy). In other words, faced with what they felt was an undeserved and unexpected level of wealth, people subconsciously worked toward becoming poorer, bringing their self-image and reality back into balance. People try to maintain equilibrium in their lives at all levels.

Since serial killers see themselves as good people, their cruelty is not tolerated by their subconscious minds. Any act that throws equilibrium off balance *will be subconsciously engaged until it is corrected.* Killers *consciously* want to be free to continue killing, but *subconsciously* want to be caught, to prevent themselves from hurting anyone else and to end their internal struggles. Killers use common expressions that reveal these subconscious battles in action. For instance, when serial killers say that they "got sloppy" or were "not as careful as before," this is a conscious explanation for their subconscious desire to be stopped.

"They got me, oh fuck. Gettin' too sloppy. I was gonna do one more, make it an even fifty. That's why I was sloppy. I wanted one more, make the big five-oh."

Robert Pickton, bragging to his cell mate that he had killed 49 women, and was trying for 50 (Cameron, 2010).

After committing murder for the first time, killers expect frantic television coverage and headlines. They expect their phones to ring. They expect sirens converging in the distance, and SWAT teams hammering on their front doors. They sit back and wait for the inevitable in nervous apprehension. But then, something even more dramatic happens: nothing.

Serial killers are astonished by how long it takes them to get caught. Because they feel unique and special, they find it hard to believe that anyone could *not* notice them. The more they kill without incident, the more personally brilliant they feel, and the more they magically believe that law enforcement will never catch them.

> "We believed we would never get caught. It was all part of a game, we thought we were better than they were."
>
> "Railway Killer" John Duffy (Clough et al, 2001)

There are numerous examples of how brazen serial killers can be, but perhaps the best example is the arrogance of "Hillside Strangler" Kenneth Bianchi. Just days after committing murder, Bianchi went on a ride-along with the Los Angeles Police Department, trying to join the force. During the ride-along, Bianchi asked the patrol officer if they could visit the Hillside Strangler sites. To Bianchi's disappointment, the patrol officer was not familiar with them. The officer suspected nothing.

Serial killers fail to appreciate that their murders are difficult to solve primarily because many of their motives – including thrill-seeking, anger, power & control – are intangible. Serial killers are not killing to avenge injustices. They're not killing out of necessity or despair. Their murders are often of people they hardly know, during moments of anger or selfish indifference.

Over time, killers gradually convince themselves that since they're superior to police they can make mistakes without repercussions. They can leave clues, take chances, and write taunting letters to the press. Cognitive dissonance forces them to make foolish mistakes.

For law enforcement officers, serial killer arrogance is a blessing. The more incompetent a killer feels that law enforcement is, the more incompetent the killer becomes.

> "I honestly believe I wanted to get caught. I started taking a lot of chances. Even the night I got caught, I had plenty of time to leave before the police arrived. What did I do? I slowly drove by the police, he took off after me and I was arrested again. I was glad it was over."
>
> Timothy Krajcir (Echols & Byers, 2010).

The list of criminals who have made foolish mistakes is a long one. It includes Ted Bundy, who used his real name – "Ted" – to introduce himself to women he was stalking. It includes Robert Pickton, who offered to dispose of bodies for his friends, should they ever need the service. It includes "Green River Killer" Gary Ridgway, who called up a volunteer hotline and offered to help look for the killer. And it includes Dennis Rader, the BTK killer.

Dennis Rader, the self-named "Bind Torture Kill" murderer, evaded capture for decades, but investigators would later discover he had been inserting himself into the investigation all along. At one point, Rader was working as a home security installer, and business was booming because of his own rapes and murders. The job not only allowed him access to premises, but also gave him inside knowledge of alarm systems. In the ultimate irony, people were calling up the murderer to enhance their safety.

At the 25th anniversary of his killings, the story of the "BTK Killer" was documented in a local newspaper, *The Wichita Eagle*. Unwilling to pass up such an incredible opportunity for self-promotion, Rader began sending letters to the press and police after a multi-year period of silence, taking responsibility for more murders and letting them know he was alive and well. In one of Rader's letters, he absurdly asked the police if a floppy disk (digital storage medium) could be traced to a particular computer. The police said, "no," hoping he'd be foolish enough to send them something. He did. Police received a disk that listed the last location used as "Christ Lutheran Church," and the last user as "Dennis." Within minutes, police confirmed that a man named Dennis Rader was congregation president. Surveillance began on Rader immediately, ultimately leading to his arrest. Rader was later quoted as saying that he didn't think the police would lie.

> "I feel pretty good. It's kind of like a big burden that was lifted off my shoulders."
>
> Dennis Rader in court on June 27, 2005. Rader had just detailed his murders to Judge Waller.

Occasionally, though rarely, a killer's inner turmoil reaches the point where it becomes unbearable. In November of 1998, for instance, a man named Wayne Adam Ford strolled up to the counter at the Humboldt County Sheriff's office and told the desk Sergeant that he had "hurt people." To prove it, Ford took a plastic bag out of his pocket containing a severed women's breast and placed it on the counter. Even after this, detectives *still* had to fight for a confession from Ford, as he realized he'd likely get the death penalty if he continued cooperating. He eventually confessed to four murders, and is currently on death row.

"Co-Ed Killer" Ed Kemper murdered his grandparents when he was just a child. As an adult, the 6'9" man spent his free time hanging out at a bar across from the local courthouse called "The Jury Room," where he'd chat with police and they would buy each other drinks. Like most serial killers, Kemper respected men in positions of martial authority, even as he looked down upon them. The bar visits gave Kemper a convenient way to find out if police were looking in the right direction (clearly they weren't). When Kemper's subconscious turmoil finally overwhelmed him, he called the Santa Cruz police department to turn himself in, only to be accidentally cut off. Not willing to give up, Kemper called back, confessing to eight murders while still in the phone booth (UPI, 1973). After the operator assured him the police would come, Kemper waited patiently to be arrested.

Being a murderer is, as author Truman Capote described in the novel *In Cold Blood* (1965), like "running a race without a finish line." It is exhausting. It's the duty of law enforcement officers to help criminals free themselves from their inner turmoil by apprehending them and obtaining their confessions.

Phillips: Were you relieved to be arrested?
Dahmer: Part of me was, and part of me wasn't (long pause).
Phillips: Explain.
Dahmer: (Sighs) I don't know, it's like...I don't believe I have a split personality, but you know the feeling where you're sort of glad about something, but on the other hand you're not? That's how it was. It was a relief not to have to keep such a gigantic secret, that I'd kept for so many years. And once I saw that I had no choice but to face it, I decided to face it head on, and, make a full confession. So, I am glad that the secrets are gone.

Killer Jeffrey Dahmer, verbalizing the mental conflict between his conscious and subconscious desires in an interview with MSNBC, 2009. In an earlier interview, Dahmer claimed he was certain he had "...no subconscious secret desire to ever be caught." Yet, in the same interview he stated that only part of him regrets being caught. He added, "Intellectually I know this is the best thing that could of happened for me and everybody else involved, because I could not stop myself" (FBI, 1992). By definition, people are not consciously aware of their subconscious desires.

PART 8:
SERIAL KILLER
INTERROGATIONS

STRATEGIES FOR LAW
ENFORCEMENT

In October of 1969, Sergeant Gutierrez of the Los Angeles Police Department interviewed Dianne Lake (aka Snake), a member of Charles Manson's "Family" cult group, using threats and intimidation (for instance, threatening she would be sent to the gas chamber). After two hours of interrogation, the only admission he obtained from Lake was that she liked chocolate bars. Later, officers Gibbons & Gardiner interviewed Dianne Lake with patience and understanding, and she admitted not only that Charles Manson had ordered the killings, but also that a member of the Family (Charles "Tex" Watson) had stabbed victim Sharon Tate.

In November of 2010, 21-year-old Cody Legebokoff was being investigated for murder at police headquarters in the northern city of Prince George, Canada. Interviewer Darren Carr, an officer with a strong British accent, told Legebokoff that the city of Prince George was small compared to his hometown of London, England. He asked Legebokoff to guess how big London is. He emphasized their differences. The entire interview lasted less than six minutes. Next came in Detective Greg Yanicki, who asked Legebokoff if he was alright and being treated fairly. Yanicki sat down to eat a sandwich with Legebokoff, and for the next hour they chatted about small towns, car dealerships, fishing, ranching, the lumber industry, hockey, girlfriends and more. Yanicki would later spent hours successfully interviewing Legebokoff.

Officially, an *interview* is a conversation with a person whose involvement in a crime is uncertain, or who may have knowledge of a crime without being directly involved in it. An *interrogation* is conducted with a suspect. In practice, the two terms are used interchangeably.

If your image of "interrogation" or "investigative interviewing" includes threats and screaming, then your view isn't an effective one. Aside from the fact that evidence obtained using excessive use of force is inadmissible in court, the information gained by it is often incorrect anyway.

The best way to get information from anyone is to ask questions and listen to the answers. Subjects who don't find anything in common with you are less likely to speak with you. Interviewing means conversation.

PREPARATION

An interrogation is very much like an investigative journalist's interview, where the guest may be intentionally withholding information, or even hostile. Successful journalists know in advance what topics they want to discuss. They prepare questions but don't stick to a script, letting the conversation flow freely. Law enforcement interrogations must have clear purpose and direction. The following techniques, employed by successful investigative journalists, are also highly effective in interrogations.

KNOW YOUR SUBJECT

Knowing the facts of the case is a necessity, but an interviewer should ideally know *everything* about the subject that it's humanly possible to know: who their friends are, what they care about, and what they *don't* care about. You should know how they take their coffee: *"Two cream and one sugar, just as you like it."* You should know what a day in the life of your subject looks like.

PREPARE YOUR GOALS

In an interview with a killer, one's ultimate goal is often assumed to be a confession. But is that the goal? And if it is, is it the goal of *this* interview? The goal of the first interview may simply be to determine the subject's relationship to the scene. It may be to understand the significance of a piece of physical evidence. Have specific goals for the interview, and work toward them methodically.

PREPARE QUESTIONS

Prepare important questions in advance, but don't expect to ask them all. Let the conversation flow, rather than moving from question to question like a grocery list. Determine exactly how you're going to ask the questions, including tone, volume, and facial expression. To put the subject at ease and ensure understanding, use language that matches the subject's lifestyle and education level. Anticipate how the subject could evasively answer your questions. If possible, do role-plays prior to the real interview. To test a subject's cooperation level, ask questions you already know the answers to. If a subject gives you a ridiculous explanation, point it out to them, and wait.

WORK ON FLOW

If the subject admits to knowledge of a crime, then what? Do you have a plan? Questions should never be prepared in isolation, but as a transition point to the next question or topic. Don't spin off into a new topic just because you have other questions on your list. Ask follow-up questions.

Subjects are, as much as their interviewers, anticipating questions and formulating answers. They're thinking of ways to manipulate and mislead you, and to appear honest and forthright while doing so. Unless you prepare more thoroughly than your subjects, you're at a disadvantage.

> "The expectation that an interrogator could walk into a room with a high-value detainee and simply employ 'techniques' to gain accurate and important information significantly underestimates the complexity of effective intelligence interviews."
>
> Intelligence Science Board, 2009

CLASSICAL INTERVIEW FORM & STRESS MANIPULATION

In the early 1900s, psychologists Robert Yerkes and John Dodson recognized that animals perform complex tasks most efficiently when in an optimal, intermediate level of physiological arousal. If their arousal (stress) levels are too low, subjects don't give tasks their best attention. If their arousal levels are too high, subjects are unable to concentrate, reducing their effectiveness.

Sales offices around the world have discovered the practical value of Yerkes & Dodson's research. In an overly casual office environment workers are ineffective, spending too much time chatting and sipping coffee. Conversely, in an ultra-high-paced environment, workers make excessive errors, bad decisions, and are prone to exhaustion. An optimal stress level lies somewhere between these two extremes, resulting in a superior level of performance.

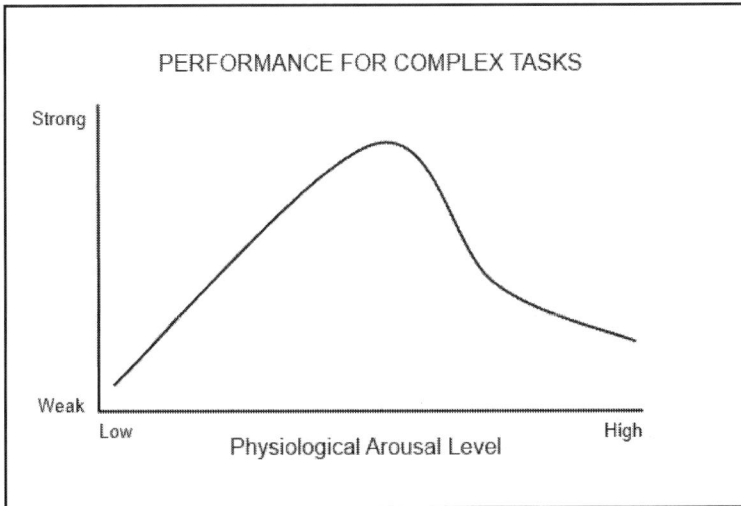

PERFORMANCE FOR COMPLEX TASKS

Strong

Weak

Low   Physiological Arousal Level   High

Long before Yerkes-Dodson's research existed, playwright William Shakespeare manipulated the arousal/stress levels of his audience. He knew his audience had to be stimulated to be entertained; yet they'd become fatigued if a high level of action or suspense were kept up for an entire play. Recognizing these constraints, he employed what is now known as the "classical" play structure. In this structure, anxious scenes are followed by relaxed ones, followed by still more anxious scenes, rising to a high point or climax in the middle of the play. Following this high point, the scenes gradually taper down to a conclusion.

In an interrogation, even telling the truth is mentally demanding. One must tell what happened, explain why, and make educated guesses regarding one's motivations and feelings. But while telling the truth is demanding, maintaining lies is *exhausting*. When lying, one must use appropriate body language and expressions, invent details and events, all while maintaining the consistency of a reasonable story and remembering the details for later.

Like William Shakespeare in his plays, an effective interviewer intentionally mixes periods of low arousal and high arousal, manipulating the mental demands of the interview to elicit information. When working with an uncooperative subject, the effective interviewer will rarely let the subject ride in the optimal arousal zone; instead, he'll ensure the subject is either mentally overloaded, or relaxed to the point of boredom. Since serial killers are adept at faking emotions, lying and deception, putting them "off their game" by manipulating their stress levels is crucial. Subjects should only be allowed to ride in the middle range if they are cooperative.

Managing the correct level of mental stress during an interrogation is a balancing act. A level that is consistently low will not create the pressure required to extract information, though it may reveal clues. A level that is too high for too long will simply cause the subject to shut down. It's important to note that "stress," in the context on an interview, doesn't refer to making threats and kicking chairs. Stress is achieved by focus, pace, and the introduction of uncomfortable topics.

Any technique that taxes a subject's mental abilities can be used to reveal deception (examples follow). It's notable that for a truthful subject, none of these techniques are particularly stressful. If you really watched a movie, how stressful would it be to be asked about the movie? These techniques are only stress-inducing if the subject is lying or knows uncomfortable information. It's not that an untruthful subject will necessarily be caught off-guard or be unable to answer the questions. It's that the mental power required to fabricate the answers will eventually become overwhelming.

TECHNIQUES TO INCREASE MENTAL LOAD

ASKING FOR DETAILS
"What restaurant did you eat at? Did you make a reservation? What did you order? How much did you pay?"
"What movie did you watch at the theatre? What time did it start? How full was the theatre? How much were the tickets?"
"You mentioned that you were knocking on the door. Was the door made of metal or wood? What color was it?"

CONFUSING THE SUBJECT'S PERSONAL PERSPECTIVE
"How do you imagine the victim's father felt about the incident? What do you think he'll do?"
"Why do you think she was chosen as a victim? What do you know about her?"
"If you were the killer, what would you have done?"

MIXING FALSE & TRUE FACTS FOR CONFIRMATION
"You mentioned you drove past Main Street and 1st Avenue at about 7 pm. There was a serious accident at that intersection that shut down a lane for about half an hour. How did you get through it?"
"We have information that most of the restaurant seating was closed for a private function that day. How did you manage to get a table?"

INTRODUCTIONS

If you were a suspect and a law enforcement officer said, "You're accused of killing women, and I'm here to find out why you did it," would you even begin talking? Seasoned cops have

180

actually began conversations like this, as if their intimidating physical presence alone would make a serial killer confess. Since an interview requires conversation, a better introduction is required. The purpose of a solid introduction is twofold. First, it introduces the topic of discussion. Second, it's a direct invitation to talk, minus direct accusatory elements. Be aware that in some state and countries, you must tell the subject what their charge is, and what the possible consequences are; even then, the introduction can still take on a friendly tone.

Introduce yourself ("I'm _____") and state the reasons why you're both here. For instance, "The purpose of this meeting is to talk about the disappearance of several women. I'm looking for information that will help us understand what happened." The subject is merely being asked to participate in a discussion. If an interviewer already has sufficient evidence against the suspect, the initial introduction may take on a more direct tone: "We have evidence that you are aware of the disappearance of several women. I'm here today to get your side of the story and clarify any misunderstandings." Don't be your subject's enemy. Be the neutral information gatherer, because that's precisely what you should be.

RAPPORT BUILDING / ESTABLISHING BASELINE RESPONSES

Any good salesperson will tell you that the best way to begin a sales conversation is to get to know your customer. At the beginning of an interview you are selling yourself. You are selling your expertise, your trustworthiness, and your professionalism. Begin the interview with simple questions that are non-combative.

The rapport building section of an interview is used to get the conversation rolling and sometimes to moderate a subject's anxiety level, which may be too high at the beginning of an interview. The opening of the interview is also the time to observe a subject's normal responses so you can compare these to reactions from stress questions later on.

Instead of "rapport building," the Office of the Director of National Intelligence (USA) prefers the term "operational accord." Operational accord doesn't necessarily include making friends with the subject, or casual informality. It denotes a respectful working relationship that "may allow an intelligence interviewer to engage with, challenge, and debate with the detainee [subject], or agree with him if appropriate, without shutting down the relationship or causing the loss of important information" (2009).

In the rapport-building phase, ask simple questions without worrying about whether or not the questions drive the investigation forward. "Can you please confirm for me your present address?" "How do you like your job? Tell me about your coworkers." Don't pretend to be someone you're not. Avoid treating subjects like criminals, or lecturing them about their ways or habits. You role is to question and learn, not to judge.

PERSONAL SPACE

The subject's attitude should determine how the furniture is set up in the interview room. For maximum stress, inducing a sense of vulnerability, it's best to have no desk between interviewer and subject – just plain chairs, facing each other. Choose a distance that feels "just barely" comfortable. One would use this configuration for a subject who has adopted belligerent attitudes or postures; for example, leaning back in his chair with his legs splayed out casually, as if relaxing at home. Another example would be a subject sitting slouched with arms crossed. A spartan setup of two chairs facing each other is usually enough to end such alpha displays.

A more common setup, inducing a lower stress level than the above, is to set up two chairs at ninety degrees to each other, with a desk in the corner (the desk would be to the left side of one chair, and to the right of the other). This configuration is common in police interviews and can be used in most situations.

For the least stress, use the traditional office configuration of two chairs facing each other with a desk in the middle. The desk forms a physical barrier between the interviewer and subject, and gives the subject a sense of security similar to a podium in front of a public speaker. This configuration is recommended only for subjects whose stress levels are already so high that they are distraught or having trouble communicating.

Walls and desks of the interview room should be clear of any distracting items that can cause a subject to "drift," or be used as cues to fabricate information. Functional items or props to be used in the interview should be prepared ahead of time whenever possible. If it's necessary to conduct an interview at a person's home, make sure their cell phone is turned off and other potential sources of distraction limited.

AVOIDING SCHEMAS

A *schema* is a mental matrix of preconceived ideas, based on experience. It's a way of organizing and interpreting information, but also affects the recall and recognition of information. A schema is the brain's way of quickly making sense of the world, and saving energy in the process.

The easiest way to describe a schema is by example. Take a moment to picture a doctor's office waiting room. What does it look like? Who is there? For North Americans, this image may include a reception desk with a female secretary, filing cabinets, simple chairs, and a selection of boring magazines to read while waiting. These are all things that may come to mind from hearing "doctor's office waiting room." For someone from rural Africa, however, the same scene may consist of an old school house with green and yellow walls, a wooden desk in the middle of a large room, and almost no medical equipment except the bag the doctor brought with him. As a further example, imagine another doctor's office in rural Africa, where the waiting room is white and chrome and sparkling clean, filled with modern office equipment for the doctor and her staff.

For interviewers, a problem with the human brain is that it "creates" images, based on context and experience, which may be inaccurate. Subjects sometimes exploit the human tendency to make assumptions by *intentionally* leading their interviewer's thoughts in the wrong direction. Interviewers may also lead their own thoughts in the wrong direction through no fault of the subject. Consider the following examples:

Officer: How do you know Susan?
Subject: I met her once at a party.

The subject uses the word "once," implying that he met Susan only a single time. In reality, they were lovers. The statement, "I met her once at a party" is true, but intentionally deceptive.

Officer: How do you know that Joe got shot at the club?
Subject: I heard from a guy who was there.

The subject leads the officer by saying, "I heard," suggesting that he was not present at the scene. In fact, he was also at the scene.

Officer: You said an off-duty firefighter helped you make a sling for your arm. What was his name?
Subject: It was a she. I didn't catch her name.

In this case, the interviewer misled herself, through her preconceived image of a firefighter.

Successful interviewing involves active listening: asking follow-up questions, clarifying information, paraphrasing, and asking for additional details. It means paying attention to every word the subject says, and not making assumptions. If you drift on to the next question while the one you just asked is being answered, you'll only hear the information you *expect*, missing the subtle words and phrases that can lead to a breakthrough. At worst, your mental wanderings will create gaps in the conversation that your brain will naturally fill – possibly with information that was never said.

Detective Loya: Okay. Where was her tattoo on her?
Bryant: Um, she had one on her ankle and she said she had one on her back and she said it had notes.
Detective Winters: Okay.
Detective Loya: Okay. Did you see the one on her back?
Bryant: Um, yes she showed me.

Detectives Loya and Winters, interviewing NBA basketball star Kobe Bryant for alleged sexual assault. Bryant uses, "she said," as if he had not seen the tattoo on the girl's back. To his credit, Detective Loya asks a follow-up question that confirms Bryant saw both tattoos. The entire interview was carried out with great skill. Charges against Bryant were later dropped when the woman refused to testify (2003, TheSmokingGun).

CONTEXT REINSTATEMENT

People recall information most accurately under the same conditions that the information was encoded. That is, one's memory of an event will be most vivid when recalled under the same conditions that the event occurred, including the mood, location and atmosphere. In most cases, having a witness or suspect relive the moment in the actual location under the same conditions is impossible: you can't, for instance, conduct an interview in a dark alley on a rainy night. You can, however, have a subject revisit the moment *mentally*.

During the interview, have the subject recreate the context for themselves by asking them cognitive and sensory related questions. Ask them about everything they saw, felt, smelled and heard. Ask them to give you the smallest details; even ones that they feel are irrelevant. Ask them what they were thinking at each moment. By mentally recreating the event, recall will be more detailed and accurate.

In dealing with sexual assaults and murders, "reliving the moment" may be too traumatic for a subject to endure. In this case, there are techniques an interviewer can use to make the interview tolerable while still maintaining accuracy.

One effective method for reducing subject stress while maintaining accuracy of recall is to have a subject relive the moment not as themselves but as 3rd person observer, detached from the scene by some distance: "If you were looking down from the building next door, what would you have seen? Tell me what happened." Having a subject become a 3rd person observers, and not the individual involved in the action, reduces psychological stress.

Another technique to reduce psychological stress is to have the subject start their narrative *before* the significant event started, and continue it beyond the event as well. If a woman was assaulted while jogging in the park, it may be traumatic for her to start her story at the park. Instead, she could start her narrative at home, filling a water bottle and putting on her shoes. Starting the narrative before the traumatic event helps lead a subject into it gradually, increasing mental preparedness and allowing them to recall details that may have been missed. If time permits, have a subject repeat their story in reverse order, which may allow them to recall additional details. If subject is lying, having them recall the story in reverse order will prove mentally taxing and may reveal inconsistencies.

"Let's try this differently. If it was a movie, you know like, how if we were to watch a movie together and we would have a beginning, and it would unfold - the story and stuff like that. Is it possible for you to kind of tell me, to think of it like a movie, and kind of tell me, step by step by step, kinda, how you, like, all through the story?"

Detective Greg Yanicki, interviewing serial killer Cody Legebokoff, November 28th, 2010. Though he stumbles, Yanicki successfully encourages Legebokoff to distance himself from the event by telling his story as if it were a movie scene. It took several attempts.

IDENTIFYING WATERLINE CONCERNS

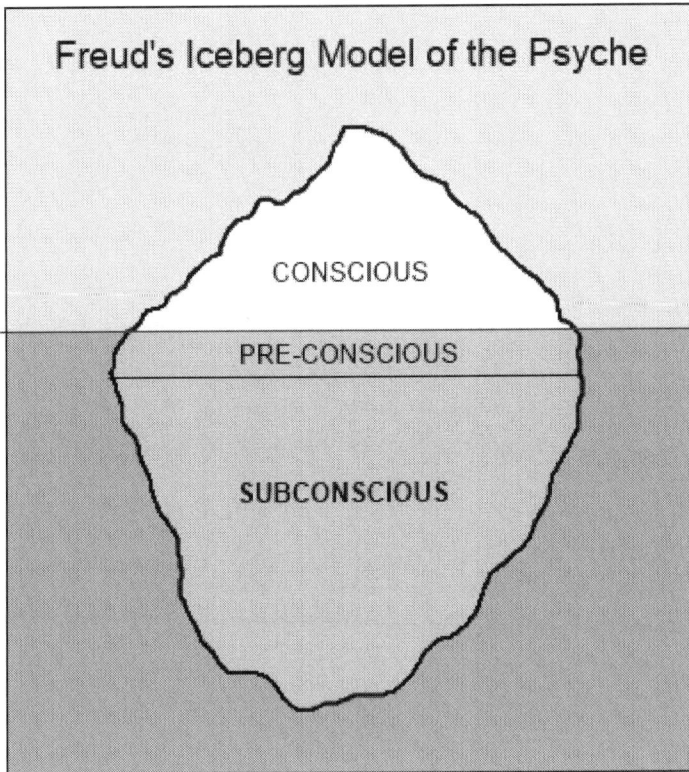

Freud's Iceberg Model of the Psyche

CONSCIOUS

PRE-CONSCIOUS

SUBCONSCIOUS

Everyone has both conscious and subconscious concerns. In Freudian terms, concerns that a person is aware of are "above the waterline" (referring to Freud's famous iceberg model of the psyche). Concerns that a person is not consciously aware of are said to be "below the waterline." For an interrogation to be maximally effective, both the subject's conscious concerns and subconscious concerns need to be identified and addressed.

Concerns that are "below the waterline" are, by definition, not consciously known to the subject and not obvious. A terrorist, for example, may express solidarity to a group not necessarily because he believes the group's doctrine, but because he has a strong need for belongingness and affiliation. *Any* group that supplies this sense of belongingness will fill his psychological need. Similarly, a serial killer who is a volunteer at his local church and gives to charity probably has a strong desire to be recognized for being a good person.

Conscious or "above the waterline" concerns are readily recognizable to both a subject and an interviewer, though the subject may not immediately realize how important his concerns are to him. A conscious concern for a killer could be, for instance, a fear that if he is incarcerated, no one will be available to take care of his pets. Or, it could be that he is worried prison food will make him fat. A conscious concern might seem trivial to an interviewer, but loom large in the mind of a subject.

When Colonel Russell Williams was arrested, his biggest concern was for his home and the needs of his wife. Williams and his wife had just purchased a new home. Williams was worried that the police would "tear the place apart" in their search for evidence, ripping up carpets and tearing down walls. The police couldn't promise to *not* search the house, but in turn for Williams' cooperation, they promised to take it easy when they did. Williams, as it turns out, was an excellent judge of his wife's character: she was paid $3000 by the Ontario Provincial Police after complaining that detectives scratched her hardwood floors during the search.

After his arrest, Israel Keyes biggest fear was that he would become infamous, and that the negative publicity would upset his mother. In his interviews with the FBI, he expressed concern that his photo would be front page news. The FBI could not legally keep Keye's information from the press, but in exchange for information they did manage to keep what could have been a media circus into a relatively low-profile affair. Keyes committed suicide while in custody nonetheless.

By recognizing a person's *subconscious* needs, an interviewer can provide subjects with the praise and respect they require, building relationships and, hopefully, leading to improved conversations. *Conscious* concerns can be used as leverage; by offering to remove a potential threat before it occurs, an interviewer can gain a subject's confidence and cooperation. As an interviewer, make sure you only make promises you can keep.

NON-VERBAL CUES

When lying, a serial killer will always touch the small indentation in the middle of his neck, just above the collarbone, with his right index finger. If a suspect touches this spot with his index finger after being asked an important question, it means he is lying. *Yeah, if only it were that simple.*

Law enforcement officers gain experience spotting lies first-hand from dealing with criminals. Experienced officers may formally study body language and interrogation. Serial killers, on the other hand, are narcissists who have been studying deception, non-verbal cues, body language, and manipulation their *entire lives*. A serial killer's very existence depends upon the successful deception of everyone around him.

Skilled interviewers are often trained to look for specific deceptive behaviors during an interrogation. However, serial killers are acutely aware of their non-verbal cues. Instead of looking for specific behaviors, I recommend looking at the overall picture of a truthful subject.

Truthful subjects make frequent eye contact with their interviewers, use natural movements and gestures, clarify information without prompting, and interject new information as they remember it. They may be nervous but will appear natural.

Deceptive subjects, on the other hand, appear "unnatural." Their stories seem rehearsed and deliberate. Their answers are controlled, sometimes only given after long pauses. They either avoid details, or throw in irrelevant and confusing ones. They try hard to build rapport: women may be flirtatious. Their reactions are over-the-top and often inappropriate.

If you are in doubt as to whether or not a subject is being truthful, compare the two descriptions above to the person in front of you. Ignore the person's attractiveness (or lack thereof), their dress, their grammar, and other irrelevant judgmental cues. If you feel that something is suspicious about a person, your intuition is probably correct.

EXAMPLES OF NON VERBAL CUES

Shifting and twitching - especially when asked a difficult question

Rigidity and limited body movements - an intentional effort to avoid shifting and twitching.

"Deer-in-headlights" reaction - momentary pausing with wide eyes (dilated pupils), when asked a targeted question.

Yawning - increases blood flow to the brain. In an interview, yawning means that the subject is trying to pay attention. Frequency of yawning tends to increase as the anxiety level of an interview builds.

Turning the body - away from the interviewer, as if getting ready to run away.

Grooming gestures - touching the hands, head, neck, and face are signs of stress.

POLYGRAPHS

> "Robinson had no conscience or remorse. He and others like him know and understand they are lying, but they don't get flushed in the face, shift their body, wet their dry lips, or look away when they lie. They'll look you right in the eye and tell you what good people they are and that they must be believed."
>
> Former FBI agent John Douglas, describing killer John Robinson and others with antisocial personalities (Douglas and Singular, 2003).

On May 27th 1991, a 14-year-old Laotian boy ran out of Jeffrey Dahmer's apartment building and onto the street, where he staggered around in a daze. The boy was naked, drugged, and bleeding from his buttocks area. Dahmer ran after him. Two neighbors who were walking down the street protected the boy from Dahmer's advances, and called the police.

When the police arrived in their squad car, Dahmer strolled up to them, said "Hello," and calmly explained that the boy was his 19-year-old gay lover. The two had been partying together, Dahmer said, and the young man had gotten very drunk. Dahmer chatted with the officers, apologizing to them for causing trouble.

The officers helped Dahmer carry the boy back to his apartment, where they saw a Polaroid photo of Dahmer and the smiling boy (taken earlier that night) that seemed to confirm his story. Satisfied, the officers wished Dahmer a good evening and left the apartment. The officers joked over the radio that they would have to be "de-loused," but didn't bother to file an incident report. Had they looked into Dahmer's bedroom, they would have seen a corpse in plain view.

If Dahmer could remain this cool and emotionless with a semi-conscious victim, suspicious police officers in his apartment, and a corpse in the bedroom, do you really think he would fail a polygraph?

The effectiveness of polygraphs is questionable at the best of times, but they're certainly useless against serial killers. Polygraphs are designed to detect the normal emotional responses that serial killers simply do not have.

Prolific killers Ted Bundy (30+ victims), Gary Ridgway (49+ victims), Robert Pickton (49 victims), and Charles Cullen (40+ victims) all passed polygraph tests. In fact, Ridgway and Cullen each passed *two*. Cullen later said he was stunned that investigators put so much emphasis on his polygraph results, completely ignoring the fact that he had attempted suicide several times, which he felt was an obvious indicator of his guilt.

"I didn't necessarily believe that I would pass it or fail. I, I didn't know whether it would prove or disprove anything. I thought on some level that I didn't want to confirm it and on other parts I didn't want to make you think I didn't do it."

The "Angel of Death," former nurse Charles Cullen, in an interview with police (NJ, 2004). In the interview, Cullen suggests he couldn't decide if he wanted to pass the polygraph and continue to kill, or fail the polygraph and be caught. Due to his indecision, his polygraph results were inconclusive; that is, he passed.

Upon learning a serial killer was on the loose in their home state of Washington, citizens Melvin Foster and Gary

Leon Ridgway independently contacted police to ask if they could be of any assistance. After background checks, both became suspects, and both were given polygraph examinations. Foster, a taxi driver, failed the polygraph and was given "special attention" by police for some time afterward. Gary Ridgway, later found to be the killer, passed his polygraph test and was moved to the backburner of the investigation.

When used against serial killers, polygraph tests will at best provide inconclusive results. At worst, they can create skepticism and doubt within the investigative team ("Maybe he isn't the guy?") or derail the entire investigation. Don't use polygraphs.

> "I was just (yawns) excuse me, I just uh, relaxed and took the polygraph. I mean, I didn't practice or anything...just relaxed and answered the questions, and whatever it came out, it came out."
>
> Gary Ridgway (Maleng, 2003).

RECOGNIZING CALMNESS

Young Edward Kemper, who murdered his grandparents at the age of 15, looked calm and cool when he met state psychiatrists for a mental health evaluation in 1972. After the evaluation, they declared him "no longer a threat to himself or others." As the psychiatrists stamped Kemper's form and congratulated him, they were unaware that he had the severed head of a high school girl in the trunk of his car.

When police officers went to Kenneth Bianchi's apartment on Verdugo Road in Glendale, California, and told him that his name had come up in connection with the Hillside Strangler investigation, he calmly asked, "Won't you come in?"

During their brief discussion, Bianchi told the officers that he admired them, and that he had applied for a position at the Los Angeles Police Department himself. Had the officers been familiar with serial killer psychology, they would have immediately recognized two red flags: Bianchi's calm appearance, and his interest in law enforcement. Instead, they took their report and filed it away.

During interviews, serial killers sometimes fool investigators by appearing relaxed. The investigators think that if a subject lacks concern there is no way he could be involved in the crime, when in fact the opposite is true. Think about it. If law enforcement officers approached you for questioning, you'd probably be worried even if you were innocent: *I didn't do anything! Why do they want to talk to me?* The very act of being sequestered is extremely stressful, known in military circles as "captive shock." Yet, serial killers are often polite, calm and cooperative, sometimes to the point of boredom.

No innocent person will look calm when being interviewed about murder.

"I walked in and like, *wow, this isn't what I expected.* All of us looked at each other and said, 'That's the guy that's been eluding everybody?' What's remarkable is that he was so normal. If you didn't know what he had done, you would like him."

Mark Prothero, defense attorney for Gary Ridgway (*Twisted - The Green River Killer*, Discovery Channel, Aired Sept.6, 2014)

RECOGNIZING "YES" or "NO" AVOIDANCE

> **Officer**: So if we search you are we going to find any dope on you?
> **Suspect**: I don't know. I doubt it.
>
> *(Cops*, Spike TV, aired Sept. 26, 2014)

"Did you kill the girl?" When a killer is faced with a direct question such as this, sometimes his subconscious mind takes over. The killer knows he must answer the question, yet also knows that if he tells the truth there will be serious consequences. And so, within a split second, he answers in a way that avoids saying, "Yes, I did it," while simultaneously avoiding a direct "no."

In the examples below, answers range from most *potentially* truthful (A1) to least potentially truthful in descending order.

Q: "Did you take the money?"
A1: "No, I didn't."
A2: "No, I didn't. I would never do that! I'm not a thief!"
A3: "I would never do that! I'm not a thief!"
A4: "Why are you asking me this?" (attack mode)
A5: "No, I didn't." (spoken while smiling, laughing, or using other inappropriate expressions)

Q: "Did you end the lives of these children?"
A1: "No, of course not!"

A2: "No, of course not! I would never do such a terrible thing! That's ridiculous."
A3: "I would never do such a terrible thing!"
A4: "Why would I hurt kids? I love kids."
A5: "I swear to God I love kids. Why would I hurt them?" (The subject invokes God to add credibility to his statement).
A6: "I knew the kids, sure, but I would never hurt them!" (The subject eases his conscience by adding a partial truth, while still avoiding a direct answer).

Direct denials – "I didn't do it!" – don't necessarily indicate that a subject is telling the truth; but the *avoidance* of direct denials usually indicates deception. Liars also tend to embellish their statements with greater detail than is necessary, as if trying to convince themselves they are being honest. Even for compulsive liars, lying is subconsciously uncomfortable.

Officer: So if we were to come in there [your property] with your permission...
Pickton: That's no problem.
Officer: and take samples from the area and that...
Pickton: Help yourself.
Officer: and we were to test it, would we find any human DNA in there?
Pickton: Hmm, if you do I mean I, I gotta give you credit because the problem is not that I'm aware of.

Police interview with killer Robert Pickton, when he was still a suspect (File #98CQ-33017). The officers in charge did not pick up on Pickton's evasive answer, and did not search his property.

RECOGNIZING FREUDIAN SLIPS

> "There – it's – you know, one of the hardest parts of my job is to connect Iraq to the war on terror."
>
> President George W. Bush on the CBS Evening News (Couric, 2006).

Back in 1901, psychiatrist Sigmund Freud noticed that people sometimes make mistakes while speaking that reflect their true feelings, which he named "Fehlleistungen" (faulty actions) in his native German, but which are now universally known as *Freudian slips*. A Freudian slip is when people say things that either a) unintentionally reveal information they wished to conceal, or b) express subconscious beliefs or desires.

An excellent example of a Freudian slip is a friend of mine who, upon meeting his new and attractive female co-worker, shook her hand firmly and said, "Pleased to mate you." Freudian slips are often this obvious, but not always. Law enforcement officers need to be attentive to spot the subtle Freudian slips that may prove vital to a case.

> "Butkovich is not one that I killed so I don't know nothing about it."
>
> John Wayne Gacey, in an interview with CBS 2 News, where he had been claiming that he has never killed anyone (May 1992).

In his initial interview with the police, suspect Robert Reldan stated, "I sure hope no more girls get killed." At the time, the bodies of the two women he was being interviewed about had *not yet been found.* As far as the public was aware, the girls were still missing persons (Muti and Buckley, 2012). Reldan's slip, revealing his knowledge of their murder, instantly made him a prime suspect.

Serial killers withhold vast amounts of painful subconscious information, as well as conscious facts they wish to keep hidden, and so Freudian slips are commonplace. When a suspect makes a slip during questioning, don't call them on it. Pointing out a slip will only make the suspect more cautious and deliberate. Instead, pretend that nothing happened, and continue questioning. If the error is not pointed out, it's possible that the suspect will make additional slips.

"She didn't say anything, then she had gotten out [of the truck] and she went over and like, she, she was trying to make a run, kind a like, kind a like, walking, like she was mad and she was hitting herself with this wrench."

Cody Legebokoff in court, Aug 2014. Legebokoff stated that his victim, a 15-year-old girl, had committed suicide by hitting herself in the head with a wrench. In cross examination, Prosecutor Joseph Temple pointed out to the jury that Legebokoff had begun to say, "She was trying to make a run for it," before he caught himself in mid-sentence.

AVOIDING SUGGESTIVE STATEMENTS

A suggestive statement in an interview "suggests" ideas to the subject during a line of questioning. For example, "What color was the vehicle? Was it blue?" or "Was he carrying a gun or a knife?" As a basic rule, it's recommended that you avoid suggestive statement questioning in your interviews.

Some interviewers use suggestive statement questioning in the same way that polygraphers do. For instance, if a blue vase was stolen, a polygrapher might state, "a red vase was stolen, correct?" and then later state, "I'm sorry, it was a blue vase that was stolen, wasn't it?" and watch for any changes in reading between the two questions. The idea is that only the guilty party would know the correct color, and respond most strongly to that question. The problem with this technique is that a subject's willingness – or unwillingness – to comply will get in the way. For instance, an honest subject will say "yes" to any suggestive question, even if he realizes a split-second later that his response was incorrect. A suggestive statement can be, in effect, a trap placed by the interviewer that has no value for the investigation. As such, facts obtained through suggestive questions may be deemed inadmissible in court.

This author realized the "trap" potential of suggestive questioning years ago, during a visit to an army surplus store. While in the military, during a multi-national training exercise, I had traded a green beret to a British soldier in exchange for a commando knife. In the army surplus store, I mentioned to the owner that I owned this commando knife. "But is it real?" the owner had asked. "There are a lot of fake ones around." I replied that mine was real. "Does it have a star at the top of the handle?" he asked. In fact, I had no idea if the knife I owned had a star in the handle. But, the way he asked the question seemed to indicate that only a genuine commando knife would have such a star, and I knew that mine was genuine because of the situation and the source. "Yes it does," I replied. "Then it isn't real," he shot back. "You got scammed." I'd been cornered into making a false statement. Don't do the same to your subjects during an interview. Don't lead subjects with suggestive statements.

Wiegert: So Steve [Avery] stabs her first and then you cut her neck? (Brendan nods "yes") What else happens to her in her head?
Fassbender: It's extremely, extremely important you tell us this, for us to believe you.
Wiegert: Come on Brendan, what else? (pause)
Fassbender: We know, we just need you to tell us.
Brendan: That's all I can remember.
Wiegert: All right, I'm just gonna come out and ask you. Who shot her in the head?
Brendan: He did.
Fassbender: Then why didn't you tell us that?
Brendan: Cuz I couldn't think of it.

Wiegert: You helped to tie her up though, didn't you? (pause) Brendan, cuz he couldn't tie her up alone, there's no way. Did you help him tie her up?
Brendan: Yeah.
Wiegert: OK, tell me what you did.

Officers Wiegert and Fassbender interview Brendan Dassey, made famous in the Netflix series, *Making a Murderer*. Dassey was a highly vulnerable witness, just 17 years old and with borderline mental disability. Yet, the investigators used suggestive statements throughout the interview (Calumet County Sheriff's Department, 2006). Dassey's conviction was overturned when it was deemed his confession had been coerced.

AVOIDING EMOTION & VALUE CUES

As dangerous narcissists, serial killers find questions regarding their feelings both confusing and annoying. Narcissists may ignore questions about feelings not because they don't want to cooperate, but because they're confused as to what a "normal" answer should be and don't want to expose themselves.

Unless adding stress is part of your interrogation plan, avoid using the word "feel" in your questions. Instead of, "How did you feel when you saw the blood?" use an alternative that uses logic: "What did you think when you saw the blood?" Using logic words instead of emotion words will make it easier for narcissists to communicate with you.

Avoid giving narcissists clues as to how they should be feeling, or what their values should be. For example, the question, "Were you scared when you saw the body?" implies that fear is the normal response to seeing a body. Similarly, the statement, "You must have been upset when you found out that your young daughter had sex," is loaded with value and emotion cues. Such a statement tells the subject that the interviewer feels sex at a young age is wrong. Dangerous narcissists, who often have no idea how they should be feeling, use such cues to manufacture socially acceptable responses. Neutral, open-ended questions without emotion or value cues are preferable: "What's it like to see a body?" or "When you daughter started having sex, what did you think about it?" Such questions expose the subject's way of thinking, without revealing the normal one.

AVOIDING UNINTENTIONAL "OUTS"

Husband: I can't believe you cheated on me!
Wife: I'm so sorry.
Husband: Has this been going on for a long time, or did it just start?
Wife: No, no, it just started.
Husband: Is this the first time you've done this? Have you cheated on me before?
Wife: No, I've never done this before, I swear. It will never happen again.

In this example the husband, who has much to lose, offers his wife several "outs" about her affairs.

Interviewing a subject about murder can be stressful for the *interviewer* as well as the subject, particularly if genuine rapport has been built. When a subject is being peppered with questions and begins to squirm, sometimes this makes the interviewer so uncomfortable that he will offer the subject a way out. That is, the interviewer subconsciously acts to spare the subject the anguish of his own interrogation.

The best way to explain this problem is to give two examples of the same scenario. In the first example below, the interviewer has conducted the interview in the correct manner and has not asked any limiting questions. In the second example, the interviewer has unintentionally given the subject a way out.

Q: Do you know why you killed her? What your motivations were?

A: No, I've tried to understand that myself.

Q: It just happened?

A: Yes.

Q: How many times has this happened prior to this? Ten? Twenty?

A: No, not even close.

Q: You're a smart guy. You wouldn't get caught soon. So how many is it?

A: Not that many.

Q: Do you know why you killed her? What your motivations were?

A: No, I've tried to understand that myself.

Q: It just happened?

A: Yes.

Q: Have you ever killed someone before?

A: No, this is the first time.

Q: You haven't killed anyone else?

A: No.

In the second scenario, the interviewer has not only provided a convenient "out" for the killer to grab hold of (that this was his first murder), but also deepened it by asking the same question again, solidifying the killer's answer. People strive for consistency in their beliefs and actions, and so from this point on, even if additional evidence is discovered, the interviewer will have a difficult time getting the killer to admit to other murders.

As empathic human beings, interviewers feel the stress and anguish of their subjects, and may try to minimize their own discomfort by offering means of escape. A well-formulated interrogation plan will minimize the possibility of using unintentional outs.

Pickton: Uh, I go to West Military Supplies uh on 1st Avenue, on Front Street.

Yurkiw: Military Supplies. What do you get there?

Pickton: I just go there just, you know just to bullshit.

Yurkiw: Do you buy any of their surplus stuff or anything like that?

Pickton: Oh we always buy something, whatever you know. What uh, what are you referring to? Like I mean uh...

Yurkiw: Oh stuff that they'd only use for military purposes. Um sometimes they have uh different style binoculars. Um what else to they have there? I'm trying to think.

Cater: Well he's already stated that he doesn't have...You don't have any weapons or anything like that?

Yurkiw: No.

In this bungled interview with Robert Pickton (later identified as a serial killer), officers Yurkiw and Cater stumble over themselves giving Pickton excuses, and even answer their own questions (File #98CQ-33017). Years later, a search of Pickton's home would reveal a machine gun (prohibited in Canada), handgun, night vision goggles and handcuffs.

AVOIDING "NORMAL THINK"

A narcissistic woman I know forced her elderly mother, who had been living with her for several years, to move out of the house and into her own apartment. A few weeks later, the woman told me she had been calling her mother every day, sometimes twice a day, just to chat. It seemed that the woman was experiencing pangs of guilt. "Why are you calling your mother every day?" I asked to confirm. "Because," she explained, "I don't want her to have any excuse to come back to visit."

Narcissists don't use the same logic as the rest of us. Their thinking is based on feelings of superiority, persecution (that *they* are being persecuted), cold logic, and above all, selfishness.

Occasionally, a seemingly inexplicable criminal act becomes understandable if one views the situation from the viewpoint of an offender. Take, for instance, the rape and murder of an elderly women perpetrated by a teenage killer. It might seem incredible that a 16-year-old would rape an elderly woman, especially if a beautiful 25-year-old woman lives next door. But consider the circumstances. A 16-year-old boy may not have any experience dealing with a 25-year-old woman. For this reason alone, he may consider her unapproachable and unobtainable. Under what circumstances would she let him into the house? A fit young woman also presents a dangerous target. What if she fights back? On the other hand, the same teenage boy may be very comfortable around an 80-year-old woman from his experience with his grandmother and her friends. As a target, an elderly woman is weak and vulnerable. She may be more likely to let a young boy into her home, considering him harmless like her own grandchildren. Sexual attractiveness would be irrelevant to a sexual predator of this sort, who would view his victim merely as a collection of parts and not a human being.

If a serial killer offers an explanation that seems to be genuine but doesn't make sense to you, probe deeper. Ask the killer, point-blank, what his rationale was for his behavior. His actions will often be well thought out and deliberate, but his motivations may be completely different from what you expected.

Fezzani: Why did you write to the police and the media about the two people who were wrongly convicted of the murder of Taunja Bennett?
Jesperson: I wanted them to know the murderer was still at large. I got bursts of adrenaline when I felt I was leading everyone.

Serial killer Keith Jesperson (Fezzani, 2015). Prior to this interview, people assumed that Jesperson wrote to the press to exonerate the two men who were wrongly accused of his crimes.

SAVING FACE
RATIONALIZATIONS, PROJECTIONS & MINIMIZATIONS

"I know you've been honest with me on the last one [interview], and I believe you because that chick, the last one, was crazy. There's no doubt about it. Fuck, they [the police] already knew that."

Corporal Paul Dadwal, intentionally demeaning victim Loren Leslie for the psychological benefit of her killer, Cody Legebokoff (Nov 29, 2010).

"Saving face" is a term used in Asian cultures to describe the efforts people put into helping each other protect their egos, particularly the way they're viewed by others. While Westerners pride themselves on dealing with the truth no matter how harsh it may be, Asians tend to ignore outright truth in favor of harmony.

Serial killers have fragile egos. They do not wish to deal with the truth. In fact, their whole lives are spent avoiding the truth. This being the case, interviewers should use every opportunity to help their subjects "save face."

Skillful law enforcement interviewers use face-saving questions and comments to help killers minimize inconsistencies between who they perceive themselves to be (good, honest), and their actions (murderous, deceitful). Skillful interviewers don't chastise their subjects for using face-saving comments, but instead encourage them.

In the successful interview of serial killer Robert Pickton, the investigators successfully used powerful questions such as, "You want to tell your side of the story, don't you?"

and "People are saying terrible things about you. You want to set the record straight, don't you?" People want the opportunity to protect their battered egos. They want to provide explanations for their behavior.

The face-savings statements of serial killers tend to be absurd. Tommy Lynn Sells, for instance, blamed the mayor of Lexington, Kentucky for his murder of a 13-year-old girl named Haley McHone. If the mayor had kept the bushes in the local park trimmed, Sells explained, he wouldn't have had a good hiding place and therefore wouldn't have been tempted to rape and kill Haley. Criminals accept such ridiculous rationalizations because they've made them thousands of times before – to themselves – and have come to believe them.

When people genuinely feel they won't be judged, and that they aren't responsible for their actions (or at least that their actions were justified) they're far more likely to discuss them.

EXAMPLES OF FACE-SAVING STATEMENTS BY LAW ENFORCEMENT

WITH A THIEF
"The people whose stuff was stolen - they were rich. And besides, they left their window open so they deserved it."

WITH A RAPIST
"With the way she acted, and the way she was dressed - she didn't look very innocent, did she?"

WITH A KILLER
"The woman who died wasn't really high class was she? And besides, it was probably an accident."

In some countries, such as England, the use of face-saving statements is considered an oppressive interview technique. Their concern is that if the severity of a crime is sufficiently marginalized, innocent subjects might confess merely to end their stressful interviews. Keeping this in mind, one should avoid dismissing the severity of a crime ("murder is no big deal") but instead highlight rationalizations the criminals themselves might use. Avoid minimizations for subjects who are showing signs of severe stress or who are vulnerable – including children, the elderly, and those with low IQs.

PART 9:
SERIAL KILLER
INTERROGATIONS

STRATEGIES USED BY KILLERS

DECLARATIONS OF HONESTY

> "To be honest..."
> "Honestly..."
> "You have to trust me."
> "I wouldn't lie about that."
> "I swear I'm telling you the truth."
> "Believe me."

In an attempt to appear honest, killers may employ the term "honestly" or equivalent expressions as an add-on to some of their statements. In the past, law enforcement officers were taught that anyone who uses the term "honestly" in a sentence is deceptive, which is unusual since so many officers use the expression themselves, especially during interrogations. In fact, there are several reasons why people use declarations of honesty, some of which indicate deception but most of which do not.

One common use of a declaration of honesty is to introduce a subject that the speaker feels is risqué or embarrassing; for instance, "Honestly, I don't like my boss very much," or, "To be honest, my wife and I are getting a divorce." Subjects who use declarations of honesty in this manner should not be considered deceptive.

Another common use of a declaration of honesty is with a statement that is inconsequential, but reveals the person's thinking: "Honestly, I haven't given it much thought," or "I have to be honest, I don't care one way or the other." Subjects who use declarations of honesty in this manner should not be considered deceptive.

The third common use of the declaration of honesty is as an interjection: "Honestly! I don't know what's wrong with that kid," or "Honestly, she's the most beautiful woman ever!" As with the two previous examples, subjects who use declarations of honesty in this manner should not be considered deceptive.

Both deceptive and non-deceptive subjects may use declarations of honesty if they feel they are not being listened to or believed: "Honestly, I'm telling you the truth!" Of course, sometimes people are not being believed because their stories are false. Using "honestly" to add emphasis is a moderate sign of deception, but *is* sometimes used by truthful subjects.

> "And honestly I really hadn't thought of it at all until you mentioned it."
>
> Israel Keyes, in an interview with the FBI, May 24, 2012. Because the statement merely reveals Keyes' thought processes, his statement does not indicate deception.

Both deceptive and non-deceptive subjects may use declarations of honesty to introduce simple statements that have important consequences: "Honestly, I never met her before that night." The purpose of this usage is to add credibility to a statement. A subject who uses this technique *frequently* should be considered deceptive.

> "I know, and I'm trying to tell you as honestly as I know how, what happened."
>
> Ted Bundy, in an interview with James Dobson, Jan 24, 1989. Bundy's interview included several statements he had previously contradicted.

OFFERING ALTERNATIVES

> **Travis**: Are you a Secret Service Man?
> **Secret Service Man**: Why do you ask?
> **Travis**: I've seen a lot of suspicious-looking people around here today.
> (Secret Service Man glances at Travis momentarily)
> **Secret Service Man**: Who?
> **Travis**: Oh, lots. I don't know where they all are now. There used to be one standing over there (points).
>
> Travis Bickle (played by Robert DeNiro) attempts to offer an alternative suspect in this scene from the 1976 movie, *Taxi Driver*.

Serial killers may offer alternatives to shift focus away from themselves. The alternative offered could be an alternative suspect (as in the lines from *Taxi Driver* above), or it could be an alternative story or motive.

On Feb. 6th, 2002, a team of investigators was searching Robert Pickton's home and grounds. Knowing the team would find his victim's personal items, Pickton preemptively offered police an explanation; he said he had been buying used vehicles from police auctions, and that whenever he found something inside a vehicle he would bring it into his home. With this one story, Pickton hoped to provide an explanation for any object the investigators might find. Unfortunately for Pickton, he didn't have a good explanation for large quantities of his victim's blood, also found in his home.

Killers rarely offer direct alternatives ("I think my neighbor did it"), but instead offer them as hints or subtle suggestions: "You should ask my neighbor if he saw anything. He sometimes goes to their garage to borrow tools." Killers know from experience that they don't necessarily have to prove themselves innocent, but merely add doubts about their guilt.

BAIT ANSWERS

Bait answers are small, relatively insignificant confessions that subjects make to appear truthful and to deflect the current line of questioning. Consider the following exchanges:

Security company interviewer: Do you use drugs?
Security candidate: I used marijuana a few times when I was a teenager.

Corporate Security: Have you ever taken anything from the bank?
Bank Employee: Well, I admit, about a year ago, I took a box of pens home.

The overwhelming natural urge for any interviewer is to follow up with a question related to the newly revealed confession: "Tell me about that!" However, to do so is to take the bait. If a subject offers a bait answer, ignore it. Subjects expect their interviewers to bite at bait answers. Ignoring the bait may raise a subject's discomfort level and lead to important disclosures. Following are the same conversations, extended by a single line:

Security company interviewer: Do you use drugs?
Security candidate: I used marijuana a few times when I was a teenager.
Security company interviewer: Okay. What other drugs are you familiar with?

Corporate Security: Have you ever taken anything from the bank?
Bank Employee: Well, I admit, about a year ago, I took a box of pens home.
Corporate Security: What else have you taken?

In the examples above, the interviewers have wisely ignored the bait answers, and instead asked follow-up questions to reveal the true information their subjects wished to hide.

On the 27th of November 2010, Constable Aaron Kehler of the Canadian RCMP noticed a truck driving erratically on an isolated stretch of highway in northern Canada. After he pulled over the truck, Kehler saw blood on the driver's chin as well as on a pipe wrench inside the truck. The driver, 21-year-old Cody Legebokoff, immediately offered bait; he admitted that he and a friend were illegally poaching deer. They had shot and wounded a deer, Legebokoff explained, and used the pipe wrench to finish it off, taking turns clubbing it until it was dead. Constable Kehler, noticing some half-empty bottles of alcohol and a childlike monkey-design backpack on the passenger seat, told Legebokoff that "taking turns clubbing a deer to death" could lead to becoming a serial killer. Kehler called a backup officer. They soon found the body of a teenage girl in the woods, and Legebokoff was arrested on suspicion of murder.

After exploring possibilities and broadening the focus of the questioning, one can always come back to ask questions related to the bait answer. But, don't grab the bait without exploring why the subject presented it in the first place. Don't chase the bait.

ATTACK MODE

"See, in their last moments, people show you who they really are...so in a way, I knew your friends better than you ever did. Would you like to know which of them were cowards?"

The Joker (played by Heath Ledger), verbally attacks his jailer in the 2008 movie, *The Dark Knight*.

When "cornered" with a difficult question or series of difficult questions, a subject may attempt to derail the interview by going into attack mode. The subject will assault the interviewer's integrity, credentials, or the topic of the interview itself. The subject may make offensive comments against the interviewer's race, religion, comrades or country. He may try to distract the interviewer, or deflect the line of questioning. Sometimes the subject will simply ask the interviewer to stop!

Examples of attack mode:
- "How long have you been doing this job?" (attacks the interviewers credibility)
- "Why are you wasting my time?"
- "How long is this going to take?" (subject suggests that his time is more valuable than the interviewers).
- "Why are you trying to ruin my life?"
- "Why are you doing this to me?"
- "Are you suggesting that I would do such a thing?"
- "You know, the police beat me when they arrested me!"
- "I feel cornered. Just stop!"
- "You are pressuring me! I can't answer with this kind of pressure."
- "Why don't you believe me?"
- Crying (usually, but not exclusively, employed by women)

Any acknowledgement of an attack, no matter how small, can temporarily stall the interview. In the first instance in the examples below, the interviewer acknowledges the subject's comment, leading to a break in momentum. In the second instance, the interviewer ignores the subject's attack and successfully continues the line of questioning.

EXAMPLE 1

Officer: Why did you go to her house?
Subject: How long have you been going this job? What are your qualifications?
Officer: I have a criminology degree, and ten years in the field. Now why did you go to her house?
Subject: A criminology degree. You think that helps? Anyone can read a textbook.

Officer: Why did you go to her house?
Subject: How long have you been going this job? What are your qualifications?
Officer: Don't change the subject. Why did you go to her house?

EXAMPLE 2

Officer: Do you recognize the person in this photo?
Suspect: It's not very clear. Do you have a better photo?
Officer: I don't think so. Just this one. Do you know the person in this photo?
Suspect: I can't see it clearly enough to say.

Officer: Do you recognize the person in this photo?
Suspect: It's not very clear. Do you have a better photo?
Officer: It's clear enough. Who is the person in this photo?

If a subject goes into attack mode, the correct response is to 1) dismiss the comment entirely, 2) call the subject out on their attempt, if necessary, and finally 3) move forward with the questioning. A subject will often try the same attack several times.

Jim Reese (FBI) was interviewing serial child-killer Arthur F. Goode, when Goode suddenly asked, "Do you have any little boys at home?" The killer grinned at Reese, as if pleased with himself. Reese said that turning his back to the killer and leaving the room was the hardest thing he had to do in the entire time he had been with the FBI (DeNevi and Campbell, 2004).

If a subject attempts to push your buttons, recognize the attack for what it is, and keep your professionalism. If you feel you're losing control of your emotions, do as Jim Reese did and leave the room. If you lose your cool, the subject wins.

> "If you put me on trial for this my tribe is going to kill you."
>
> Mohamed Rashed Daoud al-'Owhali, US Embassy bomber, to NYC Detective Wayne Parola, 1998. Al-'Owhali also threatened the interviewer's families.

SILENCE

The best way to overcome silence is to avoid it in the first place – by being fair, responsive, and non-judgmental. However, overcoming silence consistently, especially with belligerent subjects, requires more. As the US Army's interrogation manual (FM 2-22.3) states, "interrogators must have a deep understanding of the cultural norms, anomalies, and emotional triggers of the person being interrogated in order to select appropriate strategies and to interrogate effectively." A solid intelligence collection process begins long before the subject enters the interview room.

People want to talk while under duress. In the minutes leading up to the interview, a subject should only be spoken to minimally. A subject's opportunity to ask questions should begin when he meets the interviewer. If a subject's concerns and questions have already been addressed before the interviewer enters the room, he may have no reason to begin talking.

In North America, lawyers often advise their clients to exercise their right to remain silent. This probably isn't good advice for anyone except the lawyer, since remaining silent only intensifies law enforcement's focus on a person. An innocent subject has nothing to fear from speaking, and in fact can clear up any misunderstandings by doing so. If a subject remains silent or answers "no comment" to important questions, he should be reminded that if he waits until his day in court to provide answers, people will be less likely to believe his statements.

It's important for an interviewer to *continue asking* questions even if the subject refuses to answer them. Later, if can be brought to the attention of the court that the subject refused to answer these questions during the interview. If the questions were never asked, it can't be pointed out that the subject refused to answer them.

Despite all efforts, some subjects will remain silent or say "no comment" to every question. When dealing with silence, first act as if the silence were due to a misunderstanding, and ask your question in a different manner. If the subject still refuses to speak, wait. Then, wait some more. Wait until the silence makes everyone in the room squirm in their shoes. Since most people feel the need to fill silence with words, the ability to comfortably endure excruciating silence is a powerful tool. If the suspect continues to be obstinate, you may move on to another topic, but always let him know that you'll come back to the one you left behind ("OK, we'll talk about this again later"). Make sure that you do.

A final way to get an obstinate subject talking is to bring up topics that any narcissist will have strong opinions about, such as the role of the individual in society, justice, and faithfulness – preferably in a way relating to the subject's life. If the subject still does not respond to your statements, suggest an embarrassing conclusion for his silence. The goal of any interview is to have a conversation. Any conversation is a good start.

STONEWALLING

> **Yousafsai**: How would you describe the men arrested in Kenya and Tanzania [for the US Embassy bombings]? How many of them do you know?
> **Bin Laden**: Praise be to God. What I know is that those who risked their lives to earn the pleasure of God, Praise and Glory be to him, are the real men, the true personification of the word men. They managed to rid the Islamic nation of disgrace. We highly respect them and hold them in the highest esteem, and pray to God, Praise and Glory be to him, to accept them as martyrs and permit them to intercede on behalf of their kin.
>
> Osama Bin Laden, in an interview with ABC News' Rahimullah Yousafsai, 1999. During the hour-long interview, Bin Laden didn't directly answer a single question. Yousafsai was not allowed to ask follow-up questions, rendering the interview pointless.

Stonewalling is a subject's attempt to continue speaking without actually cooperating or communicating. Stonewalling includes giving vague answers, providing answers unrelated to the questions, responding to questions with additional questions, or filibustering with long narratives. Stonewalling is a passive-aggressive defensive behavior.

If a subject is rambling and not answering questions, it's perfectly acceptable to call him on it: "You seem to be getting a bit off topic. Let's get back to the question of..." If a subject's answer isn't sensible, tell him so. Narcissists pride themselves on being logical. Being called out on nonsensical answers will add to their stress levels and often cause them to revise their statements.

Overcoming stonewalling behavior means recognizing that an interrogative interview is not an everyday conversation, and that the rules of everyday conversation do not apply. Be polite, but control the conversation.

SUBSTITUTIONS for Saying, "You are lying," or "You didn't answer the question."

"That doesn't make sense to me."
"I'm not sure I understand that. What I was asking was..."
"Can you please explain that again. My question was..."
"I hear what you are saying, but that doesn't sound logical to me."
"I need you to tell me everything."
"Be straight up with me."
"Be up front with me."
"I need to hear your full side of the story."

THE CONFESSION & BEYOND

> **Williams**: I want to, um, minimize the impact on my wife.
> **Detective Smyth**: So do I.
> **Williams**: So how do we do that?
> **Detective Smyth**: Well, you start by telling the truth.
> **Williams**: (pause) Okay.
> **Sergeant Smyth**: Alright, so where is she [the victim's body]?
> **Williams**: Got a map?
>
> Colonel Russell Williams admits to murder, 7th Feb, 2010. The moment of confession is rarely as obvious as, "Yes, I did it."

A moment of drama in many interviews is when a suspect confesses to a crime, occasionally in detail, occasionally using sadistic truth. *If I'm going to make a confession,* some killers reason, *I'm going to make this as disturbing as possible.* Faced with a gruesome and aggressive confession, any interviewer will feel a surge of anger. But you can't show it.

As unnatural as it may be, the best thing to do when faced with a horrific confession is to transform your disgust into incredulity ("Wow! That's amazing!") and encourage the killer to say more. Killers think murder is fun and exciting and *cool*. When a serial killer is talking about his exploits, you want to be his college roommate, not his mother. Any negativity or look of disgust could shut down the confession.

Being non-judgmental in the face of a horrific confession will require every ounce of training and professionalism that an officer can hope to muster.

> "I'm a legend already (laughing)...the whole fuckin' world knows me. All the way to Hong Kong to everywheres."
>
> Serial killer Robert Pickton to his cellmate, following his admission to police (Project Evenhanded "E" Division File #2001E-1388, 2002).

After a confession, law enforcement officers should keep a killer updated with information regarding his case, particularly any new evidence found that supports his conviction. As dangerous narcissists, serial killers have the amazing ability to convince themselves, over time, that they did nothing wrong. Keeping a killer informed about further incriminating evidence helps reduce any regret he may have about confessing, and prevent him from developing strong levels of denial later.

Many serial killers experience a profound sense of relief after confessing. Indeed, the weeks immediately following a confession can be amongst the most enjoyable times of a killer's life. Investigators, reporters and psychologists will all want to speak with the newly discovered killer about his favorite hobby – and for the first time in his life he may do so candidly. Killers often appear to thoroughly enjoy these interviews.

In most cases, a killer will work with law enforcement officers to help them find bodies and reveal missing details. This provides real psychological benefit for both the killer and the victim's families. Many serial killers have an unspoken admiration for law enforcement. This phase of the investigation is the closest they will come to experiencing law enforcement camaraderie.

Some killers become so engaged in helping law enforcement that they come to consider themselves members of the investigative team. Gary Ridgway, for instance, actually *lived with* the investigative team following his arrest, sleeping on a mattress in the corner of their office. When Sheriff Dave Reichert asked Ridgway how it was going, Ridgway replied, "Pretty good. We've up to seventy-one victims, but there's still six sites where we haven't found the bodies" (Maleng, 2003). Clearly, Ridgway considered himself one of the guys.

Killers may experience a sense of melancholy after the initial busy period working with law enforcement and other professionals winds down. After a time, as the bright lights fade and interest wanes, they will settle down into prison life where they no longer have to keep secrets or fight their inner demons. Of course, high-profile killers will have an assortment of pen pals and groupies waiting to provide them with additional attention.

"I won't let myself out [of prison]. I will spend the rest of my life here. I don't want to hurt nobody. I have made peace with myself."

Serial killer Timothy Krajcir, to his prison psychiatrist (Echols, 2011).

CASE STUDY – ROBERT PICKTON

A SHORT BIOGRAPHY OF ROBERT PICKTON

Robert "Willie" Pickton appeared to be a simple pig farmer who lived on a pig farm – but appearances are deceptive. The Pickton farm, located in the community of Port Coquitlam about 30 minutes from Vancouver, Canada, was a busy place. Robert Pickton's brother, Dave, regularly hosted large parties where locals would drink beer, barbecue and socialize. Those who regularly visited the property included workers from Dave's demolition company, drug dealers, prostitutes, and members of the local chapter of the Hell's Angel's biker gang who owned a clubhouse nearby.

Both Pickton brothers were involved in breaking down vehicles for spare parts and scrap metal, as well as hosting illegal cockfights for the local Filipino community. They even owned an after-hours nightclub called Piggy's Palace, near the farm. The brothers were "well known to police." As the city of Port Coquitlam grew, the Picktons sold off pieces of their land to real estate developers and became wealthy.

Despite his prosperity, Robert Pickton maintained a strange, poverty-stricken lifestyle. He lived in a trailer next to a slaughtering shed. He continued to drive an old, dirty pickup truck. He ate dog food out of cans, using plastic forks. He made no concessions whatsoever to his wealth.

By the time of Robert Pickton's arrest, the pig farm was surrounded by major housing developments to the west and north, a golf course to the east, and shopping malls to the south.

Although "farm" implies isolation, the Pickton farm wasn't isolated.

Pickton's farm provided him with a ready-made, industrial disposal system to use for his victims. He'd hoist up his victims and cut them apart using equipment designed for pig slaughtering. Then, he'd bury the obvious pieces (such as the skulls) in large pits dug on the property using industrial digging equipment. Finally he'd take the flesh, mix it with fat and scraps from pigs, and bring it to the city of Vancouver in 45-gallon drums for disposal at an animal product processing plant. The fat from Pickton's victims eventually became cosmetics and soap.

West Coast Reduction Limited, the plant that Pickton used to process the fat, lies at the edge of the Downtown Eastside of Vancouver – a small geographic area with an abundance of prostitutes, drug addicts, criminal gangs and the mentally ill: it is infamously known as Canada's poorest neighborhood. In summer, tourists can be seen walking through the area on their way to nearby Chinatown, clutching each other for support upon realizing they're surrounded by people shooting heroin and talking to themselves. As Pickton became comfortable with the Eastside from his frequent trips there, he began hanging out in the area's bars, buying drinks and socializing. The area became his preferred hunting ground.

Police knew that women were disappearing from the Downtown Eastside. Since these women were mostly uneducated and destitute, the police showed less incentive to find them than if they had been urban housewives. Complicating the issue is the fact that prostitutes with drug addictions *often* go missing. Some turn up months or even years later, having kicked their habits. Others die in hospital under their real names, which are different from their street names. Was there really a problem? There was: Robert "Willie" Pickton.

Prostitute Teresa Triff was a blonde-haired blue-eyed woman, just five-foot-two and 111 pounds. Kathleen Wattley was a petite black woman, five-feet-five inches tall and "thin as a rail" (Cameron, 2010). Diana Melnick, who had attended private school prior to becoming a drug addict and prostitute, was five-foot-two and weighed about a hundred pounds. Michelle Gurney, a twenty-nine-year old native, was five-foot-four and weighed 100 pounds. Pickton targeted petite, easy to control victims – preferably drug addicts – so he could invite them back to the farm to either "party" or "come clean."

Pickton didn't kill all of the women who came back to his farm. He had sex with some of them, gave them drugs and alcohol, and then drove them back to the Eastside exactly as he promised. Some actually lived with Pickton in his trailer, for weeks or even months.

In March of 1997, a prostitute named Wendy Lynn Eistetter battled Pickton in a vicious knife fight at the farm when Pickton tried to handcuff her against her will. With a handcuff still locked on one wrist, she managed to run off the farm to the nearest roadway, where she found a passerby to drive her to the hospital. Hospital staff were surprised when a woman was brought to the emergency room with severe knife wounds and a handcuff on her wrist, but even more surprised when a male stabbing victim, dizzy from blood running out of his jugular, independently arrived moments later with the key to the handcuffs in his pocket. Charges against Pickton were dropped after Eistetter failed to show up in court, but word of the event spread throughout the prostitute community: *Willie Pickton is dangerous.*

Perhaps the most surprising thing about Robert Pickton was how many people knew (or should have known) that he was a killer. Several years prior to his arrest, police were tipped that Pickton had a freezer full of human flesh on the farm, but were unable to obtain a search warrant based on third-party hearsay. Pickton's friend Scot Chubb gossiped that

Pickton had told him the best way to kill a prostitute was to inject her with windshield washer fluid. A female friend of Pickton's actually stumbled upon him butchering a woman in his barn. Instead of calling the police, she blackmailed Pickton for drugs and cash.

Robert Pickton had been an unusual person his entire life, and this "weirdness" was his greatest asset as a killer. Many of Pickton's friends were drug addicts, prostitutes and cons who viewed the police as the enemy. Others wanted to talk to the police, but were always too high on drugs for their statements to be considered reliable.

In mid-1999, police followed Pickton in unmarked cars for two weeks, but he was cautious and they discovered nothing. DNA samples from Pickton were checked against the DNA found on three murdered prostitutes, but the results came back negative. Robert Pickton, a prime suspect, was actually looking like a dead end. By the fall of 2001, Pickton was just one of six hundred possible suspects. Then, in early 2002, police got the big break they were looking for.

Pickton's friend Scot Chubb needed money for rent, and offered to become an informant. At first Chubb offered to disclose the whereabouts of an illegal marijuana grow operation, but then he offered something better: the location of illegal firearms, including a submachine gun. The gun owner's name was Robert "Willie" Pickton.

After obtaining the long-sought-after search warrant, a team of Coquitlam RCMP and Vancouver police officers moved in. They found the illegal firearms, as well as women's clothing, jewelry, purses, two pairs of handcuffs, and a Smith & Wesson .22-caliber revolver with a dildo slipped over the barrel. In a box next to Pickton's bed they found a collection of kitchen knives. Most importantly, they found an asthma inhaler prescribed to "Serena Abotsway" – one of the missing women.

The Pickton farm soon became the largest crime scene in Canadian history.

The Pickton Farm. Robert Pickton's trailer was at the north-east end of the property; David Pickton's farmhouse (Robert's brother) is to the south-east of the property. The nearby Hell's Angel's Clubhouse can be seen in the lower-right corner of the photograph, just across the street from the farm.

Copyright Cnes Spot Image, Digital Globe, GeoEye, IMTCAN, Province of British Columbia, Map Data Copyright 2013 Google Inc.

THE PICKTON INTERVIEW: INTRODUCTION

"[City of] Coquitlam RCMP interviewed Pickton in January 2000 and a Provincial Unsolved Homicide Unit member spoke with him in March 2001. Neither interview was a well-planned step within an overall strategy to investigate the leads on Pickton. The Pickton Interview did not even meet the most basic police standards. It appeared to be completely unplanned, despite the fact that months had gone by since the first effort to interview him, the seriousness of the suspected crime, and the compelling evidence available to police at that time...I conclude that the failed interview had a devastating impact on the Coquitlam Pickton investigations, which entered a period of hibernation. Despite still being considered a priority case, police took little or no action."

Wally T. Oppal, in his 2012 executive summary, *Forsaken: The Report of the Missing Women Commission of Inquiry.* Fortunately, police would get another chance.

The Robert Pickton interview of Feb. 23, 2002 is featured in this book because it serves as an excellent platform from which to learn. Although it was a well-executed interview, it was not perfect. Police had bungled interviews with Pickton twice previously, using flawed techniques and non-existent game plans. They were not about to do it again.

Before the Feb. 23rd interview, Dana Lillies of the Vancouver Police Department informally spoke with Pickton for hours. During these chats, Pickton told Lillies his life story and most of its monumental moments (minus the killings, of course). These details would later be used to great effect in the official interview.

Immediately prior to the Feb. 23rd interview, police fact-checked their information and reviewed their notes. They created a board featuring photographs of the missing women. The interviewers prepared thoroughly and had focus. The Feb. 23rd interview marked the end of a long hunt for a man with a lethal lifestyle.

THE FEBRUARY 23rd, 2002
ROBERT PICKTON INTERVIEW:
EXCERPTS AND ASSESSMENTS

EXCERPT 1

Context: The interview begins. Sergeant Bill Fordy has just introduced himself to Pickton.

Sgt. Bill Fordy: ...Ah, one thing that I'm gonna tell you Rob is that ah, I'm gonna treat you with respect here today. Okay. Um, I'm not going to be mean with you and I'm not gonna yell at you, I'm not going to get physical with you. I'm gonna treat you with respect and I'm also gonna treat you with dignity okay. Because if I was sitting in that chair that's how I would want to be treated quite frankly. Okay. And I'm also gonna give you my word that nobody else is gonna treat you physically. Okay nobody's gonna hurt you or try to hurt you or anything like that. Alright I give you my word on that. Alright you understand that . . .
Robert Pickton: Mm, hmm. Mm, hmm.

COMMENTS: Individuals called for questioning may be expecting physical abuse and experiencing "captive shock." Fordy tells Pickton he'll be treated with respect both to gain Pickton's trust, and to create the obligation of reciprocity. Fordy kept his word.

EXCERPT 2

Context: Pickton is read his rights.

Sgt. Bill Fordy: Okay because, the law considers me to be a person in authority, right. Ah, this is a criminal matter obviously that we're here for today. And you know these are very, very serious ah, allegations. And as a police officer, as, as a, a um, you know someone who ah, is a policeman right, I can get subpoenaed to court, any court in the country for that matter. I've been in courts in different provinces, you know, different jurisdictions, different cities, different towns okay. And I can give evidence alright. I mean I can give evidence, I can get called to give evidence on what takes place right today between you and I. Alright.

Pickton: Mm, hmm.

Sgt. Bill Fordy: So it's important to me that you understand ah, that you don't have to talk to me and that anything that you do say could be given, given as evidence because we're being video recorded right. And you know what Rob, that's not only for my protection, that's (POINTING AT CAMERA) for your protection as well.

Pickton: Right.

Sgt. Bill Fordy: Alright and I'm sure you can appreciate that right, and you're probably glad it's there at some level, I would imagine.

Pickton: Well not much I can do about that anyways, I mean it's here or there.

Sgt. Bill Fordy: Yeah.

Pickton: I'm not trying to hide anything but.

Sgt. Bill Fordy: No and you know what, I thank you for that...

COMMENTS: When a salesperson asks someone to sign a contract, the salesperson rarely says, "I need you to sign the contract here," since some customers might find words like "sign" and "contract" imposing. Instead, the salesperson might say, "I just need your name down here at the bottom of the page," or something equally benign. Similarly, some police officers believe that reading a suspect his rights in straight-faced legalese will make the suspect go silent. Fordy reads Pickton his rights in a casual fashion, though his delivery is not well thought out. Fordy's casual delivery ensures that Pickton's ability to understand his rights will not be questioned in court. Fordy also thanks Pickton for his cooperation: he will do so many times throughout the interview.

EXCERPT 3

Context: Sgt. Fordy continues to read Pickton his rights. Fordy knows that Pickton has likely been advised not to speak to the police or cooperate with their investigation.

Sgt. Bill Fordy: Okay. I guess my point being is that you know, you make a decision on what you want to do, whether or not you want to talk. Your brother might say don't talk to the police, your lawyer might say you don't talk to the police, everybody might say don't talk to the police. But at the end of the day Rob, that decision to speak or not to speak is yours. Alright. As a police officer I have to give you that opportunity to tell your side of the story if you want to. But that decision to do it, to speak with, with the police or not to speak with the police, is yours. Alright, it's important to me that you understand that. I can't, I can't force you to or I can't make you say anything you don't want to say. You get your advice from people, from lawyers, from family, from friends and then it's up to you to do what you want to do. Alright. Like somebody might say to me Bill don't eat junk food, it's not good for you, it's not in your best interest to eat chocolate bars cause its gonna make you fat. And I might still eat a chocolate bar, that's my choice. Right that's like this situation you know, you're given advice alright, but at the end of the day you're the person sitting in the chair, and you're the only one who can make a decision on what you do want to do.

COMMENTS: Though suspects have the right to remain silent, in most instances they choose to waive this right. Serial killers despise unsolicited advice. By stating that silence is what "other people" want Pickton to do – possibly against his will – he entices Pickton to speak.

EXCERPT 4

Context: Fordy introduces his personal motivation(s) for his interview with Pickton.

Sgt. Bill Fordy: ...Ah, I'm a student of human behaviour alright. Ah, one of the things that I enjoy about my job is I get to talk to lots of really interesting people and I like to learn about people. Quite frankly, it's very, very interesting. You know we all have hobbies, we all have interests. One of my things that I find interesting is people and how do people end up the way they end up. Now quite frankly Rob at the end of the day here, you could be...
Robert Pickton: I'm just a pig farmer.
Sgt. Bill Fordy: You could be just a pig farmer or you could be somebody very, very important...

COMMENTS: Fordy's stated reason for wanting to interview Pickton – to learn about human behavior – is only partially true: his other reason is to obtain a confession. Fordy suggests that Pickton might be "just a pig farmer," or that he might be "somebody very, very important." That is, Fordy plants the idea in Pickton's mind that he is more important as a killer than as a pig farmer, which is strangely true. After this interview, Pickton described himself as "a legend" to his cellmate.

EXCERPT 5

Context: The rapport building phase.

Robert Pickton: I like working.
Sgt. Bill Fordy: So do I. What do you like about work?
Robert Pickton: Anything. Anything in general.
Sgt. Bill Fordy: Mm, hmm.
Robert Pickton: Framing houses all the way up to flooring, fabricating, anything.
Sgt. Bill Fordy: (PAUSE – 15 SECONDS) Mm, hmm.
Robert Pickton: That's about it, (INDECIPHERABLE) there. (PAUSE)
Sgt. Bill Fordy: Mm, hmm. So Dave's [Pickton's brother] a good, good guy, you enjoy his company.
Robert Pickton: Yeah.
Sgt. Bill Fordy: You don't ah, you were never close to Linda. Who's your best friend?
Robert Pickton: In which way?
Sgt. Bill Fordy: Any way.
Robert Pickton: Any good friend, what kind of friend are you referring to, girlfriend, boyfriend...
Sgt. Bill Fordy: Well I got some close buddies that if I was ever in a jam you know, in the middle of the night I could call 'em and say hey man, I ah, I'm in trouble, can you come and help me out? You know, they're, they're friends of mine that I know that would always be there for me. You know, good, bad or indifferent. Those are my good friends, you know, four or five guys that I consider good friends. That some I've known for a long time, some I've only known for a little while but I consider them good friends. People that you know, if they were

in a jam too, I would help them out unquestionable. No questions, they are my good friends.

Robert Pickton: Yeah, lots of friends.

Sgt. Bill Fordy: Who's your best friend?

Robert Pickton: Everybody.

COMMENTS: Despite Fordy's long introduction and rapport-building work, Pickton begins stonewalling with weak answers and irrelevant details. This is a man with things to hide.

EXCERPT 6

Context: Fordy explains to Pickton details of the search that is underway at the farm.

Sgt. Bill Fordy: ...So there's a Forensic Anthropologist for the bones, Entomologist for the bugs, they've got crime scene people there to gather in fingerprints and evidence. They've got blood spatter there, analyzing, interpreting all the different blood cause there's blood everywhere and forwarding those for analysis. Alright. They've got special lights out there you know, I'm gonna show you some pictures later on that ah, fluoresce different types of thing. Like you know blood looks one way in a certain type of light and it looks different in a different type of light. There's special lights that these experts have that helps them in their investigations. Alright. And as you know that whole property is secured now. There's policemen there ah, twenty-four hours a day, right and they're gonna probably be there for a year.

Robert Pickton: A year.

Sgt. Bill Fordy: Oh yeah. Oh yeah, what they've gotta do and it's, it's really this, and like I say, when I heard that too I said the same thing, I said a year. But what they've gotta do is because they've gotta take all the dirt down, plus it looks like, what they're gonna do is they've set the first target at twenty-five feet. So they go down, they go down to the ground level right, and then down twenty-five feet.

Robert Pickton: Really?

COMMENTS: Fordy steps up the pressure. He impresses upon Pickton the thoroughness of the investigation and the inevitability of a conviction. Fordy's speech must have had the intended effect, because shortly after this Pickton begins a string of involuntary yawning – the body's way to increase blood flow to the brain.

EXCERPT 7

Context: The mental battle between Pickton and Fordy intensifies.

Sgt. Bill Fordy: Okay, let me ask you this alright. Rob. Would it be possible for your DNA to have been in this [interview] room yesterday?

Robert Pickton: Anything's possible.

Sgt. Bill Fordy: No, that's not my question. Would your DNA have been in this room yesterday?

Robert Pickton: Possible.

Sgt. Bill Fordy: How is that possible?

Robert Pickton: Well anything can be set up or anything could be put in that's not there.

Sgt. Bill Fordy: Okay. If you have never been in this room would it possible for your DNA to be in this room? The answer's no. Right. You have to agree with me on that.

Robert Pickton: (YAWNING) Not necessarily. Could be set up.

Sgt. Bill Fordy: Okay. But I mean let's in the absence of being set up, it's not possible for your DNA to be anywhere right?

Robert Pickton: Yeah.

Sgt. Bill Fordy: Okay, good, I'm glad you agree with me on that because that's an important point. One of the things that ah, I know Rob ah, through my experience is that there is always two and there is sometimes three or four or five sides to every story.

Robert Pickton: Yeah, (YAWNING) there's more than, there (INDECIPHERABLE) there's not always one side to a story cause there's always two sides or more.

COMMENTS: Using the simplest of arguments – that DNA evidence "could be set up" – Pickton attempts to dismiss the evidence he knows will be found at his property. Fordy will later regain his composure and effectively argue that while one or two items may be set up or inconclusive, multiple layers of items and bloodstains from different victims are indisputable evidence.

EXCERPT 8

Context: Sgt. Fordy has introduced a prop to the interview – a photo board featuring women suspected of being Pickton's victims – and is reviewing it with him.

Sgt. Bill Fordy: Okay. Number twelve ever been to your place? (Pickton SHAKES HEAD "NO")

Robert Pickton: She's pretty too.

Sgt. Bill Fordy: Yeah, she is pretty. Has number thirteen ever been to your place? No? Fourteen, you've seen her around but you don't remember.

Robert Pickton: There's so many people...

Sgt. Bill Fordy: Fifteen ever been in your place?

Robert Pickton: Really none of them have, not that I know of.

Sgt. Bill Fordy: Well let's just take our time and walk through, so you're a hundred percent. Sixteen? (Pickton SHAKES HEAD "NO") Seventeen? (Pickton SHAKES HEAD "NO") ... has number eighteen ever been to your place?

Robert Pickton: She's pretty too.

Sgt. Bill Fordy: Yeah. What about number nineteen, I'm sorry did you say eighteen had been to your place or no?

Robert Pickton: No. I said I think she's pretty too, I says.

Sgt. Bill Fordy: Okay. Has nineteen ever been to your place?

Robert Pickton: No.

Sgt. Bill Fordy: What about twenty?

Robert Pickton: She's really pretty.

COMMENTS: Pickton's response to photos of suspected murder victims – saying "she's pretty" – would be bizarre if he were innocent. In all, Pickton said "she's pretty" or "she's nice looking" ten times during this portion of the interview. Pickton killed the girls he thought were the most attractive.

EXCERPT 9

Context: Pickton is explaining to Sgt. Fordy that, as a side business, he purchases vehicles at police auctions and sells them for scrap. Pickton says that he sometimes finds personal items left inside the vehicles.

Sgt. Bill Fordy: So whenever you find something in the vehicle then you always take it back to the owners?

Robert Pickton: Usually if I can find 'em, because it's not really mine to have. I don't, I don't, I don't steal from anybody, I don't have to, me myself, I try to help people out. Like people steal from me right, left, and center and I try to help and knife's in the back.

Sgt. Bill Fordy: Mm, hmm.

Robert Pickton: But now I'll still help up today.

Sgt. Bill Fordy: Well you know what, it's good to hear that you're like that Rob.

Robert Pickton: Yeah. Well the only thing is, if I had to do the whole thing over again, I'll try and help. Even if I get knifed in the back again.

Sgt. Bill Fordy: Mm, hmm.

Robert Pickton: I'll still try to help.

Sgt. Bill Fordy: Yeah. So when you take stuff back to these owner's do they ever say thanks or do they just expect you to do that because the cops had the car or how does that work?

Robert Pickton: No. No, no, no, no, no. The vehicle's from the Vancouver Police, I mean whatever becomes of them, it doesn't matter it's already been checked out. I got ah, ah, one truck I got out of from Vancouver Police Department, it was, it had the seat folded in, had a big ax in there, blood, blood all over the ax. I don't know if the police ever did find that ax, if, they try and find the weapon on that one. But I opened the seat up and there's a, there's a...

Sgt. Bill Fordy: Is it still there?

Robert Pickton: No it's gone now. Big single bladed axe, blood all over it.

Sgt. Bill Fordy: I think they found one out at your place.

Robert Pickton: An axe?

Sgt. Bill Fordy: I think so, yeah, maybe they found it.

Robert Pickton: Anyway, the thing is, that came out so ah, there, if, if, if that's the one then, they found it, then I don't know. It was at my place, it was at the house, front house.

Sgt. Bill Fordy: No, I thought it was in the workshop. Maybe I'm, maybe I was wrong, maybe it's a different one.

Robert Pickton: All I know there's supposed to be ah, I know it's a single bladed axe and it had blood, blood all over it. It came out of ah, 1989 Chev Astro. Astro Mini Van.

Sgt. Bill Fordy: Mm, hmm.

Robert Pickton: Yeah.

Sgt. Bill Fordy: Mm, hmm.

COMMENTS: Pickton tries to convince Fordy of his trustworthiness by saying that whenever he finds personal items in vehicles that he purchases from police auctions, he tries to track down the original owner(s) and return their goods. Pickton also tries to use the police auctions as an explanation for the numerous trophies he knows police will find on his property. Implausibly, Pickton says that he occasionally finds weapons in the vehicles, once including a bloody axe. Later, he will say he finds bras, clothes, and asthma inhalers (one of the most incriminating items found on Pickton's property was an inhaler with the victim's name on it). To stop Pickton's excuses, Fordy could have called Pickton out on the ridiculousness of his argument: "If several items from the missing women all ended up on your farm, from vehicles you purchased, that would be quite a coincidence wouldn't it? You need to come up with something better than that, Rob."

EXCERPT 10

Context: Pickton explains to Fordy that he owns a .22 caliber pistol that he uses to slaughter pigs.

Sgt. Bill Fordy: Tell me about your .22.
Robert Pickton: Well I had a little .22, I shouldn't be talkin' because my, my lawyer's not here.
Sgt. Bill Fordy: Mmm, it's up to you.
Robert Pickton: Yeah, cause I shouldn't be, I really shouldn't be. But the problem is I mean, I'm open and like I says, I never kept any secrets, I told everybody about everything. Dave [Pickton's brother] would come over, oh, yeah, I got one, I got a .22 and so on and so forth and the, and it's also, I got this and I got that, yeah. Only thing is ah, sometimes I use the .22, I

shouldn't be talkin' but I'll tell you this ah, I use the .22, sometimes I do big, big boars. Big boars, I mean my Hilti thing, my pin driver goes in that far, the head is very, very solid, very heavy. Very, very big boned, sometimes you have to use three or four or five shots to even bring 'em down.

Sgt. Bill Fordy: Hmm.

Robert Pickton: That's heavy, they're, they're...

Sgt. Bill Fordy: That would be a lot of work, wouldn't it.

Robert Pickton: Oh yeah, couldn't do that. Then they make a lot o'noise.

Sgt. Bill Fordy: Mm, hmm.

Robert Pickton: So the problem is I put plastic around it, just to quietin' the noise down a little bit, and I really, mean big pigs.

Sgt. Bill Fordy: Mm, hmm.

Robert Pickton: And that's why, and then I figure I, I put this here little plastic thing over the top of it, over the top but you probably know about that too right. Anyways I put that thing over the top of it to quiet it down, but I never used it.

Sgt. Bill Fordy: Ah, so you just lost me. Say that again. We were talking about your Hilti gun.

Robert Pickton: No. Talking about a .22.

Sgt. Bill Fordy: Okay. Alright, sorry.

Robert Pickton: But they are both .22 is anyways is .22 calibre and the Hilti and the .22 on the other.

Sgt. Bill Fordy: Yeah. Yeah.

Robert Pickton: But I shouldn't be talking about that. That's, that's for the lawyer. But anyways like I says, you could take as I am, you and take me any which way you want, you could drag me up and down the road here and that still doesn't make me remember anything, I remember dates, I remember this, I remember that, remember faces or whatever but I don't remember any of these people really. Really, honestly I don't. Like you can link me up with them, I'm charged, I'm you can do whatever you want to do with me, that still doesn't make me

244

a murderer, just because but I don't know 'em and as you guys can link whatever onto me I can't help that, because that's your privilege. I got nailed to the cross, I'm just a plain little farm boy, I'm just myself but again I don't do, I wouldn't change very much. If I had to do the whole thing over again, I'm myself. I'm sorry, I'm sorry for living. And ah, you know, if I can, I'll take my life for any one of those people (POINTS TO PICTURE BOARD) just to, (CRYING) just to have them alive. So...sorry.

Sgt. Bill Fordy: Can I sha, just shake my hand okay. I want to make a deal with you here right now okay. It's okay Rob, don't, don't apologize for anything, don't apologize for who you are okay. We just shook hands alright. We're gonna make a deal, you and I. Okay. (STANDS UP)

Robert Pickton: (OVER TALKING) I'm sorry. I'm sorry, I'm sorry.

Sgt. Bill Fordy: You don't need to apologize to me ever again. Alright because I accept you for who you are, I don't want you to change anything, who you are. We're gonna make a deal, you and I, right now.

Robert Pickton: I'm really sorry, I mean I can't help you any more than that. But I can, if I take my life for any one of those people, I would do so.

Sgt. Bill Fordy: Thank you for telling me that Rob.

COMMENTS: Pickton begins to lose his composure, crying and apologizing "for living." Fordy, with professionalism, tells Pickton that he accepts him and that no apologies are necessary. In this section of the interview, Pickton appears to show genuine remorse for his crimes. After the interview, Pickton would tell his cellmate that although he killed 49 women, he was disappointed that he didn't hit 50. After 50, Pickton explained, he was going to take a break before killing another 25. The search of Pickton's property revealed that the "plastic thing" Pickton says he put on the .22 as a silencer is, in fact, a dildo. On it was the DNA of one of the missing women.

EXCERPT 11

Context: Pickton keeps coming close to admitting his guilt without actually saying it. Fordy attempts to have Pickton open up by reminding him that he is a good person.

Sgt. Bill Fordy: And if I thought for one second that you were that kind of person Rob I wouldn't waste one second of my time with you, I wouldn't sit here, I wouldn't care. But I don't see you as that kind of person, I saw the way that you talked about your mother, you know, how much you love your mother and I understand that because I love my mother the same way that you love your mother. And I wish my mother was still with me (OVERTALKING) at my side everyday.
Robert Pickton: I wish she was here too.
Sgt. Bill Fordy: And if your mother was still alive and was beside you Rob you probably wouldn't be in this chair right now, dealing with these issues you've have to deal with because all of your problems started after your mom died. That's when you started killing people.
Robert Pickton: No.
Sgt. Bill Fordy: Not before hand. You telling me you killed someone before your mom died? (Pickton SHAKING HEAD "NO") Okay Rob, because we both know that you did okay. So what I want you to do is just listen to me, remember you told me you were gonna tell me the truth. I don't want you to say any lies to me, I don't want you to say anything that's not the truth. Okay. Because and you know what, I understand, let me tell you something else Rob, I understand you, your, your need to lie to me right now, because you're scared. You know, deep down inside your gut you don't know what's gonna happen.

You know, you don't know what's gonna happen Monday. All you know right now is yes, you are a big media celebrity.

Robert Pickton: Yeah, no kidding.

Sgt. Bill Fordy: You are bigger than the Pope, you're bigger than Princess Diana, you're just like fuckin' Bin Laden. You know you're on the front page of every paper in the country today. Every one.

Robert Pickton: In the paper?

Sgt. Bill Fordy: Everybody knows who you are right now.

Robert Pickton: In the paper today? They put me in the paper.

Sgt. Bill Fordy: Absolutely. This is done, you are over, okay. Only one thing left Rob, that is for me to decide what kind of person you are because there is irrefutable DNA evidence that you are responsible for taking these girls.

Robert Pickton: You, mean I'm in the paper too, today?

COMMENTS: Fordy plays to Pickton's narcissism by telling him that he's "bigger than the Pope." However, Fordy also makes a miscalculation. In this and subsequent sections, it becomes clear that Pickton hates the idea of publicity. Fordy uses this fear to add pressure to the interview, but doesn't offer to minimize media exposure in return for information. The idea of his name and photo being on the front page of the newspaper would continue to distract Pickton for the remainder of the interview.

EXCERPT 12

Context: Fordy is discussing the DNA evidence found inside Pickton's trailer – including large amounts of blood under his carpeting and mattress.

Sgt. Bill Fordy: And you're saying okay, yeah, I agree with you now, the experts are gonna say she died there. That's where she died based on the amount of blood. And you're saying to yourself but Bill how does that prove that it's me? And you're saying to yourself show me that it's me and yeah, I'll admit it, because you are a logical thinker. That's what the experts say about you, is you are logical and you think okay, show me and then you told me here today that you were a good person. Right. So you're a logical thinker and a good person so naturally what you're gonna say to me is Bill show me how that ties to me. Right, that's probably what you're thinking. And then yeah, once you show me I will accept responsibility. That's what the experts say you're gonna do, because deep down inside you are a good person, you know the difference between good and bad and let's face it. So I'm show...

Robert Pickton: So my picture's all over the front page.

Sgt. Bill Fordy: Hear me out.

Robert Pickton: Shit. ... I didn't do anything.

Sgt. Bill Fordy: You know what Rob, you did.

Robert Pickton: I didn't.

Sgt. Bill Fordy: Hear me out, please stop it. I don't want anymore lies okay. And you know what Rob, if your mom was in this room right now, with us, if your mother, whom you love, and whom you respect, was in this room right now Rob, she would want you to tell the truth...

COMMENTS: Fordy appeals to Pickton's narcissistic sense of logic by explaining how the evidence overwhelms any explanations Pickton may have concocted. Fordy also wisely calls Pickton out on his lying, invoking the good name of his mother to ask for the truth. However, Fordy also makes errors. He doesn't give Pickton any real incentives to admit his murders. He doesn't pause to let the significance of the evidence sink in. He tries to anticipate Pickton's denials, but ends up rambling. Fordy's argument could have been simpler:

"Based on the large amount of blood, the experts are going to say the women died in your place – the place where you live, eat and sleep. The women's blood is all over your place, Rob."

EXCERPT 13

Context: Now that Pickton's name is public, Fordy explains what people might be thinking about him.

Sgt. Bill Fordy: ...That's all we want is balance, we want balance (Fordy TOUCHES Pickton WITH THE FILE) and we want to be loved and we want to be respected and that's all you've ever wanted, is to be loved and to have balance in your life. That's all I want and that's all you've ever wanted and if your mom was here she would want you to tell the truth and to be a standup, responsible guy Rob.
Robert Pickton: But I didn't do anything.
Sgt. Bill Fordy: You did okay, stop it. Please don't say that anymore. I'm gonna show you. Alright and you know what, you're probably sitting there and you're, and you're wondering Jesus how do I get out of this now?
Robert Pickton: I didn't do anything.
Sgt. Bill Fordy: Hear me out, that's what you're wondering right. What's, what are you wondering?
Robert Pickton: I didn't do anything, I don't know her.
Sgt. Bill Fordy: Okay you may not know her name.
Robert Pickton: No.
Sgt. Bill Fordy: You might know her as a different name...
Robert Pickton: No. I don't know her face or nothing else.
Sgt. Bill Fordy: Well maybe she looked a little bit different but I know you remember her eye okay and you know what, it's okay for you right now to be scared. (Fordy MOVES AWAY) It's okay for you to say jeez Bill I don't know her. I don't want to accept responsibility because this is a scary time for you.

This is a scary, scary time and there are a lot of people right now that think that you're some crazy, sick, demented, wacko. There are people out there that think that of you. There are some cops in this building right now that think you're some crazy, sick, demented, wacko. I'm gonna tell you though, there are also some cops that think these girls live on the East side of Vancouver, they're out there selling their bodies, they had no self-respect, they're jamming needles into their arms, heroin, coke, up, down, speed, whatever, they are the masters of their own destiny and everything happens to everybody for a reason. I've been involved in cases where I've seen girls from the East end stealing from each other, you know, breaking into houses, stealing from innocent, good, hard working people. I've seen those kind of girls in action. Okay. There are different camps in this right now Rob, there are camps that see you as some sick, sick, demented man. Some weirdo, now I hope that's not the case. You know, you're probably asking yourself jeez, what are my friends gonna think of me? What are the people around me gonna think of me? Are they still gonna be my friends? (Pickton – HEAD IN HIS HANDS) Are they gonna leave me and abandon me, leave me on my own, to go away to jail forever and be alone? I can't work anymore, can't go back to my farm. I can't imagine what's going through your head right now, other than you're scared. Other than you're asking yourself why, why did this happen to me?

Robert Pickton: Why?

COMMENTS: Fordy suggests that although the people who make up "society" might think he's crazy, at least the police understand him. Fordy comfortingly suggests to Pickton that the heroin junkies and prostitutes he killed were responsible for their own deaths, due to their abhorrent lifestyles. Finally, Fordy plays on the narcissists' fear of abandonment by telling Pickton that if he explains himself (provides a confession) he has a better chance to be understood and may not lose his friends. Although all of these suggestions are powerful, Fordy again steamrolls Pickton with multiple comments, giving no time for them to sink in.

EXCERPT 14

Context: Pickton continues to deny his involvement in the murders, even as he accepts that he may be locked up forever. Fordy's interview is going in circles. He is replaced by Constable Dana Lillies, who has previously built rapport with Pickton over a series of informal talks.

Cst. Dana Lillies: I'll bet. It is a lot to be taken in, were you able to sleep last night? Have you eaten anything since you've been in, in custody here? (Pickton SHAKES HEAD "NO") I brought you a sandwich.
Robert Pickton: I don't like it.
Cst. Dana Lillies: You don't like it. Well what do you want to eat, cause we, we should really get you something to eat.
Robert Pickton: I didn't eat anything yet.
Cst. Dana Lillies: What, what would you like to eat Robert?
Robert Pickton: I don't know. At this stage, do I deserve anything to eat?
Cst. Dana Lillies: What's that?
Robert Pickton: Do I deserve anything to eat?
Cst. Dana Lillies: Of course you do. (Lillies PUTS TOILET PAPER DOWN) Robert, you're a human being, you're a human being who's made some mistakes, and that's why we're here to talk to you. To understand, we're not here to judge you, I told you that last week, that I wasn't going to judge you. I'm ready to listen to whatever you have to say.
Robert Pickton: I'm dead before I start.
Cst. Dana Lillies: You're not dead.
Robert Pickton: Just as well.

Cst. Dana Lillies: Like I said, you're a human being, and we're treating you like a human being. You deserve that. (PAUSE)
Robert Pickton: I should be on death row.

COMMENTS: Pickton's remarks that he "doesn't deserve to live," and "should be on death row" are his first explicit indicators of guilt, and suggest he may be close to confessing. He was not. Thirteen pages of transcript later, Pickton is no closer to confessing that he is here.

EXCERPT 15

Context: Constable Lillies is discussing with Pickton what gives him the urge to kill. Though Pickton has admitted little, if he tells Lillies what causes his urge to kill, it will be a an admission.

Cst. Dana Lillies: Was it something that's like a, a switch that just gets clicked on and, and you just react, or is it something that you planned for weeks in advance? (PAUSE 30 SEC) Or is it maybe something that, that's not planned weeks in advance, something that just you decide when you wake up in the morning that this is something you gonna do today.
Robert Pickton: See I don't know her.
Cst. Dana Lillies: That's not what I asked is it? You probably don't know her. (Lillies PICKS UP HER PHOTO AND SHOWS Pickton) Her name is Mona WILSON, she was a prostitute, and you killed her. Now whether or not you knew her isn't really the issue. The reality of the situation is that the evidence doesn't lie, the reality of the situation is her blood is all over that camper and it's mixed with your DNA. So whether or not you knew her, where she lived, who her parents were, whether or not she had children, that's not what I'm asking.

(PASSES PHOTO TO Pickton WHO PUTS IT DOWN ON THE TABLE)
Robert Pickton: I don't know her.
Cst. Dana Lillies: And you never will, because she's dead.

COMMENTS: Lillies' attempts to have Pickton discuss his motivations to kill are unsuccessful. During the exchange, Pickton implies that he has never seen the victim by saying that he doesn't "know her." Lillies catches Pickton at this attempt at *redefinition* and turns it back at him.

EXCERPT 16

Context: Constable Lillies is trying to convince Pickton that the police will never give up in their search for evidence, and so "resistance is futile." Like Fordy, Lillies is now doing most of the talking, while Pickton is responding with single-sentence answers.

(PAUSE 35 SEC)
Robert Pickton: I'd like to go back to my room.
Cst. Dana Lillies: Well, you know what, that's not gonna happen right now. Cause there's more things that we want to talk to you about. Are you absorbing this are you understanding the situation? (PAUSE 25 SEC) You know better than anybody what we're going to find at that farm and we're going to find it, eventually. It might not be today, it might not be tomorrow, it might not even be six months from now. But they're not going to leave until they find everything and until they have answers for those families. ... Robert...
Robert Pickton: I can't help you.
Cst. Dana Lillies: Yes you can. Yes you can. (Pickton PUTS HAND OVER EYES) Why do you say no? Robert why do you

253

say no? Is it because you're afraid or is it because you just don't care?

COMMENTS: Constable Lillies, showing her frustration, belittles Pickton by offering him two negative choices, similar to words in a spat between lovers: "Is it because you're afraid or is it because you just don't care?" To his credit, Fordy asks Lillies to leave immediately after this exchange and once again takes over the interview.

EXCERPT 17

Context: Fordy and Pickton are discussing an asthma inhaler in an expensive case, found on Pickton's property and belonging to one of the victims. Pickton had earlier claimed he found the inhaler in a vehicle he had purchased at a police auction. He had also claimed that whenever he found expensive personal items, he tried to return them to their rightful owners. Here, Pickton is explaining that, in order to find the owner of the inhaler, he had called his friend, "Dr. Lee."

Sgt. Bill Fordy: Well obviously you took the inhaler out cause it was worth four hundred dollars
Robert Pickton: Yeah, yeah looks ah, looks expensive so I says I'm gonna open that and that's it.
Sgt. Bill Fordy: So you phoned up Lee, what's Lee's last name? The Dr, the dentist, the PHD.
Robert Pickton: I can't, can't help you with that.
Sgt. Bill Fordy: Okay, what's her phone number, I'm sorry?
Robert Pickton: I can't help you with that neither.
Sgt. Bill Fordy: Okay, you can't remember it.
Robert Pickton: Ah, she moved to a different ah, different place.
Sgt. Bill Fordy: Okay where, where did she work?

Robert Pickton: She doesn't.

Sgt. Bill Fordy: I'm sorry what was this? Okay, you told me she had her PHD.

Robert Pickton: No, she, she's up there pretty high.

Sgt. Bill Fordy: Ah okay, and what company was she working for?

Robert Pickton: She's doesn't. She doesn't work.

Sgt. Bill Fordy: Ah, okay but she's got ah, like a Master Degree or PHD or something? In what, do you remember?

Robert Pickton: Of any, any I mean anything, doctor stuff yes.

Sgt. Bill Fordy: Okay. How do you spell her first name?

Robert Pickton: Lee, L-E-E.

Sgt. Bill Fordy: And her, her last name? Just think about it for a second.

Robert Pickton: I'm been trying to think about it all day.

Sgt. Bill Fordy: Ah, okay cause she can maybe help your story out a little bit. Um, and what's ah, her phone number? Where did she li, where did she work?

Robert Pickton: She didn't.

Sgt. Bill Fordy: Okay, where did she live?

Robert Pickton: Off of Harris Road.

Sgt. Bill Fordy: Off of Harris Road okay, what colour was the building?

Robert Pickton: You're asking me the impossible.

Sgt. Bill Fordy: Well I mean she's obviously a very good friend of yours, somebody that you call about something important like this so.

Robert Pickton: Yeah, but that's before ah, a everybody know her address everything else, so she wants, she wants to keep herselfs quiet.

Sgt. Bill Fordy: Yeah, this is, this is the most important day of your life. Let's be honest.

Robert Pickton: I don't know what her last name is.

Sgt. Bill Fordy: Okay. So you don't know Lee's last name.

Robert Pickton: I don't know if she's using a married name or her maiden name neither.
Sgt. Bill Fordy: Let's, let's be honest you don't want to tell me Lee's last name.
Robert Pickton: No I don't, know...
Sgt. Bill Fordy: Okay. (OVER TALKING)
Robert Pickton: He, he got ah, she got a son named Rocky.
Sgt. Bill Fordy: Rocky. Make movies about guy's like that. Ah, okay. So you found the inhaler in the glove box...

COMMENTS: As Fordy relentlessly presses Pickton for details, the lies become obvious. Pickton ludicrously claims that his friend, "Dr. Lee," is an unemployed Ph.D. with a son named Rocky, that Lee is her first name, and that he doesn't know her phone number or where she lives. Although this line of questioning appears directionless, it lets Pickton know that if he manufactures details, he'll become stuck in a frustrating quagmire of questions he can't answer.

EXCERPT 18

Context: After watching Pickton's interview once again going in circles, Staff Sergeant Don Adam takes over. Adam is discussing Pickton's former friend, Lynn Ellingsen, who witnessed Pickton skinning a corpse in his barn. Instead of going to the police with this information, Ellingsen had blackmailed Pickton instead.

S/Sgt. Don Adam: We know that Lynn was blackmailing you, alright. You've told people that and we've got those statements and you know what, she is going to screw you again, like, everything she's done to you, she is gonna screw you again Willy. And that's one of the things you could stop. You choose to tell the truth here tonight, and that choice is yours alright.

256

But you could screw her right back because if you talk before she does, there's no need for us to make a deal with her, we could be down there arresting her later on tonight if you tell the truth about what was going on, do you understand? Don't you get tired of being beat up by people, and abused and used Willy? Aren't you tired of it? Isn't it time you did something just for me, just for yourself? Don't let these people beat you up, make you into a monster, use you, walk away from everything they've done, laughing and what, selling their story to CNN, so they make money on it. You know how it goes. That's all in the palm of your hand, alright. Are you gonna be made a fool of by these people, don't do it Willy. Don't do it.

COMMENTS: Adam plays into a common pet peeve of serial killers: that loved ones and friends will make money off their misfortune by becoming co-authors and talk-show guests. Adam tells Pickton the truth: that he should tell his own story, and that that this is his chance to finally take control of his life. Pickton did not take Adam's advice. Lynn Ellingsen would testify against Pickton in court, appear in a documentary, and walk away a free woman.

EXCERPT 19

Context: Sergeant Adam compares Pickton to other killers.

S/Sgt. Don Adam: ...And I don't believe that right into the core of your being you are as much of a monster as people are gonna portray you to be. Because if you were, you would have killed or hurt some of these other good people who are out there. You live in [the city of] Port Coquitlam, there's schools near by alright. I just finished talking to a guy who was dragging women into a van and raping them alright and he was caught at a Coquitlam schoolyard, planning the next attack on a little girl. Willy are you the same kind of guy as that? Have you ever hurt anybody like that? Okay, those are the things that you can talk about, Willy I talked to a guy years ago who killed his two little babies, killed his wife and lit a fire to burn his five year old son to death because he wanted to have sex with another woman. Cause he was bored. Willy are you like that? Would you kill your family, do you see what I mean? So Willy, the mistakes that you made alright, they're, they're driven by certain things. They're driven I think by anger, and stuff that's happened with you. But you're not at a school yard Willy are you, you're not trying to grab little girls off the street. There's absolutely no indication you've ever done anything like that and if you tell me that you haven't I will believe you. Can you look me in the eye and tell me that Don, I have never done anything like that?

Robert Pickton: I haven't done anything like that.

COMMENTS: Adams compares Pickton favorably to child killers and pedophiles, and argues any crimes he may have committed were due to circumstances and not really his fault. Since Pickton would have told himself the same excuses over the years, he probably found Adams' confirmation comforting.

EXCERPT 20

Context: The confession begins.

S/Sgt. Don Adam: How many do you think you've done [killed]?

Robert Pickton: I don't know. (TAKES A DRINK)

S/Sgt. Don Adam: Would it be twenty?

Robert Pickton: I don't know.

S/Sgt. Don Adam: You've got an idea though Willy. You're, you're, you're a guy who knows the dates of things, you're, you know. You've a good idea. Fifteen, twenty, where, where do you think it is, or thirty. It doesn't matter, just tell the truth.

Robert Pickton: I don't know.

S/Sgt. Don Adam: Well, I can put about twelve to you right now, okay, so there's those twelve, right. Ah, shall we start from sort of the most recent and go backwards? You did Sereena, we know that Willy, agreed?

Robert Pickton: Sereena...

S/Sgt. Don Adam: Sereena Abotsway, I'd have to and I apologize because I, because I'm not a front line investigator, like I'm a manager, should I get in, somebody in here who knows these girls and, and we can discuss it or would you just want to talk to me. (Fordy COMES IN AND GIVES HIM A PIECE OF PAPER THEN LEAVES) So this, this is Sereena, alright. Okay, so we know that you, you know, you did take her life, alright. Just tell me about that, let's start, let's take little steps alright. I think you know right now, unless their pictures are so different you're not sure, I think you could, you could make a choice and just reach out and touch the ones that ah, that you've done Willy you know the ones that...

Robert Pickton: (LAUGHING) You're making me more of a mass killer than I am.

S/Sgt. Don Adam: Well how bad is it, how big is it?

Robert Pickton: I don't know.

S/Sgt. Don Adam: Well is it ten, twenty.

Robert Pickton: I don't know.

S/Sgt. Don Adam: Well is it five, tell me you've done more than five, we're gonna be spending millions of dollars. Well it's more than five, we both know that. Agreed?

Robert Pickton: I don't know.

S/Sgt. Don Adam: Willy, come on. We don't need to play games with each other. Are you just not quite convinced yet you want to tell me the details of the killings? Is that, that's what it is isn't it? Come on, tell me the truth. Are you still thinking what's in it for me?

Robert Pickton: What's in it for me?

COMMENTS: Faced with the overwhelming physical evidence that police are discovering at his property, Pickton finally starts negotiating. At this early stage, Pickton doesn't really confess to murder, so much as stop denying his involvement.

EXCERPT 21

Context: The confession continues. Pickton begins this section by admonishing Adam for the time it took to catch him, and suggesting that the police were incompetent (a frequent complaint from serial killers).

Robert Pickton: That's right. Bad policing your guys behalf. Right. It took so long.
S/Sgt. Don Adam: Pardon.
Robert Pickton: Bad policing on your behalf because its been so long.
S/Sgt. Don Adam: Yeah, cause it took so long to catch you. Yeah. Yeah, you're right. Yeah, and ah, I know a lot of policemen feel bad for the families of these people. Did you ever think of quitting?
Robert Pickton: Yeah.
S/Sgt. Don Adam: Was it, is it that drive we talked about, like does that accurately describe it, cause I would like to know, cause obviously someday I'll be sitting with somebody else Willy, it would be nice to...
Robert Pickton: Yeah, it'll all, it'll all come out. It'll all come out.
S/Sgt. Don Adam: These guys that lecture to us, talk about it fantasy, the fantasy of the killing and that, is that, (Pickton SHAKING HEAD "NO") no it's not like that. Is it anger?
Robert Pickton: Who said that?

S/Sgt. Don Adam: Well...

Robert Pickton: Fantasy, what do you mean?

S/Sgt. Don Adam: That, that serial killers have fantasies about what they want to do to their victims and that they, for you nothing like that.

Robert Pickton: No. No.

S/Sgt. Don Adam: Anger? Well you, you sort of said it was anger. Would I be right in, in saying Willy, that you had reached the stage where you just no longer sort of really viewed these girls as being worth anything.

Robert Pickton: Mm, hmm.

S/Sgt. Don Adam: And you killed...

Robert Pickton: But ah, no, no, that's not. I had one more planned but that was, that was the end of it. That was the last I was gonna shut it down, that's why I was just sloppy. Just the last one.

S/Sgt. Don Adam: You were gonna do one more.

Robert Pickton: (INDECIPHERABLE) that was the end of it. That's why I got sloppy because the other thing never got that far.

S/Sgt. Don Adam: Like why didn't you just drag that mattress that you, where killed ah, Mona, why didn't you just drag it out and burn it. I mean that would have been...

Robert Pickton: I don't...

S/Sgt. Don Adam: ...did you not realize there was blood underneath it? Like you don't have to say anything? Like if you'd a burnt it Willy, just sloppy.

Robert Pickton: Sloppy like I just told you.

S/Sgt. Don Adam: Let me ask you a question? They talk about a, people keeping trophies.

Robert Pickton: No.

S/Sgt. Don Adam: So when you kept the women's ID in your place that was just...

Robert Pickton: No.

S/Sgt. Don Adam: ...again sloppy.

Robert Pickton: Yeah.

S/Sgt. Don Adam: Jesus Willy, you must be kicking yourself, like...

Robert Pickton: I know.

S/Sgt. Don Adam: You gotta be, you gotta be saying like why. All you would have had to do...

Robert Pickton: I know.

S/Sgt. Don Adam: ...is go through that, clean up.

Robert Pickton: I know.

S/Sgt. Don Adam: And you'd still be on the street.

Robert Pickton: I know.

S/Sgt. Don Adam: Oh, it must piss you off.

Robert Pickton: I know.

S/Sgt. Don Adam: It must eh?

Robert Pickton: I know.

S/Sgt. Don Adam: Like that mattress all you had to do was burn it. Well you would have had to washed the walls right.

Robert Pickton: Sloppiness.

COMMENTS: Like many serial killers, Pickton talks about being caught because he "got sloppy," indicating his subconscious desire to stop killing. Adam directly asks Pickton why he didn't burn the bloodied mattress to destroy the evidence, but Pickton is at a loss to explain why. In their search, police found weapons, a blood-soaked mattress and carpet, bloody hand prints, IDs from victims, and flesh in freezers. Pickton's home and property were overflowing with evidence, much of which was in plain sight.

EXCERPT 22

Context: Having purged himself of pressure by confessing, Pickton now appears to be enjoying his interview. He is refusing to provide details, taunting Adam with riddles

("Giving your head a rattle am I?") and answering "no comment" to questions.

S/Sgt. Don Adam: I have to try and understand you. And I have to talk lightly about what you did, because otherwise I'm gonna shut you down, and you won't talk to me. Alright, but all the time I'm seized with the fact that while you and I are talking about this [the murdered women] as if it's so many ah, you know, used cars.
Robert Pickton: Well.
S/Sgt. Don Adam: That there are people who's are, hearts are being broken and...
Robert Pickton: What can I say?
S/Sgt. Don Adam: Well I just want you to know how much it bothers me to have to sit here and act as if this is just a chess game.
Robert Pickton: It's not a chess game but the problem is I'm just only asking you for everybody get their life back together. That's all I'm asking for.
S/Sgt. Don Adam: Alright. Let me think about that, I'll be back in a sec.
Robert Pickton: Do I get to go back to my cell?
S/Sgt. Don Adam: Yeah, let me ah, talk to my ah, people and I'm sure we can arrange that. (Pickton PICKS UP PICTURE BOARD OF FARM – SITS BACK YAWNING) (Adam LEAVES ROOM 4 MIN 16 SEC LATER, Fordy RE-ENTERED THE ROOM)
Sgt. Bill Fordy: Rob, how you doin?
Robert Pickton: Oh, ...
Sgt. Bill Fordy: What's that?
Robert Pickton: (INDECIPHERABLE)
Sgt. Bill Fordy: Um, Don asked me to come and ah, just take you back to your cell.
Robert Pickton: Yeah, no problem.

COMMENTS: After hours of interviewing, Adam loses his cool with Pickton's cat-and-mouse approach to revealing information and his cavalier attitude toward human life. Adam wisely leaves the interview room and has Pickton taken back to his cell. There, Pickton will brag about his murders to his cell mate, then masturbate before falling asleep, snoring throughout the night. The weight of the huge secret he had been carrying was gone.

EPILOGUE

As a result of this interview and other evidence, Pickton was sentenced to 25 years in prison with no possibility of parole, the longest term then available for an offender in Canada.

Following Pickton's conviction, Doug LePard of the Vancouver Police Department issued an apology to the families of the deceased, saying, "I wish from the bottom of my heart that we would have caught him sooner. I wish that, the several agencies involved, that we could have done better in so many ways. I wish that all the mistakes that were made, we could undo" (LePard, 2010). The Vancouver Police Department made classic mistakes in their investigation: they denied the existence of a serial killer in their jurisdiction, even against the protests of local residents who recognized their must be one; they didn't dedicate sufficient resources to the investigation, possibly due to the nature of the victims (prostitutes); and, their early interviews with Pickton lacked planning. These are lessons to be learned for all law enforcement agencies.

A WORD ON PSYCHOLOGICAL PROFILING

In the movies, criminal profilers are so accurate they can successfully determine a killer's occupation, what the killer looks like, and even the exact address of the next victim's home. In real life, criminal profilers have a conundrum. The more specific a profile is, the more useful it is to law enforcement. However, the more specific it is, the more likely it is to contain errors and therefore be misleading. As a result, psychological profiles tend to be frustratingly vague. The dirty secret of the profiling world is that most psychological profiles are so vague as to be basically useless.

"...we hypothesized that the suspect would have a late model car and would be employed at a job with limited responsibility... We predicted that the killer would keep a fetish [trophy], frequently a body part, a lock of hair, underclothing or jewelry.. We predicted that the murders would continue and that sexual molestation would be accompanied by sexual mutilation... The perpetrator would likely only select male victims..."

An example of a typically vague psychological profile (Turco, 2008). The killer's three previously discovered victims were boys. All three had been sexually molested and mutilated.

When studies have been done concerning the accuracy of detailed psychological profiles, the results have been laughable. One study (Kocsis et al, 2002) asked groups of police officers and sophomore chemistry students to prepare psychological profiles based on the evidence from a real case. The chemistry students outperformed all the police groups on accuracy, including the senior detectives. In fact, the profiles completed by the most experienced officers were the *least* accurate. Another study compared psychological profiles created by a number of groups including professional profilers, police officers, psychics, and college students studying either science or economics. There was no difference in overall accuracy (Kocsis et al, 2000). Yet another study (Hodges & Jacquin, 2008), found that while a background in psychology improved the accuracy of profiles completed by females, it did nothing for males. The researchers, both women, curiously suggested that perhaps the most intelligent males don't pick psychology as their major.

Investigators must avoid the trap of devoting resources toward determining a killer's thoughts and motivations, even if that information will have limited investigative value. A psychological profile *can* be used to provide focus for an investigation, but should *never* be used to eliminate suspects. The eyewitness information, tips, and other clues used to construct a profile are always flawed to some degree. Psychological profiles are rarely accurate enough that, armed with one, an officer would be able to spot the killer walking down the street. More likely, the killer would walk past unnoticed.

In the book, *Criminal Shadows* (1993), psychologist David Canter explains what he calls "The Electrician and Ladder Principle." Few electricians are injured by electricity, even though they work with high-voltage electricity every day. Instead, they have accidents related to the unplanned moments of their work that require no special skills, such as falling off ladders or tripping over cords. Similarly, serial killers are unlikely to reveal themselves while killing, since these moments are the result of longstanding fantasies and planning. Instead, serial killers might reveal their criminal nature by violently assaulting a spouse, threatening a neighbor, committing a robbery, talking about killing to impress a friend, or writing an enraged letter to the editor of the local newspaper. Killers reveal themselves during spontaneous moments that haven't been given forethought and planning. They reveal themselves in ways that most people overlook. Good investigators recognize that a comparatively minor act may reveal a darker, hidden nature.

Gumshoe police work, including knocking on doors, questioning neighbors, and gathering forensic evidence has always been the best way to catch killers – including serial killers. Knowledge of the characteristics and habits of serial killers, as outlined in this book, will aid in the successful recognition of likely suspects.

VICARIOUS TRAUMATIZATION

"The guilty soul of Mrs. Grinder has been sent to the judgment bar of god. At exactly 1:15 o'clock this afternoon the judge's sentence, that she be hung by the neck until she be dead, was executed. The scene was a sad, solemn and deeply impressive one. The only person present who seemed to be not in the least affected was the murderess herself."

From "The Execution of Mrs. Grinder," *The New York Times*, Jan. 21, 1866. The only people who don't think death is a traumatic event are murderers.

Serial killer investigations require looking at shocking crime scenes, listening to survivor testimony, dealing with grieving family members and hearing gruesome confessions. As a result, professionals may experience *vicarious traumatization*.

In the investigation of killers Fred and Rose West (which involved rape, murder and incest), not only the police were negatively affected, but also the West children, the defense lawyers, and even the legal secretaries who had to type up the case material.

Law enforcement officers should never dive headfirst into a prolonged first-person identification with a killer without taking time out. Maintain a healthy routine, including good food, exercise, and rest. *Expect* to be frustrated by the investigation. If you try to relax but are unable to, do the opposite: run, work out, watch an action movie, or any activity that matches your level of physiological arousal. If your negativity and agitation persists, seek professional advice. Don't be one of the many law enforcement professionals who experience a heart attack or stroke well before their time.

For those involved in serial killer investigations, vicarious traumatization is a normal reaction. It should be expected.

BIOGRAPHIES

BERKOWITZ, David

Nickname: "The Son of Sam," "The .44 Caliber Killer"

Born: June 1, 1953
Died:

Number of victims: 6
Preferential victims: young couples
Job/Career: army soldier, postal worker
Primary killing method: shooting with a .44 caliber revolver
Primary disposal method: leaving the bodies *in situ*

Other notable facts: Berkowitz targeted young couples on dates, particularly those in parked vehicles. During the summer of 1976, Berkowitz' murders terrified the people of New York and vicinity so badly that they often stayed home at night, refusing to leave. Berkowitz was originally called the ".44 Caliber Killer," due to his use of a Charter Arms .44 caliber bulldog revolver in the murders; however, Berkowitz wrote a letter to the press and signed it "Son of Sam." The press began using the new name. After his arrest, authorities were concerned that Berkowitz might profit from movie and book deals. In response, NY State legislature enacted the "Son of Sam" laws, stating that a killer may not profit from his crimes. Since then, other states and countries around the world have enacted similar legislation.

BERNARDO, Paul Kenneth

Nickname: "The Scarborough Rapist," "Ken" of the "Ken and Barbie Killers"

Born: August 27, 1964
Died:
Number of victims: 3+
Preferential victims: teenage girls
Job/Career: accountant, cigarette smuggler
Primary killing method: poisoning and strangulation
Primary disposal method: dismemberment and encasement in concrete, for disposal in remote locations

Other notable facts: Prior to becoming a killer, Bernardo committed at least 11 rapes. Brought in for questioning due to his similarity to a circulating composite sketch, police concluded that the well-spoken, polite young man could not possibly be responsible. Bernardo and his trendy girlfriend (later wife), Karla Homolka, became known as the "Ken and Barbie" killers.

BIANCHI, Kenneth Alessio

Nickname: "The Hillside Strangler"

Born: May 22, 1951
Died:

Number of victims: 12+
Preferential victims: teenage girls, young women
Job/Career: security guard, ambulance driver, and others
Primary killing method: strangulation
Primary disposal method: dumping the bodies in the hillsides of California, near Los Angeles

Other notable facts: Bianchi and his older cousin, Angelo Buono, were killing partners. Bianchi's mother was an alcoholic prostitute who gave him up for adoption shortly after his birth. After Bianchi and his older cousin had a falling out, he moved from Los Angeles to Bellingham (near Seattle, Washington) to be with his ex-girlfriend and her son. He continued to murder on his own, but was arrested after the neighbor of one of his victims identified him. Bianchi unsuccessfully pleaded not guilty by reason of insanity, while faking Multiple Personality Disorder.

BUNDY, Theodore Robert (Ted)

Nickname: "The Campus Killer"

Born: November 24, 1946
Died: January 24, 1989, by electric chair

Number of victims: 14-35+
Preferential victims: slim girls and women with straight hair
Job/Career: law school student and others
Primary killing method: bludgeoning and strangulation
Primary disposal method: partial burial in remote forest or swamp locations

Other notable facts: Also known as Theodore Sandy and Theodore Cowell, Bundy graduated from the University of Washington with a major in psychology, and later studied law. First arrested in Salt Lake City, Utah, for failure to stop for a police officer, Bundy escaped from custody by jumping out of the 2nd floor window of a law library during his hearing. He was captured a week later, but the slim-built Bundy escaped yet again through a 12-inch hole in the ceiling of his cell, underneath a light fixture plate. Bundy literally walked out the front door of the jail. He committed additional murders before he was apprehended two years later in Florida. During those two years, Bundy was on the FBI's most wanted list. The FBI reports describe him as having clear blue eyes and "wirey" hair that, when washed, appears "afro-like."

BUONO, Angelo Jr.

Nickname: "The Hillside Strangler"

Born: Oct 5, 1934
Died: Sept 21, 2002, due to heart attack

Number of victims: 12+
Preferential victims: teenage girls, young women
Job/Career: auto upholstery shop owner and others
Primary killing method: strangulation
Primary disposal method: dumping the bodies in the hillsides of California, near Los Angeles

Other notable facts: Buono and his younger cousin, Kenneth Bianchi, were killing partners. In 1977, the pair gave a ride to a female hitchhiker who they learned was Catherine Lorre, daughter of actor Peter Lorre. Peter Lorre had become internationally famous starring in the German movie, *M*, in which he played a serial killer. Buono and Bianchi let the girl go, not wanting the publicity that would come from killing someone with a famous father. After years of "successful" murders, Buono was arrested after Bianchi moved to Washington and almost immediately bungled his first murders there, leaving multiple layers of evidence.

CULLEN, Charles Edmund

Nickname: "The Angel of Death"

Born: February 22, 1960
Died:

Number of victims: 22-45+
Preferential victims: hospital patients
Job/Career: male nurse
Primary killing method: drug overdose, usually using insulin
Primary disposal method: leaving the bodies *in situ*

Other notable facts: Cullen was sexually abused by his father. The first time Cullen attempted suicide was at the age of 9, when he drank the contents of his chemistry set. He later joined the US Navy, but was discharged after multiple suicide attempts. When Cullen was arrested for murder and brought into the courtroom for sentencing, he kept saying, "Your honor, you must step down," over and over, until the judge finally had him gagged with duct tape and a towel. Cullen continued saying the phrase, muffled through the towel, even as he was duck-marched in chains out of the courtroom. Cullen is serving 18 consecutive life sentences. He has not committed suicide in prison.

DAHMER, Jeffrey Lionel

Nickname: "The Milwaukee Cannibal"

Born: May 21, 1960
Died: Nov 28, 1994, murdered by a fellow prison inmate

Number of victims: 15+
Preferential victims: multi-ethnic boys
Job/Career: chocolate factory worker and others
Primary killing methods: bludgeoning, strangulation
Primary disposal method: Dahmer dismembered his victims and dissolved them in acid

Other notable facts: As a teen, Dahmer said he collected road kill "for curiosity." Dahmer served in the U.S. military as a medical specialist (269th Armor Division), where he became a sharpshooter with an M-16 rifle, and a marksman with a 1911 handgun. Dahmer was forced to enroll in a rehabilitation program for alcohol abuse. His documents from the time read, "PFC [Private First Class] Dahmer has been showing no desire to be rehabilitated and has been involved in several incidents, is not willing to control his alcohol intake. Recommend he be declared a failure at this time." His access to classified material was revoked, and he was given an Honorable Discharge the same year, at the age of 20. During the *manic curve* phase of his killing spree, Dahmer murdered almost a victim a week: all males. He ate his victim's body parts, particularly their hearts, storing the leftovers in his refrigerator. After his arrest, when asked by the FBI what type of men he prefers, Dahmer replied, "Chippendales," referring to a famous male striptease group. The FBI hilariously misunderstood; in all their literature, they write that Dahmer likes men who look like "Chip and Dale," the cartoon chipmunks.

DUFFY, John Francis

Nickname: "The Railway Killers," "The Thriller Killers"

Born: 1959
Died:

Number of victims: 3+ (in addition to multiple rapes)
Preferential victims: young women
Job/Career: carpenter, rail worker
Primary killing method: strangulation
Primary disposal method: leaving the bodies *in situ*

Other notable facts: Mulcahy is the partner of John Duffy, together known as the "Railway Killers."   They were also known as the "Thriller" killers, from their habit of listening to the Michael Jackson album of the same name while trolling for victims. Duffy first came to the attention of law enforcement in 1985 when he attacked his wife in a bout of domestic violence. In 1986 he was arrested after he was noticed carrying a knife near a train station, but was released due to lack of evidence. He was arrested for the final time, also in 1986, for stalking a woman in a park.

GACY, John Wayne Jr.

Nickname: "The Killer Clown"

Born: March 17, 1942
Died: May 10, 1994, by lethal injection

Number of victims: 33+
Preferential victims: teenage boys
Job/Career: construction company owner and others
Primary killing method: strangulation
Primary disposal method: burying victims beneath his home

Other notable facts: Gacy got his nickname from his volunteer work as a children's party clown, calling himself "Pogo." During his first marriage, Gacy created a "club" for teenage boys in the basement of his home, ultimately resulting in his first prison sentence for sexual assault. After his release, Gacy started a modestly successful construction business and remarried. His second wife divorced him due to his moodiness and obsession with pornography. Gacy was once photographed with First Lady Rosalyn Carter (U.S. President Jimmy Carter's wife) for his volunteer work as an organizer of Chicago's Polish Day Parade. After his arrest, twenty-nine bodies were found in the crawl space beneath his home.

HOMOLKA, Karla Leanne

Nickname: "Barbie" of the "Ken and Barbie Killers"

Born: May 4, 1970
Died:

Number of victims: 3+
Preferential victims: teenage girls
Job/Career: student, veterinarian's assistant
Primary killing method: strangulation
Primary disposal method: dismemberment and disposal in concrete or remote locations

Other notable facts: Homolka was the girlfriend (later wife) of serial rapist Paul Bernardo. Together, they became known as the "Ken and Barbie" killers. Homolka is particularly infamous for striking a plea bargain with police, prior to their discovery of home videos in which she appears to be a willing participant (as opposed to a victim) in the murders the pair committed. She received only a 12-year sentence, and was released in 2005. She has moved and changed names frequently since her release. In 2016 Homolka was identified living in Montreal, Canada under the name "Leanne Teale."

KEMPER, Edmund Emil III

Nickname: "The Co-Ed Killer," "Big Ed"

Born: December 18, 1948
Died:

Number of victims: 10
Preferential victims: female student hitchhikers, family members
Job/Career: college student, highway department worker
Primary killing method: shooting and bludgeoning
Primary disposal method: dismemberment and shallow burial in remote locations

Other notable facts: At the age of 15, Kemper shot and killed his grandmother, just to see what it would feel like. Knowing that his grandfather would be angry, Kemper shot him as well. He was committed to state hospital as a minor but eventually released, at which point he began murdering female students. Kemper's final two murders were of his mother and her friend. Kemper decapitated his mother, then spent hours throwing darts at her head before smashing her skull in with a hammer. Kemper is a huge man: 6 ft 9 inches tall and about 300 pounds.

KEYES, Israel

Nickname: none

Born: March 17, 1942
Died: December 2, 2012, committed suicide in jail

Number of victims: 3-11+
Preferential victims: women
Job/Career: construction contractor and others
Primary killing methods: shooting and strangulation
Primary disposal method: hiding dismembered bodies in remote locations

Other notable facts: Israel Keyes came from a strict Mormon family, and was home-schooled. Although Keyes primarily worked in Alaska, he also committed burglaries and bank robberies all over the United States. Keyes' favorite weapon was a Ruger® 22 Charger pistol with bipod, and he was unusually proud of the fact that he had built an effective handgun silencer for it at home. He was arrested in Texas after using the debit card of one of his victims.

KUKLINSKY, Richard Leonard

Nickname: "The Iceman"

Born: April 11, 1935
Died: March 6, 2006, in prison

Number of victims: unknown
Preferential victims: contract hits, anyone who annoyed him, and random passersby
Job/Career: mafia hitman, drug and arms dealer
Primary killing method: shooting, strangulation, and poisoning
Primary disposal method: various

Other notable facts: Kuklinsky's older brother was beaten to death by their abusive father. Kuklinsky's first admitted murder, at the age of 18, was to burn alive a man who insulted him in a bar. Kuklinsky claimed that he killed random people for amusement by pretending to sneeze as he passed by them, simultaneously spraying cyanide from a spray bottle into their faces. He got his nickname, "Iceman," both from his cold demeanor and from his habit of freezing his victims to disguise their time of death. He was 6 ft 5 inches tall.

LEGEBOKOFF, Cody Alan

Nickname: none

Born: January 21, 1990
Died:

Number of victims: 4+
Preferential victims: girls, female prostitutes
Job/Career: auto mechanic
Primary killing method: shooting and bludgeoning
Primary disposal method: disposal in remote locations

Other notable facts: Legebokoff was one of Canada's youngest serial killers, convicted at the age of 24. During his trial, Legebokoff testified (unsuccessfully) that the murders were actually committed by his drug dealer and two accomplices, whom he called X, Y, and Z. In court, Legebokoff laughed whenever the prosecuting attorney caught him lying.

MANSON, Charles (Charlie)

Nickname: none

Born: November 12, 1934
Died:

Number of victims: 10+
Preferential victims: famous people, or those who got in his way
Job/Career: cult leader, petty thief
Primary killing method: strangulation
Primary disposal method: leaving the bodies *in situ*

Other notable facts: Manson was not a serial killer *per se*, but a hippie cult guru who led a group of killers known as the "Family." Prior to his conviction for conspiracy to commit murder, he had already served time for burglary, armed robbery, assault, grand theft auto, and forgery. Manson has spent nearly his entire life in prison. A historically interesting fact is that for several months in 1968, Manson and his groupies were living in the home of Dennis Wilson, a member of the Beach Boys rock group. After Wilson met two of the "Family" girls hitchhiking, Manson and the remaining girls simply moved into Wilson's home. Wilson even paid for studio time so that Manson (a guitarist and singer) could record some songs. Though the quality of Manson's songs was reasonable, they were not commercially successful.

During his trial, Manson tried to burn down the county jail by setting his cell blankets and towel on fire before leaving for court. No mention was made of how he obtained the matches.

METHENY, Joe Roy

Nickname: "The Cannibal"

Born: 1955
Died:

Number of victims: 4+
Preferential victims: men and women
Job/Career: truck driver, forklift driver
Primary killing method: strangulation and stabbing
Primary disposal method: shallow graves

Other notable facts: After his arrest, Metheny told his attorney that he had been raised in tough, "foster-like" homes, and that both his parents were dead. He also claimed to have become addicted to heroin while serving in Vietnam. Metheny's mother (very much alive) said that he had never been in foster homes, and added that she did "not recall him having served in Vietnam." Metheny lived in a one-room trailer next to the pallet factory where he worked. He was arrested after one of his victims escaped and called police. Asked in court why he killed, Metheny answered, "I had no real excuse why other than I like to do it." Metheny is an obese man, weighing 450 pounds, and is a necrophile.

MULCAHY, David

Nickname: "The Railway Killers," "The Thriller Killers"

Born: 1959, month and day not available
Died:

Number of victims: 3+ (in addition to multiple rapes)
Preferential victims: young women
Job/Career: plumber, mini-cab driver
Primary killing method: strangulation
Primary disposal method: leaving the bodies *in situ*

Other notable facts: Mulcahy is the partner of John Duffy, together known as the "Railway Killers," since they hunted victims at or near train stations.   After a series of murders, British psychologist David Cantor was brought onto the case, forming the beginning of psychological profiling in the U.K.   In 2008, Mulcahy made headlines again when he received injuries in prison after being bludgeoned by a fellow inmate with a tin of carrots.

PICKTON, Robert William ("Willie")

Nickname: none

Born: October 26, 1949
Died:

Number of victims: 49
Preferential victims: female prostitutes
Job/Career: pig farmer, scrap metal dealer and others
Primary killing method: strangulation
Primary disposal method: gutting, cleaning, and dismemberment (like livestock)

Other notable facts: The Pickton farm became such a large and complex murder site that forensic anthropology students were brought in as volunteers to help police. Inside a freezer on the property, they found skulls with the victim's feet stuffed inside them. Pickton was a cannibal. In 2016, Pickton made headlines again when it was discovered that he authored a 144-page book entitled, *Pickton: In His Own Words*. Pickton had given the manuscript to another inmate to smuggle out of prison. The book, which was riddled with spelling mistakes, appeared online briefly before sales were discontinued. In it, Pickton unsurprisingly claims he is innocent.

RADER, Dennis Lynn

Nickname: "The Bind Torture Kill (BTK) Killer"

Born: March 9, 1945
Died:

Number of victims: 10+
Preferential victims: petite women
Job/Career: city compliance (by-law) officer and others
Primary killing methods: strangulation, stabbing
Primary disposal method: leaving the bodies *in situ*

Other notable facts: Rader desired fame. Though he became known as the BTK killer, Rader had also suggested to the press, via letter, the names "Wichita Strangler," "Poetic Strangler" and "The Wichita Hangman" among others. In his free time, he was congregation President of his church. Rader was sentenced to 175 years in prison without chance of parole. In 2014, Rader wrote a letter to *The Wichita Eagle* newspaper, saying that he was sorry to hear about Ken Landwehr's death from kidney cancer: "He was respected and I'm sure, a good family man, just doing his job." Landwehr was the homicide task force commander who had hunted down Rader and arrested him.

RAMIREZ, Ricardo (Richard)

Nickname: "The Night Stalker," "Ricky Rabon (the thief)"

Born: February 29, 1960
Died: June 7, 2013 of lymphoma (cancer)

Number of victims: 13+
Preferential victims: anyone
Job/Career: burglar
Primary killing methods: shooting, bludgeoning
Primary disposal method: none (he left the bodies *in situ*)

Other notable facts: Ramirez suffered two serious brain injuries as a child, once when a dresser fell on top of his head at the age of two, and another when he was hit by a swing in the playground and knocked unconscious. After the second incident, Ramirez began suffering seizures. Ramirez' relatives were role models of deviance for him as a child: his father was abusive, his cousin shot his wife in the face and killed her while Richard was present, and his sister's husband taught Richard how to be a peeping tom. Ramirez was arrested after a crowd of local citizens pursued him and beat him up after recognizing him from a newspaper photograph. In 1987, actor Sean Penn was in L.A. County jail for parole violations when he received a scribbled note from Ramirez asking for his autograph; Ramirez was in a cell across the hall. While in prison, Ramirez was known for masturbating in front of young girls who came to visit their relatives, including his own niece.

RELDAN, Robert

Nickname: "The Charmer," "The Susan Strangler"

Born: June 2, 1940
Died:

Number of victims: 2-8+
Preferential victims: teenage girls
Job/Career: handyman/landscaper
Primary killing method: shooting and strangulation
Primary disposal method: dumping in remote locations

Other notable facts: Reldan was convicted and incarcerated for rape and assault two times prior to his final conviction. He arguably received light sentences due to his "all-American college boy" good looks, which made jurors think he could not be dangerous. Reldan has tried to escape from custody multiple times. He once escaped from a courthouse by spraying an officer with teargas and then stealing a car, but was re-arrested an hour later. Another time he complained of stomach pains and was taken to hospital. Reldan's girlfriend was caught waiting in the hospital lobby with a sawed-off shotgun and disguises in her shopping bag. Reldan was eligible for parole in July of 2008, but was denied. The parole board noted that Reldan made little distinction between "things stolen and lives taken," that he continues to think of himself as a victim, and that he is a manipulative narcissist.

RIDGWAY, Gary Leon

Nickname: "The Green River Killer"

Born: February 18, 1949
Died:

Number of victims: 49+ (Ridgway claims 75-80)
Preferential victims: female prostitutes
Job/Career: truck factory painter and others
Primary killing method: strangulation
Primary disposal method: dumping the bodies in or near the Green River, Washington

Other notable facts: Ridgway was arrested primarily due to advancements in technology; a saliva sample (DNA) he provided as a suspect in 1987 led to his arrest in 2001. Ridgway was spared the death penalty in return for helping police locate the bodies of his victims. He is currently serving 49 consecutive life sentences. According to Department of Corrections records, Ridgway is a model inmate. Ridgway seems to be concerned about his legacy; in 2013, he complained to the FBI that everyone knows serial killer Ted Bundy (also from Seattle, Washington), but not him.

RIFKIN, Joel David

Nickname: none

Born: January 20, 1959
Died:

Number of victims: 9-17+
Preferential victims: female prostitutes
Job/Career: landscaper and others
Primary killing method: strangulation
Primary disposal method: dismemberment and disposal in remote locations

Other notable facts: Despite a reported IQ of 128 (above average) Rifkin was repeatedly fired from jobs due to his chronic absenteeism, poor hygiene, and "general ineptitude." For most of his adult life he lived with his parents. In 1993, Rifkin was pulled over in Long Island for driving without a rear license plate, and police noticed he had a thick layer of eucalyptus cream on his moustache (used by morgue workers to avoid the stench of dead bodies). They discovered a decomposing female corpse underneath a tarp in the back of his truck, and arrested him for murder. Twenty years later, in 2013, police found a severed head on a golf course in Hopewell, New Jersey. It was identified as Heidi Balch: Rifkin's very first victim.

ROBINSON, John Edward Sr.

Nickname: "Slavemaster"

Born: December 27, 1943
Died:

Number of victims: 8+
Preferential victims: young women
Job/Career: x-ray technician, insurance salesman and others
Primary killing method: bludgeoning
Primary disposal method: putting the bodies in barrels

Other notable facts: As an adult, Robinson likely stole and embezzled from every company he ever worked for, including the theft of 6200 postage stamps from Mobil Oil. In 1977, Robinson was named "Man of the Year" for this work with the handicapped in Kansas City. He achieved this feat by forging recommendation letters to the mayor commending his generosity and importance to the community. After winning, he held himself an awards luncheon. When it was discovered he had forged the letters, he left Kansas City in disgrace. Another of Robinson's many frauds was killing the mother of a 4-month-old baby, then selling the baby to his in-laws who were looking to adopt (they were unaware that their lawyer's fee was going to Robinson himself).

SHAWCROSS, Arthur John

Nickname: "The Genesee River Killer"

Born: June 6, 1945
Died: November 10, 2008 in prison, due to heart failure

Number of victims: 13+
Preferential victims: boys, girls, female prostitutes
Job/Career: Army soldier, burglar and others
Primary killing method: strangulation and bludgeoning
Primary disposal method: dumping the bodies in or near the Genesee River

Other notable facts: After having served 15 years in prison for the murder of two children, Shawcross was released in 1987 and spent the following two years murdering prostitutes. The prostitutes who survived Shawcross' attacks said he was impotent. Shawcross made a number of wild claims about his life and exploits – for instance, that he was a special assignment soldier in Vietnam who killed enemy prostitutes – none of which have been substantiated. After his final arrest, Shawcross unsuccessfully faked Multiple Personality Disorder and Schizophrenia.

SWANGO, Dr. Michael Joseph

Nickname: None

Born: October 21, 1954
Died:

Number of victims: unknown
Preferential victims: hospital patients and coworkers
Job/Career: doctor
Primary killing methods: poisoning – usually arsenic
Primary disposal method: leaving the bodies *in situ*

Other notable facts: After having skipped from hospital to hospital in the United States due to performance concerns and investigations, Swango fled to Zimbabwe, Africa, where he again worked as a doctor and killed patients. He was on his way to a new job in Saudi Arabia when he was arrested at Chicago's O'Hare airport. Swango claims to have fathered a boy and girl while in Africa (from two different women), who now live in Zambia.

WILLIAMS, David Russell

Nickname: none

Born: March 7, 1963
Died:

Number of victims: 2+
Preferential victims: women
Job/Career: Air Force Colonel
Primary killing method: strangulation
Primary disposal method: leaving the bodies *in situ*

Other notable facts: In addition to his conviction for murder, Williams is serving 82 one-year sentences for burglary. Police found dozens of women's bras and panties stashed in his home, as well as numerous photos of himself wearing them. During his time in the Canadian Air Force, Williams piloted the Canadian Prime Minister and the Queen of England. After his conviction, the Canadian military burned Williams' uniforms and crushed his medals.

WUORNOS, Aileen Carol

Nickname: "Damsel of death"

Born: February 29, 1956
Died: October 9, 2002, by lethal injection

Number of victims: 7+
Preferential victims: johns (men soliciting prostitutes)
Job/Career: prostitute
Primary killing method: shooting
Primary disposal method: dumping bodies in secluded areas along major highways

Other notable facts: Prior to her arrest for murder, Wuornos had been charged with assault, fraud, robbery, resisting arrest, obstruction of justice, and prostitution. Wuornos' lesbian lover was aware of her first murder, but did not go to the police with the information; she believed that the killing had purged Wuornos of her hatred for society. Wuornos' story has been made into a comic book, a Halloween TV special, several movies (one starring actress Charlize Theron), and an opera.

BIBLIOGRAPHY

Aamodt, M. G. (2015, November 23). *Serial killer statistics.* Retrieved September 19, 2016 from http://maamodt.asp.radford.edu/serial killer information center/project description.htm

A&E Television Networks, LLC. (2003) *Biography: Aileen Wuornos* [Video file]. Retrieved from http://www.biography.com/people/aileen-wuornos-11735792/videos/aileen-wuornos-full-episode-2103569732

ABC News. (n.d.). *Angelina Jolie: Billy Bob, Knives and Sex* Retrieved from http://abcnews.go.com/2020/story?id=123685&page=1#.UVK TZknn_IU

Afshar, T. (2012). *Adapting an Evolutionary Framework in Defining the Construct of Psychopathy* (unpublished essay). Simon Fraser University, Burnaby, Canada.

Alpert, G.P., Rivera, J., & Lott, L. (2012, May) Working Toward the Truth in Officer-Involved Shootings: Memory, Stress, and Time. *FBI Law Enforcement Bulletin*, 1-7.

Anonymous (2010, Sept 19th, 12:53pm) "...I realize that I'm different..." Retrieved from www.sociopathworld.com/2008/11/do-sociopaths-know-they-are-sociopaths.html

Anonymous (2015, February 12, 3:29pm). "I've often found that in carrying on an act of normalcy..." Retrieved from

https://www.blogger.com/comment.g?blogID=1385403660762
757699&postID=3953106421830170978&isPopup=true&bpli=
1

Appleby, T. (2011). *A New Kind of Monster: The Secret Life and Chilling Crimes of Colonel Russell Williams.* Toronto, Ont: Random House Canada.

Artwohl, A.A. (2002, Oct) Perceptual and Memory Distortions in Officer-Involved Shootings. *FBI Law Enforcement Bulletin*, 18-24.

The Associated Press (1999, January 02). World's Most Wanted Terrorist: An Interview with Osama bin Laden. *ABCNEWS Online*. Retrieved from http://cryptome.org/jya/bin-laden-abc.htm

The Associated Press. (1999, May 14) Jesse Ray came forward nearly 13 years ago with report on dad, FBI says. *Amarillo Global News*. Retrieved from
http://amarillo.com/stories/1999/05/14/new_forward.shtml

Bates, B. (2013, January). Interview with "Honey," a street prostitute in Oklahoma City. Retrieved from
http://johntv.com/category/video/ and
http://www.youtube.com/watch?v=BSRd9xYvFls

Bergler, E. (1958). The Psychology of Gambling. London W.1: Bernard Hanison Limited.

Biography.com (2014). Joel Rifkin Biography. Retrieved from www.biography.com/people/joel-rifkin-11030477 (accessed September 10, 2016).

Blatchford, C. (2014, August 30). Christie Blatchford: Accused serial killer's testimony leaves little mystery in murders. *Postmedia News*. Retrieved from http://www.vancouversun.com/news/metro/Accused+serial+kil ler+Cody+Legebokoff+testimony+leaves+little/10161465/story .html

Blundell, N. (2010). *Serial Killers: The World's Most Evil.* Barnsley, South Yorkshir: Wharncliffe True Crime.

Boutilier, G. (2014, June 23). [Interview].

Brandes, B.J., Meiwes, A. & Moore, J. (2008, January). My Dinner With Antrophagus. *Harper's*. Retrieved from http://harpers.org/archive/2008/01/my-dinner-with-antrophagus/

Broomfield, N. (Director). (2002, October 8). *Life and Death of a Serial Killer* [DVD].

Bugliosi, V. & Gentry, C. (1974). *Helter Skelter: The True Story of the Manson Murders.* New York, NY: W. W. Norton and Company.

Calumet County Sheriff's Department. (2006, March 01). *Interview of Brendan Dassey by Inv. Mark Wigert & Special Agent Tom Fassbender. Complaint Number 05-0157-955.* Retrieved from https://www.reddit.com/r/MakingaMurderer/comments/3y5pak/ transcripts_of_brendan_dasseys_interviews_ht/

Campbell, J.A. (1996, June) *Bernardo Investigation Review: Summary Report of Mr. Justice Archie Campbell*. Toronto, Ont: Solicitor General and Minister of Correctional Service. Retrieved from

https://www.attorneygeneral.jus.gov.on.ca/inquiries/cornwall/e
n/hearings/exhibits/Wendy_Leaver/pdf/10_Campbell_Summar
y.pdf

Cameron, S. (2007). *The Pickton File*. Toronto, Ont: Alfred A.
Knopf Canada.

Cameron, S. (2010). *On the Farm: Robert William Pickton and
the tragic story of Vancouver's missing women.* Toronto, Ont:
Alfred A. Knopf Canada.

*The Cannibal Gives an Interview (Kannibale darf Interviews
Geben).* (2006, November 14). *Stern Magazine*, from
Frankfurter Allgemeinen Zeitung. Retrieved from
http://www.stern.de/kultur/film/armin-meiwes-kannibale-darf-
interviews-geben-576344.html

Canter, D. (1993). *Criminal Shadows*. Irving, Texas:
Autherlink Press.

Capote, T. (1965). *In Cold Blood: A True Account of a Multiple
Murder and its Consequences.* New York, NY: Random
House.

CBS 2 Vault: John Wayne Gacy Speaks (Aired 1992, May 11
at 10pm). *CBS.*
Retrieved from: http://chicago.cbslocal.com/2012/01/20/cbs-2-
vault-john-wayne-gacy-speaks/

Citizen Staff/Prince George Citizen (2014, September 15).
Exhibit Cody: PG Citizen - Legebokoff Interview 1-7. [Audio
files] Retrieved from
http://www.princegeorgecitizen.com/news/legebokoff-
trial/exhibit-cody-1.1358562

Cleckley, H. (1988: 1st ed. 1941). *The Mask of Sanity: An Attempt to Clarify Some Issues About the So-Called Psychopathic Personality*. Augusta, GA: The C.V. Mosby Company.

CNN. *Inside the Mind of Serial Killer Gary Ridgway, CNN Larry King Live* (2004, February 14). Retrieved from: http://transcripts.cnn.com/TRANSCRIPTS/0402/18/lkl.00.html

Confessions of a Serial Killer: Interview conducted with Jeffrey Dahmer by Stone Phillips (1994, Feb). Portage, WI: Columbia Correctional Institution. *CNN*.

Coquitlam RCMP Serious Crime Section (2000, January). Statement of Robert Pickton, taken on 00.01.19 at 7:30 p.m. by CST. R. YURKIW and CST. J. CATER - in the presence of G. HOUSTON: File #98CQ-33017. Retrieved from www.vancouversun.com/pdf/picktonstatement.pdf

Cough, S., Alleyne, R. & Laville, S. (2001, Feb 03). They were like two bodies with one brain, raping and killing for kicks. *The Telegraph*. Retreived from http://www.telegraph.co.uk/news/uknews/1320832/They-were-like-two-bodies-with-one-brain-raping-and-killing-for-kicks.html

Couric, C. (2006, September 06). Transcript: President Bush, Part 2. *CBS Evening News*. Retrieved from http://www.cbsnews.com/news/transcript-president-bush-part-2/

Crosson-Tower, C. (2003). *The Role of Educators in Preventing and Responding to Child Abuse and Neglect*. Retrieved from U.S. Department of Health and Human Services website: https://childwelfare.gov/pubPDFs/educator_29.pdf

Cullen, C. (2004, Sept 12). Charles Cullen: In his own words. *NewJersey.com* Retrieved from http://www.nj.com/news/ledger/index.ssf?/news/stories/nurse_20040912_confessions.html

DeMarban, A. (2012, December 07). Alaska investigators say Keyes felt a high from serial killings. *Alaska Dispatch News.* Retrieved from: http://www.adn.com/article/alaska-investigators-say-keyes-felt-high-serial-killings

DeNevi, D. & Campbell, J.H. (2004). *Into the Minds of Madmen: how the FBI's Behavioral Science Unit revolutionized crime investigation.* Amherst, NY: Prometheus Books.

Dewar, G. (2013). *Myths about bedwetting: What the research really says.* Retrieved from www.parentingscience.com/bedwetting.html

Do Psychopaths Know They're Psychopaths (n.d.) (2011, April 21). "As if knowing I'm a better person..." Quote retrieved from comments section of http://www.psychopathicwritings.com/2011/04/do-psychopaths-know-theyre-psychopaths.html

D'Oro, R. & Cohen, S. (2013, January 27). Trying to unlock secrets of dead serial killer. *The Associated Press.* Retrieved from: http://bigstory.ap.org/article/trying-unlock-secrets-dead-serial-killer

Do sociopaths know they are sociopaths? (n.d.) (2011, December 04). "I realize that I'm different..." Quote retrieved from comments section of http://www.sociopathworld.com/2008/11/do-sociopaths-know-they-are-sociopaths.html

Douglas, J. E. and Munn, C. (1992, February, Volume 61, Number 2). Violent Crime Scene Analysis: *Modus Operandi*, Signature, and Staging. *FBI Law Enforcement Bulletin.*

Douglas, J. & Olshaker, M. (1995). *Mindhunter: Inside the FBI's Elite Serial Crime Unit.* New York, NY: Mindhunters Inc.

Douglas, J. & Olshaker, M. (1999). *The Anatomy of Motive: the FBI's legendary mindhunter explores the key to understanding and catching violent criminals.* New York, NY: Mindhunters Inc.

Douglas, J. & Singular, S. (2003). *Anyone you want me to be: A true story of sex and death on the Internet.* New York, NY: A Lisa Drew Book/Scribner.

Dutton, D. G.; Aron, A. P. (1974). "Some evidence for heightened sexual attraction under conditions of high anxiety". *Journal of Personality and Social Psychology* 30 (4): 510–517. Retrieved from: https://gaius.fpce.uc.pt/niips/novoplano/ps1/documentos/dutton&aron1974.pdf

Eagle County Sheriff's Department (2004, June 08 - Original interview 2003, July). Kobe Bryant Police Interview: NBA star's graphic account of the hotel room encounter, finishing move. *The Smoking Gun.* Retrieved from http://www.thesmokinggun.com/file/kobe-bryant-police-interview?page=0

Early, P. (2012). *The Serial Killer Whisperer: How One Man's Tragedy helped unlock the deadliest secrets of the world's most terrifying killers.* New York, NY: Touchstone, a division of Random House Inc.

Echols, Lt. P. & Byers, C. (2011). *In Cold Pursuit: My Hunt for Timothy Krajcir-The Notorious Serial Killer.* Far Hills, NJ: New Horizon Press.

Express. (2010, June 29). *Angelina Jolie speaks out about her battle with self-harm, aged just 14: Angelina Jolie recalls the horrors of her past - and reveals why Brad Pitt is 'extraordinary.'* Retrieved from http://www.ok.co.uk/celebrity-news/view/23506/Angelina-Jolie-speaks-out-about-her-battle-with-self-harm-aged-just-14/

FBI Records: The Vault. (2009). Multiple files (1-19) retrieved from https://vault.fbi.gov/jeffrey-lionel-dahmer/

Festinger, L. (1957). *A theory of cognitive dissonance.* Stanford, CA: Stanford University Press.

Fezzani, N. (2015). *Through the Eyes of Serial Killers: Interviews with Seven Murderers.* Toronto, Ont: Dundurn Press.

Fuhrman, M. (2001). *Murder in Spokane.* New York, NY: HarperCollins Publishers Inc.

Gibb, D.A. (2011). *Camouflaged Killer: The Shocking Double Life of Canadian Air Colonel Russell Williams.* New York, NY: The Berkeley Publishing Group.

Graeber, C. (2013). *The Good Nurse: A True Story of Medicine, Madness, and Murder.* New York, NY: Hachette Book Group.

Gudjonsson, G.H. (2003). *The Psychology of Interrogations and Confessions: A Handbook*. Chichester, West Sussex: John Wiley & Sons Ltd.

Harrelson, L. & Gerow, N.J. (1998). *Lietest: Deception, Truth, and the Polygraph*. Ft. Wayne, IN: Jonas Publishing.

HBO. (1990). Child of Rage: A Story of Abuse, by Ken Magid. [Video file]. Retrieved from: www.youtube.com/watch?v=g2-Re_Fl_L4

Hedegaard, E. (2013, November 21). Charles Manson Today: The Final Confessions of a Psychopath. *Rolling Stone Magazine*. Retrieved from http://www.rollingstone.com/culture/news/charles-manson-today-the-final-confessions-of-a-psychopath-20131121

Hess, C. & Seay, D. (2008). *Hello Charlie: Letters from a Serial Killer*. New York, NY: Atria Books, a Division of Simon & Schuster.

Hitchcock, J. A. (2013). *True crime online: shocking stories of scamming, stalking, murder, and mayhem*. Medford, NJ: CyberAge Books.

Hicks, S.J. & Sales, B.D. (2006). *Criminal Profiling: Developing an Effective Science and Practice*. Washington, DC: American Psychological Association.

Holt, David G, official court reporter. (2005, June 27). State of Kansas vs. Dennis L. Rader, Case No. 05 CR 498.

Horvath, I. (Director). (1984). *Murder: no apparent motive* [DVD], Orlando, FL: Rainbow Broadcasting Company.

Inside Edition (1993, Feb 08). Jeffrey Dahmer [Video file].
Retrieved from
https://www.youtube.com/watch?v=RtvmGdzgdLM

Intelligence Science Board. (2009, April). *Intelligence
Interviewing: Teaching Papers and Case Studies*. Retrieved
from Federation of American Scientists website:
https://fas.org/irp/dni/isb/interview.pdf

Keppel, R.D. & Birnes, W.J. (1997). *Signature Killers*. New
York, NY: Pocket Books, a division of Simon & Schuster Inc.

Keyes, A. (2011). My Testimony. Retrieved from
www.thechurchofwell.com/autumn-keyes-trudeau.html

Klinger, E. (2004). *Into the Kill Zone: A Cop's Eye View of
Deadly Force*. San Francisco, CA: Jossey-Bass, a Wiley
Imprint.

Kocsis, R. N, Hayes, A. F., & Irwin, H. J. (2002). Investigative
experience and accuracy in psychological profiling of a violent
crime. *Journal of Interpersonal Violence*, 17, 811–823.

Kocsis, R. N., Hayes, A. F., Irwin, H. J., & Nunn, R. (2000).
Expertise in psychological profiling: a comparative assessment.
Journal of Interpersonal Violence, 15, 311–331

Kosuga, T. (2008, December 31) *Vice News: Who's Hungry?*
[Video file] Retrieved from
http://www.vice.com/en_ca/read/whos-hungry-502-v16n1

Lankford, S.M. (2002). *Born, Not Raised: Voices from Juvenile
Hall*. San Diego, CA: Humane Exposures Publishing, LLC.

Larry King Live, Interview With Father and Stepmother of Serial Killer Jeffrey Dahmer (Aired 2004, June 17). *CNN*. Retrieved from: http://transcripts.cnn.com/TRANSCRIPTS/0406/17/lkl.00.html

LePard, D. (2010, August). *VPD Missing women investigation review*. Vancouver, BC: Vancouver Police Department. Retrieved from http://www.cbc.ca/bc/news/bc-100820-vancouver-police-pickton-investigation-review.pdf

MacDonald, J.M. (1963). The threat to kill. *The American Journal of Psychiatry*, Vol. 120, No. 2 (August): 125-130.

Makin, K. (2006, June 20). Performance anxiety drove him, Bernardo told police. *The Globe and Mail*. Retrieved from www.theglobeandmail.com/news/national/performance-anxiety-drove-him-bernardo-told-police/article18452272

Maleng, N. (2003). Prosecutor's Summary of the Evidence: State of Washington vs. Gary Leon Ridgway. No 01-1-10270-9 SEA. Retrieved from murderpedia.org/male.R/images/ridgway_gary/reports/summary.pdf

Mancini, L. (nrn). (2012, December 10). Luka Magnotta Dedication: A Luka fan site. Final Blog Post. [Web log post] Retrieved from http://lukamagnottaobsession.wordpress.com/

Manson, C. (2013, November 20). "lying-ass district attorney..." [Quote]. Retrieved from http://mansondirect.com/

Manson, C. (2012, February). "Air my Sun God..." [Quote] Retrieved from http://mansondirect.com/dear%20air.html

Max, T. (2010). *Assholes Finish First*. New York, NY: Gallery Books, a Division of Simon and Schuster Inc.

McClintick, D. (2013, September 03). Serial Killer J.R. Robinson's Sinister Alter Ego. *Vanity Fair*. Retrieved from www.vanityfair.com/news/2001/06/jr-robinson-serial-killer.

McNab, C. (2010). *Serial Killer Timelines: illustrated accounts of the world's most gruesome murders*. Berkeley, CA: Amber Books Ltd, Published in the US by Ulysses Press.

Mellon, J. (2011). *The Judge: A Life of Thomas Mellon, Founder of a Fortune*. New Haven & London: Yale University Press.

Milne, R. & Bull, R. (1999). *Investigative Interviewing: Psychology and Practice*. West Sussex: Wiley.

Morton, R.J. & Hilts, M.A. (Eds.) (2005, Aug 29-September 02). *Serial Murder: Multi-Disciplinary Perspectives for Investigators*. Quantico, VA: Federal Bureau of Investigation, NCAVC. Retrieved from https://www.fbi.gov/stats-services/publications/serial-murder/serial-murder-july-2008-pdf

MSNBC (2009, October 25). Confessions of a Serial Killer. Retrieved from http://livedash.ark.com/transcript/the_confessions_of_a_serial_killer/5304/MSNBC/Sunday_October_25_2009/101692/ (accessed November 30, 2014).

Muti, R. & Buckley, R. (2012). *The Charmer: the true story of Robert Reldan - rapist, murderer, and millionaire - and the women who fell victim to his allure*. Green Bay, WI: TitleTown Publishing, LLC.

Naifeh, S.W (2011). *Van Gogh: The Life*. New York, NY: Random House.

National Forensic Technology Centre. (2013, September). *Crime Scene Investigation: A Guide for Law Enforcement*. Largo, FL. Retrieved from National Institute of Standards and Technology website: https://www.nist.gov/sites/default/files/documents/.../Crime-Scene-Investigation.pdf

Nielsen, C. (2011). *The Pig Farm* [DVD]. Toronto, Ont: CTV Television Network, Barna-Alper Productions, Studio 1.

O'Brien, D. (1985). *Two of a Kind*. New York, NY: Carroll & Graf Publishers, an imprint of Avalon Publishing Group Inc.

The Ottawa Citizen. (n.d.). (2010, October 20). *Evidence: Letters from Russell Williams*. Retrieved from: http://www.ottawacitizen.com/news/Evidence+Letters+from+Russell+Williams/3701143/story.html

Ottawa Police Service (2010, February 07). Transcript of Taped Interview, Russell Williams. Interviewed by Detective Sergeant J. Smyth. *CNEWS*. Retrieved from cnews.canoe.ca/CNEWS/Crime/2010/10/20/Edited_Williams.pdf

Psychopath: Language and the Meaning of Words (n.d.). (2015, January 09). "Ive found that in carrying on an act of normalcy..." Quote retrieved from comments section of http://www.psychopathicwritings.com/2015/01/psychopath-language-meaning-of-words.html

Pudinski, W. (1984). California crimes and accidents associated with hitchhiking. *California Highly Patrol, Operational*

Analysis Section. Retrieved from
https://www.ncjrs.gov/pdffiles1/Digitization/18834NCJRS.pdf

Real Crime: Interview with a Serial Killer [Arthur Shawcross],
Season 1, Episode 1. (2009, September 16). [Video file]
Retrieved from:
http://www.youtube.com/watch?v=02Lm74JqkGs

Redstall, V. (2011). *Serial Killers up close and very personal:
my death row interviews with the most dangerous men on the
planet.* Bramber Road, London: John Blake Publishing Inc.

Ressler, R. K. and Burgess, A. W. (1985, August, Volume 54,
Number 8). Crime Scene and Profile Characteristics of
Organized and Disorganized Murderers. *FBI Law Enforcement
Bulletin.*

Reuters. (2014, October 31). Congo crowd kills man, eats him
after militant massacres: witnesses. BENI Democratic
Republic of Congo. Retrieved from
http://www.reuters.com/article/2014/10/31/us-
congodemocratic-rebels-idUSKBN0IK1RN20141031
(accessed Oct 31, 2014).

Rule, A. (2000). *The Stranger Beside Me.* New York, NY: W.
Norton & Company, Inc.

Scott, H. (2005). *The Female Serial Murderer: A Sociological
Study of Homicide and the 'Gentler Sex.'* Lewiston, NY: Mellon
Press.

Shepard, C. (1999, March 15). Evidence Item #265. Retrieved
from http://acolumbinesite.com/quotes1.html

Simons, A.B. & Boetig, B.P. (2007, June) The Structured Investigative Interview. *FBI Law Enforcement Bulletin*, 9-20.

Sociopath utopia? (n.d.). (2009, February 05). "As much as I'd like to meet other sociopaths..." Quote retrieved from comments section of http://www.sociopathworld.com/2009/02/sociopath-utopia.html

Stambaugh, H. & Styron, H. (Eds.). (2003, January). *Special Report: Firefighter Arson.* Arlington, VA: Department of Homeland Security.

Starr, D. (2010). *The Killer of Little Shephards: A True Crime Story and the Birth of Forensic Science.* New York, NY: Borzoi, a division of Alfred A. Knopf Inc.

Stewart, J.B. (1999). *Blind Eye: How the medical establishment let a doctor get away with murder.* New York, NY: Simon and Schuster.

Terry, D. (1994, November 29). Jeffrey Dahmer, Multiple Killer, Is Bludgeoned to Death in Prison. *The New York Times*. Retrieved from http://www.nytimes.com/1994/11/29/us/jeffrey-dahmer-multiple-killer-is-bludgeoned-to-death-in-prison.html

Turco, R. (2008). Criminal Profile Construction and Investigative Procedures: Study of the Westley Dodd Serial Sexual Murders. In R. N. Kocsis, (Ed.), *Serial Murder and the Psychology of Violent Crimes* Totowa, NJ: Humana Press.

United Press International. (1971, Feb 16, No 167). Susan Atkins to Resume Testimony. *Desert Sun Newspaper.* Los Angeles, CA: Retrieved from http://cdnc.ucr.edu/cgi-

bin/cdnc?a=d&d=DS19710216.2.23&srpos=1&e=-------en--20-
-1--txt-txIN-Susan+Atkins+to+Resume+Testimony-------1

Watson, T. as told by Ray, C. (1978). *Will You Die For Me?: The Man Who Killed For Charles Manson Tells His Own Story.* Colorado Springs, CO: Cross Roads Publications Inc.

Wenzl, R., Potter, T., Kelly, L., & Laviana, H. (2008). *Bind, Torture, Kill: The Inside Story of the Serial Killer Next Door.* New York, NY: Wichita Eagle and Beacon Publishing Co.

Wenzl, R. (2015, March 07). A serial killer's daughter struggles to forgive her dad. *The Wichita Eagle.* Retrieved from http://www.thestar.com/news/insight/2015/03/07/a-serial-killers-daughter-struggles-to-forgive-her-dad.html

Wenzl, R. (2015, February 21). When your father is the BTK serial killer, forgiveness is not tidy. *The Wichita Eagle.* Retrieved from: http://www.kansas.com/news/special-reports/btk/article10809929.html

Williams, S. (2004). *Karla: a pact with the devil.* Toronto, Ont: Cantos International.

Yerkes R.M. & Dodson J.D. (1908). The relation of strength of stimulus to rapidity of habit-formation. *Journal of Comparative Neurology and Psychology* 18: 459–482. Retrieved from http://psychclassics.yorku.ca/Yerkes/Law/

Yeschke, C.L. (1997). *The Art of Investigative Interviewing: A Human Approach to Testimonial Evidence.* Woburn, MA: Butterworth-Heinemann.

Zanor, C. (2010, November 29). A Fate That Narcissists Will Hate: Being Ignored. *The New York Times.* Retrieved from

http://www.nytimes.com/2010/11/30/health/views/30mind.html
?_r=0

Zipper, P. & Wilcox, D.K. (2005, April) Juvenile Arson. *FBI Law Enforcement Bulletin*, 1-9.

Zuckerman, M. (1979). *Sensation Seeking: Beyond the optimal level of arousal.* Hillsdale, NJ: Erlbaum.

Printed in Germany
by Amazon Distribution
GmbH, Leipzig